The Alchemies
of ISIS

Embodiment through the
High Priestess

Carmel Glenane B.A. Dip. Ed.

The Alchemies

of ISIS

Embodiment through the
High Priestess

Carmel Glenane B.A. Dip. Ed.

Big Country Publishing, LLC

CONTENTS

DEDICATION TO ISIS

All Light Beings and all those who love Isis created this dedication through me.

Isis is now creating in you a joy-filled vibration as she responds to your call to be heard by her.

In my heart, the mother Isis lives.
In my heart, the mother Isis listens.
She hears my aching heart, and it is her heart that aches too.
Isis, my mother, listen to my call for help,
I am afraid, dear mother.

I hear you my child, you are forever in my heart,
as I wash your wounds in love.
I know love. I am love, and I bring to you now "the call",
My call, for you to awaken from your fear of love, to embrace "Me."

Come my child; come, come, come unto me,
I am "She", and "She" is me.
All life comes from me, all life moves through me,
All life is released through me.

In my arms you now sleep,
In my arms you now heal,
In my arms you find love.

I am with you till the end of time, as I am the end of time.
Breathe me now into your heart,
Forgive every living thing,
And you too, can be with me.

~Carmel Glenane

Introduction The Alchemies of Isis

Who is Isis?

Isis's temple is found on Isle of Philae, Aswan, Egypt. The outer court of the temple was erected by the Ptolemies in the last two centuries B.C. and by the Roman Emperors (Augustus) in the first three centuries A.D.

Isis will allow your "soul" to grow through loss and pain and she brings "life" back to you when you are letting go of the past. She waits for you to be ready for her, and she brings patience to you when you are in a space of despair. She allows you to renew yourself through her. Hope, restoration, and magic are yours when you lovingly embrace Isis. She knows the value of balanced passion and she will bring to your life all that you desire to create a mate and keep the fires glowing between you and your beloved.

Isis offers restoration of harmony after losses; she understands loss and tragedy, and the pain of relationship loss. Isis knows how to allow you to really go into the heart of yourself through the grieving process, and then let it go. Isis is ideal for balancing and restoring emotional equilibrium.

"Strong, healthy relationships come from yourself and through you.
You can really allow the magic of the Alchemies of Isis –
The Magician to come to you."
~ Carmel Glenane

About This Book

The Alchemies of Isis, Embodiment through the High Priestess is a combined teaching of The Alchemies of Isis, The Magician and The High Priestess, A Blueprint for Living through the Feminine Heart. My final Rite of Passage was completing this book, a companion volume to The High Priestess Transmissions. All humans deserve to be given the gift, and allow themselves the love, that their High Priestess and Isis have for them.

If you are looking at furthering your relationship with the High Priestess and drawing on the archetypical force behind the High Priestess as a model for your humanness, then I invite you to develop your relationship with the High Priestess through these transmissions from Isis.

Isis brings now the frequency of truth for all of life in relationship patterning. For your life and world now you are embracing a new way of being human and this is to consider yourself first in everything. Isis creates through balanced love.

Through the essence of balanced, heart-centered love, you can begin to really delve into yourself and ask yourself why you don't consider yourself "first" in everything. For your relationship with *The Alchemies of Isis* to develop in your consciousness you must just consider why it is such a challenge to consider YOU in your journey with yourself.

The Isis ray will begin to strengthen your relationship with yourself. Your High Priestess "her" self grows as you are drawing on the source energy, which goes beyond time and space to embrace the Black Isis.

- Introduce yourself to *The Alchemies of Isis* to help you control your own hormonal balance.

- "Isis elixir of life exercises" open you to the power and mystery of your own body's ability to restore and nourish your feminine.

- For anyone who would like to feel POWER TO RENEW YOURSELF WITH ENERGY.

Isis holds the key to the feminine mysteries because she helps you change your relationship with your feminine. Your feminine essence is enacted when you begin to embrace the living energies of Isis, for she is the Great Magician. The embracing of your own sexual powers to heal, renew, and change consciousness belongs to Isis. For Isis heals through the alchemy of the sexual energy.

What is the sexual energy through Isis?

Isis brings the sexual energy to the frequency of passion that is heart-balanced. She brings the balance back into the rejuvenation qualities sexual passion creates. Sexuality creates rejuvenation. The tissues, cells, and endocrine (hormonal function) are all under Isis protection for she RULES THROUGH THE MOON and the moon's powers belong to her.

PART I
THE ALCHEMIES OF ISIS

The Moon and Your Feminine

You must remember the feminine arts are the moon's magic. Through the effects of the moon and the water element, the energy of sexuality is brought to the heart to heal and renew. If sexuality is not connected to the heart, it destroys because it burns the essence of the feminine with its power.

ISIS LOVES BEING IN THE COMPANY OF THOSE WHO CAN APPRECIATE AND SUPPORT LOVE. WHERE THERE IS NO UNDERSTANDING OF LOVE OR APPRECIATION OF LOVE AS A WAY OF BEING HUMAN, ISIS CANNOT STAY.

YOU MUST INTONE DAILY:

"I NOW ALLOW MYSELF THE APPRECIATION OF LOVE. THE APPRECIATION OF LOVE MAKES ME WHOLE AND FEEDS MY IMMORTAL SOUL."

ISIS BRINGS YOUR BODY INTO A STATE OF ALIGNMENT WITH YOUR TRUTH.

YOUR TRUTH IS A BAROMETER FOR LOVE AND YOUR TRUTH REVEALS LOVE TO YOU IN ITS PUREST FORM.

Isis teaches you to nourish your body and keep it in a state of renewal, because your relationship with your body is a statement about how you cherish your emotions.

Your emotions reflect your relationship with your body. Your body is a barometer of your emotions and their well-being. You must just feel the emotional energy and find where in the body emotional energy is held.

You must allow yourself this peace, knowing Isis rules the relationship WITH THE BODY AND THE EMOTIONS. THEY ARE NOT SEPARATE.

Find a space within yourself to create with this energy. You must first seek to allow yourself the knowledge that you have a right to begin to create the conditions for your love of the alchemical processes, which give the body vigor, life force, and magnetism.

For the body to have the magnetism to bring power, radiance, and inner beauty, Isis suggests you begin to really allow the body to absorb the energies of nature, especially the natural world by being near bodies of water where the moon's powers can magnetize water. Taking moon-energized water internally and bathing in moon water brings the magnetic power of renewal to you now.

In the second section of this book, you are furthering your relationship with the High Priestess and drawing on the archetypical force behind the High Priestess as a model for your humanness. This section can be read as fiction or in any way you choose to deepen your awareness of your "self" as being part of the totality of being human.

"You" First
Isis brings now the frequency of truth for all of life in relationship patterning. For your life and world now you are embracing a new way of being human and this is to consider yourself first in everything.

For your relationship with The Alchemies of Isis to develop in your consciousness you must just examine why it is such a challenge to consider YOU in your journey with yourself.

Isis creates through balanced love. Through the essence of balanced heart centered love, you can begin to really delve into yourself and ask yourself why you don't consider yourself "first" in everything.

Strong Healthy relationships come from you, and through you. You can really allow the magic of the Alchemies of Isis-The Magician to come to you.

The Isis ray will begin to strengthen your relationship with yourself, your High Priestess herself grows as you are drawing on the source energy that goes beyond time and space to embrace the Black Isis.

You are now opening up your new pathways in this emerging relationship with Isis. This relationship will forward your intent for a new way of being human. Isis is your representative as the source energy for this new way of viewing your feminine.

It is now an experience that will take you to a new part of yourself, rather like going to a totally unfamiliar region in a part of yourself that hasn't been discovered before. You must trust that the source energy, the source guide or teacher will confer on you all the benefits you need for your journey in being human.

Isis is the representative of power over the limited mind. The limited human consciousness who knows only one thing: Control over love and control over others.

You are challenging yourself at a core level to really go into a part of yourself that knows only one thing: Love.

"All Love" is the vibration, the frequency of the Isis ray, and you are now fighting your limited mind to embrace this concept of "All Love" through Isis as a way of being human. Your identity is now going to be reshaped totally as you merge with Isis, as a way of being human. Isis will bring to you your "core" feminine identity (regardless of gender). This "core" feminine identity must have at its heart the belief that "All Love" is the result of your relationship with "Her" and yourself.

Core Relationship Identity
Isis now brings to you the ability to really let go of all relationships which you feel can't be managed in your life. You need now to really examine a relationship you struggle with. The living energies of Isis are at your disposal now for you to embark on this inner crusade. This inner crusade brings you now to a space of real awakening to her mystery.

Isis reveals herself to you now as you bring into focus your relationship with your "core" relationship identity. When a relationship is not right, it will reflect itself back to you, and you will need now to examine this pattern. Allow this to be taking place now.

Isis brings now to you her magical power to really examine your role with a person who you have chosen consciously or unconsciously to have in your life. You are constantly monitoring relationships and you need to really examine why you are allowing your sacred self to be compromised by your lower self in maintaining unhealthy relationships.

You must choose who "you" (your sacred Isisian self) want to have in your life. You must be ruthless in your self-examination here.

You are free now to really open up yourself to the Isis Alchemies.

Let's begin:
"Who do I choose to have in my life, consciously or otherwise?" i.e. Who keeps "popping" into your head at odd times, when "you" are relaxing, day dreaming, etc.? You need to observe: Why this person has appeared on your inner landscape, and why have you allowed yourself the belief that you are drawing this person's energy to you for a reason. Observing your emotional reaction to this person in this space will give you valuable insight into why you have drawn this person into your inner world.

By observing your inner landscape in this way, you are opening up to a new way of looking at relationships.

Ask yourself:
"Why am I here?"
"Why are you here?"
"Why are you here now?"
"What do "you" have to tell me about myself?"

Evoke the person's Higher Self: Ask Three Times...

In the name of love and light...
"Why are you _____(use persons name) here?"
"What are you telling me?"

This exercise will put you into alignment with what your emotional agenda may be for this person. We get many of our unmet needs met through creating fantasy relationships with various people from our past. This is an important technique to weed out these projections/fantasies and see them as weeds, choking your garden of goodness. It is very important to look now, at how; you must observe your emotional agendas for people.

When you feel you have sourced the karmic connection with the person, you then need to make a decision.

"Why you are recreating a relationship which cannot serve you now?"

Ask yourself:
"Who is it in my life that is serving my truth, my divine feminine truth?"

Ask your Heart's intelligence three times:
"In the name of love and light and in the name of my absolute divine truth...

Does ____(use the person's name) serve my truth at this point in my journey?"

By feeling the energy in your heart, opening it, and asking three times you will begin to allow yourself to eliminate old emotional agendas you may have for other people in your life.

The Enchantress
Isis the magician is the enchantress. The enchantress is a woman who brings magical intent to all of life. The essence of Isis in her frequency as an enchantress brings to you now a sense of real magic in your own power to feel and control the chaotic forces around you.

Enchanting yourself with Isis is a gift you can give yourself now, for Isis brings out the secret side of woman, the secret side that can be displayed when "she" wants to create magical intent. Draw now a circle around yourself with either a crystal wand, shell, or your hand will do. Use your right hand, and intend that you are weaving a magical spell around all your creations. Feel the power of your own essence grow as you strengthen the circle with your intent to be the enchantress and you can bring out your secret magical essence.

By allowing yourself this space to communicate with Isis, she can come to you in all her wonderment for "she" is the great magician. She is the great Isis.

Enchantment is a gift Isis offers now. For when you are able to enchant yourself, you become enchanting to others. Try it. Today I am allowing myself the secret gift of Isis to come to me. This is the gift of the enchantress. The enchantress will bring out my secret essence and my secret essence will allow others to see me as an enchantress.

The Secret "Self"

Allowing the secret self to emerge is one of drawing down the vibration of Isis in your world. This is time to just really feel and allow the vibration to infuse your cellular memory with new frequencies. Isis is the energy of absolute beauty in the self; the self, becomes a wonderful thing to experience. Allow yourself now the true experience and expression of yourself through just allowing the essence of all love through Isis to infuse every cell. Isis now allows the essence of your truth to be made magic. You are witnessing a part of yourself that brings to you all you need for your life. Isis allows the essence of your magical intent to create with you at every moment and her love of you and your humanity leads you closer to the mystery of feeling exactly who Isis really is. This is a time to just find Isis in your soul and allow yourself to be gently led by her to bring your world into resonance with your truth.

Isis heals through the energy of the heart and it is the heart she will heal when you need to feel love. Isis knows love and she is available for your grieving heart. You are experiencing the essence of

"All Love" through Isis when you align to her frequency to heal and renew your pained soul. She is there to bring your truth home to you.

Believing in the secret essence of Isis allows you to really connect in truth to the mystery. The essence of the mystery allows now for a sense of peace and renewal. You are opening up now to your own secret magical essence. The essence of your own secret magical self brings to you the sense of beauty in all of life. This beauty must be trusted. The trust of all of life brings you to a state of awareness for the mystery encoded in all of life. Isis is the frequency of allowing this precious alchemy to take. The precious Alchemies of Isis are being infused in your cellular memory now as the world of "her" matches or aligns with your own. The secrets belong to you as you open up yourself to the energy she represents.

The energy of Isis is one of "All Love" for the mystery. You are one in essence with the mystery of true allowance of spirit with "her" now as her vision is being superimposed on yours.

You will now allow through the Alchemies of Isis a belief in their totality of your feminine regardless of what you imagine your feminine to be. The Alchemies are a gift from Isis to your spirit and you must allow yourself a sharing and merging with all of life. Allowing the essence of "All Love" to bring you to a space of peace and truth for the mystery is being encoded upon you now. You are love.

Cellular Rejuvenation
The Alchemies of Isis are a process, which will bring renewal in the process of cellular rejuvenation. When you can rejuvenate your cells you are reversing the aging process. All of life brings to you now the purpose of renewal, for all of life is constantly renewing itself.

Nature renews, heals, and supports our journey as humans without us even being aware of it, and we constantly need to remind ourselves that nature and the natural world is the best healer.

Throughout history practitioners of health have recommended nature as a cure for all human aliments, because forces of nature bring rejuvenation and joy to your cells. Your cells are a barometer of your stability both inner and outer. When you feel your body not in harmony and there are blockages, you must evoke nature, and nature spirits, to heal and renew you. A nature bath is essential for youth. Natural living is living close to nature.

You are allowing the forces of the natural world to really bring to your world your expression of your abundant youth-filled life. For nature is just beginning to support your journey now, so acknowledge to nature… "Nature help me today." Find a particular place in nature to be in every day and consciously evoke nature to heal and renew you. Your cells become activated in the mountain streams, the oceans, a park, the desert, or forest. Your garden and patio must be seen to be a haven for your own ability to renew yourself.

Breath and the Elements
Breathe in the renewing energy of your breath now as you allow yourself the essence of "All Love" to surround you. You must attend to the most important requirement of living and this is to breathe in lovingly for yourself.

The sacred breath is the most precious gift you can give yourself, and you must bring to your world this sacred breath. Aligning yourself to create with the breath brings the mystery of love even closer to you. You are aligning yourself to the breath when you allow yourself the time to acknowledge the essence of the breath to heal and renew you. Allowing sacred space to bring in the breath brings you to a space of love and acceptance of yourself, and the forces of nature combined with the breath bring cellular rejuvenation and youth. Align yourself now to the breath and feel it coming in through the element of air. What is the element of air? The element of air is composed of billions of energy molecules all with life-giving nutrients. Visualize these life giving molecules all around your skin; your skin is sucking in these nutrients. Feel that now. Every cell is responding to the vibration and healing of these molecules.

Allow these vibrations to completely surround you, and align yourself now to deliberately, consciously drawing them in through your nose. Honor your nose. This organ is in sympathetic resonance with the lungs, and together they harmonize to bring life-giving prana to your entire being.

As you begin to align yourself to the elements, you will be creating in your life a direct relationship with the Isis vibration, for the elements fuse the human experience into completeness.

Your experience with the breath and the expression of how you honor yourself with the sacred breath will reinforce in you a belief that all of life is there to protect and support your journey.

You are always allowing yourself the sacred experience of the breath when you allow yourself to really merge in oneness with all of life. Allowing the sacred experience of the breath protects and supports you against disease and mental conditions which destabilize your being.

For, to be human is to love the elements and to really see them as intelligent forces ready to create with you. You can align to these sacred forces at any time to bring you back into balance with who you truly are. You need now to really feel the essence of the breath, create a new and wondrous world for you. This world is your world, and only "you" can control this world. The magical essence of life-giving prana just aligns you to all who can assist you in your world.

"I breathe in to bring to my world my absolute belief that all of life can support me."

All of life is a living intelligence, and offers itself to me when I ask lovingly through the breath. Ask through the breath for everything I require for my life and world.

Desire

Isis (pronounced zees the Egyptian pronunciation) is one you can attune to for your growing relationship with me.

You now need to feel the love I have for you as you begin to question the very nature of love itself. You need to reinforce the patterns that keep re-occurring which take you to a place and space of no love. Where may you ask is there evidence of love around you with people? Where is it possible to feel this power and love? As a human you are pre-disposed to accept love as a gift, a present, something you must have.

Like a child you hungrily and greedily seek it out in many forms and in many ways.

Food addictions feed your emotional hunger. Sex addictions, cravings keep bringing you back to look for love through pleasure. Love is about the power to change consciousness. It represents the forces of all life creating with you, not your own unmet needs struggling to find an outlet in attention seeking.

Attention-seeking behavior only reinforces old patterns, which bring you to a space of denial of your true capacity to love. Isis is now bringing you to a space of purity in loving. Pure food, uncontaminated, pure sex, not polluted by desire and ego. Just the feeling of completeness, without an agenda brings you to a space of purity to allow love to take root.

As humans, when you release desires you bring in love. Love cannot stay where there is desire and greed in any part of the human condition. I bring you love, and your peacefulness, radiance, and joy will allow you to really partake in the journey of love.

Isis, could you please explain/expand on desire? What is desire?
Desire is need. Desire is a need which humans project out on to others to satisfy an inner craving. When you desire something, someone, you are projecting out on to the object or person, (that there is) something in him or her, which you cannot meet within yourself.

Your desire must be heart-centered for your truth. Your desire then becomes your truth not an unmet need. Unmet needs must always be observed. Why do I desire this person, money, etc.? If the desire is not to forward your true purpose, it creates an imbalance that needs to be addressed. You will begin to desire less and less when you open up your heart wider. Your desires are only aspects of unmet needs.

Beginning your path to your heart through Isis creates in you a relationship with one person and that is yourself. "Yourself" has all you need for a life of completion. A complete person is balanced in the heart, for it is the heart that is the seed bearer for truth. Beginning now to allow the heart to open to yourself allows the precious Alchemy of your truth and your destiny to be your guide.

As you move through the Alchemies of Isis you will begin to perceive yourself addressing parts of yourself that have been locked away, disused, and hidden. You are now realizing that this hidden part must be discovered. If you project out to others your unmet needs you leave these hidden parts of yourself unexplored and disused.

Identity
Believing in your ability to create a new identity through the vibration of the feminine energies now reinforces the energy and essence Isis brings. You are now needing to just allow the frequency of "All Love" to surround you as the Isis frequency is evoked. The frequency of "All Love" holds the Isis vibration as you begin to really open up yourself to the mystery she represents.

Isis brings home to you now, the essence of belief in your own ability to maintain equilibrium over emotional instability, creating in you a new identity.

You will be undergoing much purification now as your old patterns are mirrored back to you. Isis allows a sense of wonder in your ability to relate to yourself through this cycle. This is one of the most important cycles in being human, and Isis offers you now strength for your continued maintenance of yourself through this transiting time. You are now bringing to your world the allowance of yourself as vibrating to "All Love" to bring your world into resonance with your truth. Isis will bring you home to yourself now as you open up the essence of being human to yourself.

You are in wonder now as you open up to the new frequency Isis brings. She brings home to you a sense of your ability to really create in love through her essence.

Natural Magic
Isis now brings you to a space within yourself, which knows only one thing, as this is to serve the great principle of truth through her. She brings to you now this truth through the process of natural magic and the magic of the natural world, for nature is under the vibration of Isis.

All forces of nature and the natural world belong to me in the balancing and renewing aspect. The vibration I represent is one of real knowing and truth for what a human is capable of. For what you are capable of is to transcend the limitations of your human existence and take yourself to another dimension within yourself.

Isis teaches you that your journey in human form must be able to part the veil and take a peek at what is behind the illusion of "Being in a Human Form." Your duty to your Higher Self/Soul is to lift the veil off your self-imposed exile from your true self.

There are many such selves, and if you don't allow yourself to reveal yourself to your Higher Self/Soul self, you begin to experience disease, mental breakdown, addictions, and mass fear. Your cultures are experiencing this right now as you collectively journey to your truth through your heart.

Purification
You are undergoing a ritual purification when you begin to feel the Alchemies of Isis, the magician working through you. You are evoking me now in my purest form and you may receive shocks,

setbacks, and many other unpleasant events occurring in your life. These trials are part of the initiatory process, and must experience them to see me in my pure form. Isis will observe you through the process and guide you in a general way, but you will need to be vigilant with your emotions as you travel through this landscape.

Just now you must prepare yourself for the next dark moon to meet Isis in her pure unmanifested form. To do this you must ritually purify yourself by abstaining from stimulants, coffee, tea, sex, and polluted food for 12 hours prior to the ritual.

This ritual's intent is to allow yourself to travel to meet Isis in the void. I have met Isis in this void in the pyramid of Giza, where I was teaching a group of students. As we finished our hour in meditation and chanting in the pyramid the group departed, except for one student who had an operatic soprano voice. I invited her to stay with me, so I could hear her singing in the grand gallery.

The grand gallery is an extraordinary acoustic center. Sounds literally can be heard in a way I cannot describe. She sang for some time, an aria, and as she did so, I left my body where I travelled through the abyss and found my consciousness beholding Isis herself.

How did I know this was Isis? I just asked her. "Is that you Isis?" My consciousness received a quick reply. "Yes, I am Isis." She was in blue. There was no fear in this space, only complete dissolution of me as anything at all.

I communed with Isis, remarking on my need to stay in the space and never returning to Earth at all. (Despite my responsibilities to a group of students waiting outside of the pyramid, the guide and bus ready to return to the hotel.)
"Her" reply was short and succinct:
"You must return."
"Why?" I was begging Isis.
"Until you forgive every living thing."
I responded, "Every living thing, Isis?"
In my heart I knew the true nature of forgiveness at that moment.

"Every living thing." The interview was over. Isis had gone, and I was hurtled back into illusion on the cold granite floor of the grand gallery.

As a way of connecting with Isis, the words "Forgiveness of every living thing" became a mantra for me at that moment. It stays with me reminding me that release to nothingness brings peace and oneness with everything. For when we forgive every living thing, we become every living thing. When we become every living thing, we merge into the pure empty space of the void, where we dance with the spirit of absoluteness ready to return again to the vibration of form once again.

For the ritual of meeting Isis in the void you will need at least one hour of uninterrupted time on the Dark Moon. Go outside if possible, if not, stay inside in a dark space with no interruptions. Prepare your offerings to Isis, and leave the offerings in front of you on a tray. Offerings can include a flower, shell, incense, pure water, unpolluted food, or essential oil.

Dark Moon Ritual
Dear Isis my Mother,
Tonight on the Dark Moon I offer you the gift of myself to find your essence. Allow yourself to breathe deeply, powerfully and rhythmically. Really concentrate on the breath into your very being. All you are concerned with at this point is the breath. Continue breathing this way for four minutes to establish your link with your Higher Self.

When you feel completely peace filled, allow yourself to just feel the energy of a soft velvety black cloak around you. Immerse yourself in the folds of the cloak enveloping you in the texture of the material, its sensuousness and softness, reminding you of a baby's shawl. Now imagine you are a baby. You are out in the dark alone, but the soft texture of the shawl keeps you safe and protected. Really feel at this moment, you are safe and protected in your shawl, and no harm can come to you. Keep in mind; this shawl is your protection.

Anubis protects your soul on your journey to meet his Aunt Isis. His mother Nepthys is Isis's sister. Anubis is the jackal-headed God of Ancient Egypt; who is a protector of souls as they journey into the underworld. Anubis is also handy for more mundane matters as well like finding lost objects.

You will be in the presence of Isis energetically. If you constantly attune to her vibration and have a pure heart to "meet" her, you will feel a gentle presence of Isis herself at some point. If you don't experience anything tangible or real in your mind, do not concern yourself, for it is the intent to meet Isis and allow yourself the courage to be in her presence that brings you to her.

This is an important evolutionary step in your soul's journey and is allowing you to open your mind to the possibility of being in the presence of Isis the Mother.

Record your experience, in whatever form Isis appears to you and you will know you have begun an important new beginning in your journey, to self-realization.

If this ritual is conducted on the Dark Moon every month, you will establish a strong and vibrant relationship with Isis.

Bless and dismiss your guides and end this ritual. Ground yourself by eating something to earth the experience. Make sure the experience is earthed and your offering is left outside for Isis.

All the deities have this aspect, which must be encountered, and surrendered to at some point in your spiritual journey.

Recoding Cellular Memory

Right now you will allow the sacred essence of Isis to really be part of your totality energetically. You are opening up to the core identity you hold within yourself, and Isis is now part of this new identity. Because you have energetically travelled into the heart of your/our great mother herself, you are now going to really begin to feel your life change. Your cellular memory is being recoded to accept new frequencies that the Isis frequency brings. Isis will begin to restructure your DNA for emergence into the pure light and energy "she" represents.

Isis is spirit made manifest in human form. She is a deity of great compassion and pure intent for your journey, and "her" understanding of the human condition brings a depth and pure love for the human experience. Isis knows what it is like to be human. Isis knows the experience of humanness in a very real way.

Bringing this experience to your world now will add real meaning to being human. Allowing "her" this sacred role in your life brings now the essence of "All Love" to you as a way of being human. Bring now the essence of Isis to you now for you have met her in her home. You have travelled there to meet her. She will envelope you in her rich blue robe of protection.

Within the depth of your soul you know the energy of your newly emerging self, with Isis brings a new sense of ownership of yourself as a separate individual. You are now challenging core beliefs about your role as a human, as you are really opening up to the identity of your human hood, and why you chose to be a human.

For to be a human embodies the essence of Isis, and brings to you the power of Isis in her manifested form (to you). For Isis embraces you now and she develops your feminine identity. She gives you a blue print for the qualities she embodies.

Isis embodies the essence, the kernel of truth in your womanhood. She seeks to ask you for a definition of this. She seeks to have you really determine what you want from your core womanhood in all its aspects. As women we sometimes forget to call upon this power to really renew and rejuvenate our planet and ourselves and heal. We are responsible for balancing the relationship energy within ourselves. We have this energy within ourselves to grow and bring peace to our world. Our world is "your" world. You must be strong like Isis, to keep fighting for love. Always Isis teaches us to fight for love, and to never give up on love. This heart-centered love must be balanced.

CARMEL GLENANE

Balance this love and you will be opening up your heart to Isis. Isis cannot stay if love is not seeking to be balanced. Isis seeks to restore harmony in the heart and bring this love back. She is the true champion of love.

Restoration of Love

Isis evokes through your consciousness a sense of true peace and hope for your world, its people, and nature. Isis is the champion of restoration. Where you need to restore something, you are offering to give it a second life, a new chance, a new beginning.

This "new" beginning now, is allowing "you" to bring to your world this restoration of hope. Allow yourself now to mentally visit a bombed city. Feel and see the despair, there are people lost, hurt, dead. They are in limbo. The buildings are shattered, homes lost, nature destroyed. Birds don't sing. The trees cannot give nourishing prana to the community. Stench and decay abound.

Now imagine the energy flowing back to this community, through the Isis vibration. Try now to feel how this community will come alive again. Isis restores the feeling of hope again. She brings hope and love to the people, first so they can begin to awaken from their shock. You must begin now to really feel this hope inside you for restoration of harmony after loss. Always evoke Isis for restoration of hope after loss of any sort.

As Isis restores life to her dead husband Osiris, by patiently hunting for his lost parts, reassembling them and lovingly breathing new life into them, so you can embrace the challenge of living through the Isis frequency.

Living through the Isis frequency brings hope to you when you have lost something precious. You can begin to feel the resurrecting qualities of Isis; her work begins immediately after a shock or loss in any way. There will have been many times when you will have felt the shattering blow loss brings. This destruction must be acknowledged and felt.

I have lost my husband, my child, my friend, my parent, pet, property, etc. It is now gone, I cannot go on. I cannot restore myself alone, because it is too painful.

You must just feel this loss, and despair, even if it has been a long time ago. Grief goes on and on if the loss isn't acknowledged fully to yourself. You must unlock this pain and really let the contents of it spill out, just watch it all come out of your heart. Really pull it out, and now evoke Isis to fully help you release it, and restore your hope in loving again. You must surrender to the force of Isis to sweep away the pain so you can re-find your lost soul parts again.

Isis restores your lost soul parts, returns them to you so you can begin to hope again. This is the role of Isis as a deity. Quite simply, she brings your lost soul parts back again, so you can begin life anew. No matter how long ago the grief occurred, if there are lost soul parts, Isis will bring them home to you again.

Isis and Loss

To begin to locate the pain of lost love is part of the function of being human. You must feel the lost part and know the human experience is loss in love. Every human experiences it in some way. Every human lives through the agony of losing something precious. There is no escape. There is not a human who will survive being human without this loss.

All humans need resources for this pain, and you should acknowledge to yourself at some point that it will happen. For many reading this now, they will know this pain already. How does one prepare for loss when one is happy and feeling content?

You must acknowledge to yourself daily, that every moment is precious with another human being. Every second is precious. By holding onto the precious loving moments, you are remembering that the love is timeless and this love cannot be taken from you. You cannot have love taken away once it has been established as a way of being human.

Just now go into a relationship you have lost, and feel an emotion about it. You must just now allow yourself to connect to this emotion, and feel the loss. Do this now.

You must just now recreate all the loving moments; feel every wonderful moment, every single precious moment. When you can re-create these wonderful feelings, you have found the love, the beauty of love. This part can grow. Yes, I am going to take this love, this moment and cherish it. I am going to give it form. This becomes a symbol for all good things. Breathe the precious loving moments into your heart, and know you are able to cherish this lost part of yourself.

Love is Real

Isis brings now to your life the belief that love is a really attainable objective in your life. It is not an illusion, it is anything but illusion. All emotion that is not channeled to the heart is an illusion. Emotion not brought up to the heart becomes the greatest barrier to love, for it creates nothing but pain. When you are seeking to find love, you must do a heart reality check. This heart reality check goes like this, and can be used as an exercise in strengthening your capacity to love from the heart.

Begin to locate an emotional desire. I have an emotional desire for a person, holiday, object, etc. (painting, furniture, car, etc.) I think I feel it in my heart but I am not sure. I need to just stop and examine this emotion. Whatever you do, stop and examine the emotion at this point. Don't proceed any further until you have just located exactly "where" it is. If it has come from the heart you will receive (from your heart) the "go ahead." If not, you are feeding an emotion and playing back an old karmic pattern.

Check with your heart by asking, three times:
"In the name of love and light and in the name of my heart if I may be given the go ahead to proceed with this…"

You will receive a confirmation. If you are not sure, do the exercise again when you are less pressured by the emotion.

Your Higher Self as your Guide

By acknowledging your higher self every day, (sometimes more if you need to) you are allowing a part of yourself, "your soul," to be with you on your journey.

Imagine not bringing a guide with you when you are in a foreign country, which has no bearing on your previous existence. If you rely on your mind only, it will bring up past patterns, and act on old worn-out belief patterns. Open your eyes wide to the existence of a supernatural you. The real you, not the illusory one trapped here on Earth in a human body.

You are drawing to yourself now the belief in your ability to really allow the essence of all life to flow through you.

Your higher self has access to your soul's blue print and brings to your awareness opportunities and events beyond the mind's ability to even comprehend. You must nourish your selves in the expression and experience of "All Love" being at your service.

You are serving "love." There is not a loving mother or father who will not help a child who earnestly and lovingly wants something to forward their soul's pain.

Imagine yourself now a loving parent. You are sitting with your child, who is a gifted musician (or whatever). The teacher is saying your daughter/son has such talent. This gift must be nourished. She/he will be an internationally talented performer, etc. As the parent, you know your past patterning is yelling. "We cannot afford… the violin, or tuition, to go to university, etc." You have others in the family. What about them? The list goes on.

Then imagine the parent saying, "Yes I believe if my child really needs this, I will be provided with the resources to supply it." This is all you need to say. Release your need to excuse anything when your child, "your higher self" needs something important to fulfill their life on Earth.

Earth our Home

Earth supplies us with all we need for our journey, and to be on Earth is a special privilege. Earth as a space offers infinite possibilities wherever you live, whether it is in a snowy wasteland, boiling desert, or tropical rain forest. Why do you persist in destroying the very home that you must have to survive? When humans become separated from the source of "All Love" they begin to find fault in what they have created. They have no real control over the weather patterns, Earth faults. It is a dangerous paradise, when humans who are constantly striving to create something out of nature, which they think is better than nature itself. It is an inhuman act, for to be human is to live with nature not against nature. Isis abhors those who cannot love nature, and she will prevent the forces of evil destroying your world, if you give her an offering and salute her sacred elements and their quarters every day. Isis knows that without nature balanced in your world you cannot have the harmony needed for growth and balance in your world.

Being one: with nature is a sacred creation, an epiphany of spirit made matter. Isis is the mother of nature and the natural world. By really focusing on nature and its most essential role in your life, you are bringing yourself into alignment with your truth.

You are aligning to the forces of the natural world when you take in nourishing prana, hear the birds calling, attune to the ocean waves, listen to the wind rustling the tree branches and leaves. When you observe the symmetry of a tree, a flower, a leaf you are actually attuning to the forces of the natural world to heal and renew you.

By feeling this, and allowing it to take place in your life, you are Love, and Love pours into your heart. Isis will always stay where the forces of light through nature are worshiped. By worshiping nature, you are worshiping yourself, because it is through nature that you are in harmony with all of life.

Love is Born

Bringing forth a birth in love is Isis' message now. Love being born awakens in you now. You are on a special calling. You are on a special mission to create this love now. Birthing a new love can open you up unbelievably regardless of whether you are in a relationship or not.

If you are in a relationship, you can call upon a new aspect of this relationship to clear karmic debris, which may have accumulated and toxic thoughts, which may have build up over time. You are cleaning out old stored rubbish between you both and bringing in the new. Imagine you now getting a new room built on to your home for a new part of your relationship together. First, look at your old home (relationship) and give it a makeover.

Ask yourself this question:
"Where are we getting stale, what areas of our life need enhancing?"

See all old buried fears go, as you awaken to the great potential this new love with your partner/lover etc. will give you.

Why bother doing this? I am married; we have been together for years, etc. First, love gives more energy. It balances the hormonal function, it feeds the soul, and you begin to glow from the inside out. It makes you feel healthy, alive, and abundant. Love feeds the soul, so it is essential if you are in a relationship to do this love test regularly.

If you are reluctant to do this or it is distasteful, you are not willing to change. This puts you in danger of the relationship eroding and becoming diseased.

You have to answer. *"Yes"* or *"No."*
"Am I willing to clean out my old store house of emotions, grievances that build up over time and start on our new room? Or I can't be bothered?"

Assuming that now you have decided to create a new depth in your relationship, you can begin to construct your new identity in Love. It's like making room for a new baby coming into your life. You must really want the benefits, so outline them to yourself, and ask if this will serve your higher purpose together.

Sometimes a relationship has grown all it can and cannot cope with or want a new aspect. If this is so you must just accept this. Decide what you both want here. This is challenging, but we live in challenging times. Truth must win in everything and must be above your own ego, which wants satisfaction by staying in a stagnant relationship.

Let's be very clear about your intent here now. My intent is to enhance my relationship by creating a new aspect of love, embracing a new depth and meaning. I am now encoding my cellular memory to accept new frequencies in Love.

I am now allowing myself the experience to deepen my relationship to embrace a balanced heart-centered relationship, first with myself and with my partner.

This new love will bring us a sense of heart-centered balanced passion. We will feel alive, healthy, balanced in our hormonal function, with more energy and most importantly, this love, this passion will feed our souls, so we can truly be the miracles of creation we are meant to be.

This love is needed not only by yourselves, but also by your whole civilization. Everyone on the planet benefits through the love between couples. It elevates the whole consciousness of the planet and it releases the powerful love hormones out into others.

To create this new view of reality when you are single, is equally important, perhaps more so in some respect. A woman undergoing a life- transforming experience of loss in relationship or purification from old karmic addictions in love is at an important crossroad. She will need to examine her need for sex for security or desire, also her relationship patterns where she is being taken advantage of, betrayed by her own fear and need to feel safe with someone, who knows this fear and takes advantage of it.

An offering to Isis for this important new chapter in your life is required, and ideally you can begin this new ritual on the full moon. Give yourself one full month, from full moon to full moon to experience this new beginning in love.

You can call upon Isis to help you in all aspects of this emerging new identity in love. Affirm your human right to experience love in all its aspects, you deserve to have the best experience a human can embrace in love. It is your right to have this feeling, as it feeds your immortal soul, and brings you closer to your truth.

Once you have stated your intent, and are prepared to commit to it, you will offer Isis a gift. Purchase a spray mist of oils which Isis favors; rose, Egyptian essential oils, a scented candle (especially for her), or a daily flower. Offer it to her as a token of your commitment to receive this new vibration in love. Once you have established this intent, you are now on your way to create the love you need in your life to expand your view of love.

"You" the Magician
Isis is a magician. The essence of magical workings under Isis is to acknowledge to yourself that in this next exercise you are under Isis magical guidance.

Magical rituals can hold certain old fears in some of us. Religious, cultural, family, teachers, and friends from the past can contribute to fear of a magical ceremony. To bring something to you that the old you may still cling on to. First, it is important to rid yourself of this judgment of yourself as being a ceremonial magician under Isis and being called by "her" to create magic for love.

When you feel you have released all these old excuses for not bringing a new aspect of love to your life, (and have your own higher self involved in the exercise), you can only draw from the power you will receive through Isis. You deserve to follow your own spiritual path to find your truth and to know that love and truth go hand in hand. When you open up to embrace this new aspect of love, you are also embracing the essence of a truthful life.

Once you have "allowed" this aspect of your core identity to become manifested, you can begin to see yourself as a magician, and a magician under the guidance of Isis. This is an important new admission of your new identity. This new vibration can make you very tired and you must acknowledge this to yourself. You will find that people who were once important in your life are not interested in you, more importantly; you are not allowing yourself to be undermined by people who cannot embrace your new reality.

Astral Love Temple
You are beginning to open up a new aspect of love, a love, which embraces an additional element of freedom. Begin now to get ready for creating your astral love space with your "beloved." Intone his/her name, and the vibration of it before you settle into your routine for pre-sleep. Allow the vibration of this name to resonate in your heart. If you do not know the name, you can just intone "Horus" or my "High Priest" or a name, which has a vibration that feels loving. You breathe your intent into the ritual by stating your intent.

From this full moon to the next, I am allowing my heart to open to myself. I am allowing myself this new experience of love. Begin to play music that resonates with your intent. Bathe and anoint yourself ritualistically, knowing Isis the great magician is overseeing your creation, and will be with you.

After you have bathed and anointed yourself with essential oil, such as Black Musk, White Musk, Rose, etc. you now begin to allow yourself to feel the presence of your "beloved." Imagine you are joining hands. You place one palm down left and one palm up to receive, visualizing him there. Open your heart, feel it opening and draw an infinity symbol over your hearts. Breathing in 8 times in succession. You have established your link. As you rest in your sacred space, before sleeping you construct your temple of love by outlining every detail of the space. It may be a house on an island overlooking the ocean or a forest retreat, a desert landscape with a temple. You are constructing a magical temple to love. This magical temple has its own power now to reshape your new identity in love.

Describe to yourself now exactly what you are seeing. Where is this place? Locate the country and the region. Get as much detail as you possibly can to bring its essence to you. Really feel the atmosphere of what you want to create. Where is the sun? How is it placed on the Earth? Which element has the greatest impact? Getting as many details as possible brings you to a space of love for yourself.

Begin this journey now. Begin to really construct this space for your dream love space. This space is an all important sanctuary and retreat from your world. You need to feel now the presence of the house spirits, or guardians of this property, whether it is a house, temple, or whatever. Ask the guardians to keep you connected to the new aspect of love you are creating with your "mate." You need to feel the space begin to develop "atmosphere." This atmosphere is like a spider web, strong but gentle. It will begin to develop a palpable feel when you come in. Imagine an atmospheric environment, with soft music, candles, and incense. Create it paying particular attention to the elements and their quarters in the space. As you open up, you are feeling the essence of "All Love" envelope you and protect you.

You are now ready to construct your interior. It may be sparse or furnished in a style that pleases you and your "mate." Don't over clutter it. Keep it Zen-like, simple, pure, and loving. Find the house's heart, and offer a gift to the heart of the house. This heart is where you will build your temple to love and it will provide a special atmosphere all on its own. Feel that now. Make this space beautiful and comfortable with what you need to create the magic of love.

When your space has been constructed, you will begin to feel safe in this space and you can begin to lie on the bed or sofa or on the rugs and just get to know yourself in this new sacred love space.

It is your astral temple to love, and you have constructed it with your thoughts of love for your magical world. This is good. Allow this to be taking place now. There will be great barriers to you ever doing this at all. The journey into the heart of yourself creates fear and you must be courageous with yourself. Feel this now. Where are my blocks? Why am I even bothering to do this anyway? List your reasons for not allowing yourself the opportunity to bring to you this magical experience of love.

Endless Love

Mostly we fear abandonment when we are opening up to something new. You need to allow this special new relationship with yourself and love to envelope you so you can become one in your own essence. You are going deeper and deeper into your heart every time you explore your new relationship with yourself in this endless loving space.

For you right now, you must just allow this essence of your own love for yourself. To really allow the essence of all life to be one with you in this space.

Allow yourself now to merge with your power as you open up yourself to really contact that masculine self that will give you power energy and life force in your life. You need to really feel yourself embracing the space of your new astral temple to love, for whom you create with in this temple will be part of your life forever, at some level, as you have embraced love. So, it is a responsibility to yourself and to the energy of your soul mate that you are bringing this part of yourself into harmony with yourself.

When you begin to merge with this new aspect of yourself in a regular ritualistic way, you are opening up your world to multi-dimensionality, as a way of being human and you are abandoning yourself to this new view of your humanness. For your humanness becomes a plastic thing which can change its form. You are now opening up to the world of feeling this love, and your energy life force becomes one with your beloved.

You will begin to create endless possibilities together. You will begin to feel the power, essence, and spirit of the world of Bliss where "All Love" is.

When we take away the pain associated with love, we discover the true meaning and potential love gives us. You need now to merge into space and find the true joy of this love for yourself.

Truly trusting now yourself to explore this self brings endless rewards. It is safe to begin this journey for your soul's evolution right now, and you must feel now the joy of knowing whatever happens in your life with love, you have found this space of bliss and completeness. All is well in this world you have created and your magical world of your love temple brings you now to a space of forgiveness is a very important new aspect you are bringing to your reality right now.

Say to yourself:
"I forgive myself for my humanness. I will never self punish myself in the quest for this perfect love."

"I will now allow myself to not only forgive myself but every living thing for what I have put myself through in order to find love."

"I must now stop trying to believe in anything else but myself in love. I know by allowing myself this love this act of love for myself I am releasing my past completely, and I am acknowledging to myself I deserve to love."

The Universal Heart
"I am now bringing to my world this deservability, and I am now free to live completely through the essence of love. In doing this I feel free to take myself into the heart of myself and then I will become 'one' with the universal heart."

"The universal heart knows now to bring me to this space of forgiveness of myself in love. This space only knows one thing and this is truth for your journey. By exploring your power to love, and demanding to be shown how to get to the heart, you merge in oneness with all of life."

To begin this journey, it will require a complete review of every single thought you have ever had about love and what it means to you. You may like to explore your connection with yourself and love, and what messages you were given subliminally when growing up about love. Very few humans are really allowed to explore the full potential of love as a child and when growing to adulthood. Their views become stuck with the old model shown them, and they shape their lives believing it must be attached to one thing in particular, i.e. Love is marriage. You can only find love by being married, getting engaged, and so forth. All cultures regulate the loving between people to some degree, some more than others. Religions then tell you what they require to have, and a human who is needing to find their core identity through self-love, and through this self-love radiate out their own self-love to another; however, this view of love is not explored. It isn't until the psyche has been damaged, the core identity smashed that you can begin to discover why you are on the planet. You are here to learn to love. The strength of love brings you into alignment with your truth.

You must allow your core identity to be redefined in love, and you must allow this core identity to bring you now to a space of purity in all there is. Every human must fight hard for love, and the great Isis knows this is essential. Every thought must be directed toward this self, this pure loving self and nothing must stand in the way of this loving act toward the self. Allowing the space of purity and love to be around you now is an acknowledgement of your self worth, and you must bring only one thought to yourself every day. "How can I love myself enough to help another for his/her love too?" Believe in this treasure, your love allows you to really connect in truth for "All Love" is: You are love.

Forgive the Past

Isis speaks now of forgiveness.

The trust required to forgive yourself creates in you now hope. Hope that you can heal the wounds your old identity has created in you. All forgiveness is about the ability to be strong and trust that part of yourself which has been enslaved to your old self. For forgiveness now implies the very thing you need to let go of: The pitying self, the one that does not want to hear the past. Your past is the only thing you must consciously deliberately forgive every day, and this past is a child-like self-pitying one. When you develop yourself enough spiritually, you will begin to look forward to forgiving the past. The part of you that only knows one thing, the pure love of forgiveness. When you forgive yourself, you are engaged in the act of love, true love for yourself. You are prizing off the self-pitying me, the clinging, crying, abandoned child. You now need to bring this child into mergence with your core self. This is adulthood, and spiritual maturity.

Isis and Nature

The vibration of Isis is one of acknowledging that you have a special role in your world. This is to bring to yourself the ability to know that you and your world are one, and that the forces of the natural world will comply with your vibration. For when your vibration matches Isis's vibration you will be drawing to you the magical relationship with all those in the world who too are vibrating to this frequency. This includes all creatures in the world, plants and minerals, for the effects are ever encompassing. As the natural magician I am, I embrace the vibration of the Earth's energies and use them for my magical work. The world of nature is my domain and is at my command.

I can command the forces of nature to assist me in my work for my own being, my love, and the ability to restore love to its rightful place after losses; i.e. relationship losses. I use the forces of the natural world to do this; I employ these elements and their vibrations. I command their very essence to assist me.

Why can I do this? I can do this because I am naturally one with them and respect them and they in turn are one with me and respect me.

For me the water element is the best receptor for my energy work because the water element holds the key to all life. When humans begin to discover the power of water and how it can change the molecular structure in the body, they will respect its force and power to change consciousness, heal, and renew.

Bringing the power of the water element to your consciousness allows the sacred essence of all life to be one with you. There is a knowing that you and the water element create together in love for all there is. Believing in the sacred essence of water to heal, renew, and restore allows the Alchemy of Isis to bring you all you need for your life. Water changes everything. Its magical power heals and renews. Your relationship with water brings you into resonance with all of life.

The essence of this sacred special element is under my protection and guidance. The essence of this sacred element binds you to your earth in a most extraordinary way. It allows the truth of all life to be revealed to you, and it brings you home safely to yourself when you are releasing the past.

A water exercise goes like this:
I allow the sacred waters of life through the Goddess Isis to bring me to a space of renewal, peace, and love in all of life. Water can be used as a ritual of purification. Water releases emotion. It shifts stuck emotion, and brings the essence of all life home to you. Allow the sacred essence of water to be used as a purification ritual every day for clearing out stagnant, stuck energy in your emotional body.

Water is the shape shifter. It changes consciousness and brings you to a space of truth for all there is. It is time now to always remember the clearing, restorative, and renewing properties of water by allowing yourself to connect to its truth through acknowledging the Goddess Isis. Her home in Egypt is surrounded by water. Bring the healing powers of water to your life to heal and renew.

Trust

Isis is now feeling your devotion to her growing, and she will now offer you the gift of illuminated truth. For the gift of illumination brings to your world the pure delight in knowing that the world and its energies, its sacred quarters, and elements support your journey. This is a magical time to just feel the presence, light, and power of Isis all around you. You are now allowing the sacred pure energy of Isis to become one with you, for when you begin to feel this love and power you are coming home to yourself.

The essence of Isis lives through the heart of "All Love", and she now allows the spark of "All Love" to become one with you now. Isis is just going to pour her grace on to you now as you feel and become one with her magical essence. The magical essence of Isis is bringing home to you your power to heal, renew, and find peace and power.

Isis finds in you, trust in this magical process of what she is bestowing on you now. For Isis now offers you her gift of trust in her as a force to heal you and bring love to your pained soul. You are now receiving the Alchemies of Isis through this trust and she is conferring on you this trust.

Say to yourself now:
"I lovingly trust the mother Isis to bring me the ability to trust her, to show me what she can bring me now in my life."

Ask yourself now:
"What do I need right now?"

I need love, and the ability to know that I can trust Isis to bring me this love. I must trust Isis to give me this gift of love, and I must now allow this gift of love to be mine. You must feel the sacred trust of Isis envelope you now, and bring you home safely.

Trusting in Isis is trusting in the flow of life to bring you all you need for your life right now. To trust in the essence of all life is to trust in Isis herself, for she is the Great Mother. Isis the Great Mother is the greatest river, the most mighty and powerful. Fill up your heart with her river, the Nile. The great Nile has the energy of Isis encoded in it, and the Nile is like a soothing balm caressing your tired and weary spirit. The Nile heals and renews, and you are reminded of the power of the Nile as she courses her way through your life, bringing to your life, the rich, luxurious release from pain and abandonment. Bringing to your life now is a need for this release.

You are attuning to all the rivers, oceans, and lakes. All water formed on the Earth's surface brings to you now the need to really trust that you are safe and not abandoned. Isis is all this and so much more. To allow yourself to experience this is thrill seeking because it takes you to a new view of your reality where the total self can be given a gift. This gift is knowing that you have surrendered and trusted the Great Mother herself. The Great Isis.

For now just breathe into your total self, trust and surrender, and know that "you" and the Great Mother are one, truly one in this trust and surrender. This is your birthright, and your truth and comes before everything else. I now allow the true beauty of surrender to Isis to bring me all I need for my life. I am life.

Mergence

Simply by being attuned to the energy of Isis brings to you now, the total trust and mergence surrender brings. This mergence allows for the spirit of oneness to be made manifest in you, so you are complying with only one reality and this is the reality of pure peace in the mysteries. By being in this mergence now, you are allowing the sacred essence of which you are to bring you to a space of knowing. This knowing allows the trust of yourself to grow and bring you all you need for your life. I am in trust and oneness with myself now, because through Isis, the Great Mother, I am allowing the sacred alchemy of who I am envelope me. I am in a space of purity for this knowing, and it and I are one. We together "share" in the circle of safety that the vibration of Isis brings.

For my circle of safety now I invite all those who wish to partake in a ceremony of self-love. Why do I create a reality, which does not support this identity, and this new mergence? What am I to do to bring this new reality about? For me now to embrace this new reality I must lovingly surrender my fear of myself. For it is "me" that I am most fearful of, and it is "me" that I must fight every day. Every day I must fight the aspect of myself that won't allow me to feel peace, filled, and loved. I gather a circle around me now, and draw the people to me who want to share in the celebration of my mystery. For I am the celebration, when I lovingly allow myself the mystery. The mystery of myself lies in this powerful space within my heart.

Right now gather your circle of people around you who want to share in the celebration of your heart. It is important that they must truly be "there" for you.

Do this now:
Gather friends, loved family, colleagues, Isis, and all those who have ever loved you from the heart to share in the mystery of your heart. The mystery of your heart is your passport to your truth, and you must surrender to this truth. Feel this love now from everyone who has this love for you.

Isis now brings down the message of hope for your world today. For today is the beginning of your new mergence to truth. This is the time to feel this mergence and flow with it. The mergence is an acknowledgement that you are flowing with the gift of yourself and this "self" now needs acknowledgement that "you" are beginning to feel the power and change truth brings. Truth is a refreshing thing. A truth-filled person is just so delightful to be around, and truth makes you feel safe. It takes enormous courage to be truthful, so to be truthful is an act of courage. Breathe the feeling of courage to you now, as the vibration of truth surrounds you. Your message is one of truth. Isis's message to you is to obey the law of truth. For the truth-filled woman is courageous. To be courageous is to be truth filled.

Isis Gifts You with Her Story

My story is the story of all women who love. My story begins with the myth of Isis and Osiris. The legend surrounding my need to resurrect my husband from the cruelty and betrayal he was exposed to. A dead man cannot resurrect himself. It takes a woman to resurrect a dead man, and bring him to life again. My story is the story of grief. Grief whose outlet is one of hope, that love, which is timeless, can re-assemble in a new form. For if you truly love someone, the love is timeless and can be re-assembled again and again. Never give up on love. Love is not to be possessed or held on to. It is to be returned to its space of purity, held there, and then reformed again. If you truly love, and have "lost" a loved one, you are resurrecting him by honoring the love you had, and can use again and again. Its just love. Love is the essence binding the cosmos. The infinite oneness of who and what "we" are.

Love is my story. Resurrect your lost 14 parts now, as you search for your lost soul bits. Find them, wherever they may be in the world, in the solar system and beyond. Find them; impregnate yourself with my love, and you, like my husband Osiris will be reborn again. Horus our son is the divine flame, the union of our uniting. Your 14 soul bits are now being united into one whole.

You need now to assemble yourself, knowing I; the Mother Isis waits patiently, grieves, and hunts for your soul bits and performs my magic to return "you" home to me. We become one and bring the flame of our love to heal the world.

The precious gift of Isis is in the magical intent of who you are, and the magical intent of what you are becoming at any moment. You must be open to the gift of knowing who you are at any moment and share this gift with all you meet. You must just feel the precious gift of magic bring you all good things as I allow your spirit to bring you the knowing that you are capable of the truth within you. For you are the holder of the key to the mystery and it is the key of the mystery inside you that unfolds around you and brings you all you need to love.

Your love must be pure and truthful in your enfoldment, right now, as you allow your precious gift of "All Love" to be your guide. The message of truth brings to you the energy of all truth to any living situation. You are exposing yourself to the living essence of a Devi (a Goddess) in me, and this living proof of who I am, reinforces all aspects of your being. Allowing your love and truth to be your guide reinforces the frequency of Isis in your cellular memory. You are one in this essence and truth now as you expose and explore your identity to your truth.

Your love for yourself must go beyond time and truth to bring you all you need for your life of love for the mystery. Bring now to your cellular memory the absolute knowing that you and all those you love benefit from the message of truth and trust that Isis brings. Breathe in now this energy, and do not be afraid of exploring this sacred aspect of yourself.

Forgiveness

Isis loves your belief in forgiveness of yourself right now and she is showing you that any relationship that is out of balance with another is one of "you," your forgiveness of yourself. This is the hardest and most hurtful thing you must face about an unbalanced relationship in you, with them. Vainly we seek to find this by not addressing the absolute core essence in ourselves. "What did I do to cause this? Why have I unconsciously drawn this to me?" Yes, ouch, it really hurts. Yes, me, I am suffering because I have drawn to me something in this person I have created.

Now you must just stop and face this. Just stop, get out of your environment, your comfort zone, and really examine "you." OK, I accept that I must have done something to bring this imbalance about. I don't have to know exactly what it is; I just have to accept that it is me that is the problem. This is my problem, every single particle, and every single thought.

Breathe deeply, powerfully, and lovingly to yourself. Breathe me in, the Isis blue ray and feel me deep in your cellular memory, burning the blue light of my illumination on to yourself, the part of you that must forgive this past pattern that has created the imbalance.

It is safe and important to do this, and a truly creative, self-loving person will acknowledge that they need to forgive themselves. Allow yourself this forgiveness now. You truly deserve the belief in what you create at any moment brings you to a space of renewal and peace for your life right now. You are now just seeing how magical and powerful your new identity is becoming with me. This identity is beginning to shape your view of yourself and your new world is opening up unbelievably. You are now beginning to just find the essence and power of your new identity merge in oneness with all of life. Your identity is shaping itself around you, remolding you, and you will appear to others to be different, more detached and less vulnerable emotionally. You need to feel this view of yourself, this new reality begin to take form, and you will allow the essence of who "you" are, bring to you all you need for your world of true love and passion.

You are bringing home to yourself your belief in love as a way of being human, and you are now just allowing this special love to envelope you, and bring you all you need for your magical world of absolute wonder in your own ability to feel and connect to all there is.

Magical Happenings
Allow yourself this day to count up all the magical happenings. You begin by evoking Isis to make all the magic happen. Just do this now.

"I evoke you Isis to make my life one of magic and renewal. I ask you to bring your state of pure magic to me now, so I can just see and be a witness to your presence every day."

"I ask you my dear Isis to allow me your gift of seeing your presence everywhere in my day, and before I go to sleep tonight, I will count up all the magical happenings in my day. So be it. In love and light for my journey now."

Isis believes that in you now, you will begin to forward your truth with me by allowing the special occurrences throughout your day to bring you one step closer to knowing who you are and what you are capable of. By noting the magical occurrences every day, you strengthen your commitment to having me in your life and this will bring you closer to who "you" truly are. The essence of who you are lies in the mystery, the mystery of "All Love" as a way of being human. This is a magical and exciting time for you now, as your human possibilities are endless. You must share in these endless possibilities with me every moment you can to forward your journey in being human.

Forward your identity now, by allowing yourself the joy and magic truth brings. Bringing the world of endless possibilities lies within your reach now, you only have to step into a new dimension; a new reality and you are there.

You must now prepare yourself for this exercise:

Breathe deeply, powerfully, and rhythmically several times to maintain your link with your higher self. You begin to allow yourself the magical intent the breathing brings.

Breathe in deeply, powerfully, rhythmically 8 times, in the method outlined earlier in this book.

Now imagine visiting a sacred space — one you love.

Stay still and imagine now it is a doorway to another dimension. Hold the energy for this intent and just imagine you are entering into another realm, one beyond your previously held definition of what your current reality is.

Take yourself into a space of pure love for your new self as you allow yourself to connect to this new reality, this new belief about yourself. Right now you are opening up to the essence of "All Love" as you transport yourself to a new way of viewing your humanness. Believing in your ability to really connect in truth for all there is only reinforces the love and purity of your life.

This is a time to allow the sacred essence of who you are to open you to the world of endless possibilities. The world of endless possibilities makes you one in essence with all of life, and all of life now respects and supports your journey. Breathe in this sacred essence to bring you back into resonance with all of love and who you are. You are now allowing your truth to merge into oneness with all of life, and all of life respects and supports your journey. You are now carrying the sacred flame to your new identity. A shared sacred one of absolute wonder, in all of life, for all you are and shall become.

The Quickening

Isis brings all this to you and more. I know as you develop your relationship with me, you are beginning to change. Your whole physicality will begin to transform, and you will feel that you are capable of feeling absolute love for yourself. You are beginning to merge with this new identity and you are shaping yourself through it now.

Whilst Isis is opening you up to your potential, you are listening to a voice inside you that you must allow yourself to listen to. This is the inner self that is calling you to begin to awaken to your potential. Allowing this essence to become part of you, brings to your world your ability to really know you are part of the essence of everything. Your ability to be able to create this essence in yourself brings you to a point of just connecting to the essence of yourself.

Your "self" is the vibration of the quickening of your "self" and your planet. It can be heard and felt all around you, and one of the symptoms of the quickening is the feeling of releasing old emotional pain in your energy matrix. Old emotional pain will be surfacing very quickly as you bring to your world your ability to really allow the essence of who you are to grow.

You must feel a connection with old emotional pain as it surfaces. You must just go into the pain, and feel it, and in this feeling, you must allow the precious gift of yourself to emerge. Why? You are restoring a broken part of your life. Look at your life now, as being like a house, one part has been badly damaged, i.e. a door, room, rooms, or half the house. Which part of your emotional life is broken?

Does it feel like half the house or just the door? Whatever it is, just see it as now being torn open, then repaired. Your repair work must begin on this emotional pain now.

To be able to recognize when your old emotional patterning is creating disorder and chaos in your life, leaves you open to experience your life through a new lens.

It is important that you begin the process, as soon as you find yourself disconnected from your true purpose. Your true purpose is to serve your own heart and to be in alignment with your heart. When you are disconnected, you begin to fragment. It's rather like watching a space shuttle lose its extensions. You are not really whole. Just consider the house again. What parts are really damaged? Listen to yourself. Look and examine exactly why you didn't want to acknowledge that "the door was falling off," "the leak was coming down from the ceiling rotting your walls," etc. You remember looking, you knew what was happening.

Ask yourself:
"Why was I not 'present' when all of this was going on?"

Ask yourself again and again and again until you have the answer. Stay still and peaceful in this moment. Don't, under any circumstances, blame or punish yourself, but simply write down to yourself exactly how you were feeling at that time. Yes, I remember. I know what was happening, but I didn't give myself enough time to explore all options, my financial state wouldn't allow it, I felt if I left the person at the time I wouldn't cope, etc. Just be brave and honest and you will find the answers.

Isis brings tranquility to your raw emotional state when you are processing such savage emotions around your past. You know at some level you allowed such a thing to happen, and yet you were unable to do anything at the time. You are punishing the part of yourself that was split off, disconnected; it just couldn't see the other options at the time.

You may have been under powerful psychic attack that you may not have been aware of, and you may not have even known this evil around you could have been systematically robbing you of your light. These feelings will surface from time to time when you begin to examine your past. Say, for example, you were a child who was attacked psychically and physically by a family member who was evil. You, as a child couldn't do very much, because the force of evil was too strong around you.

You must stop and say:

"I know what has happened. That person didn't have the knowledge I have now. I know I was that person, but I am not her/him now. I know I was under the influence of great evil because I was vulnerable physically, emotionally, and my will to change wasn't strong at that time."

You must accept and surrender and give yourself heaps of love for this trauma and say:

"May the Mother Isis heal this wound and allow me to be fully integrated. So be it."

And you will never revisit that past again. It is finished.

Believing in your own ability to change creates a new sense of power and respect; you will have for yourself, as you allow this old forgotten past to be reactivated. Most people are afraid to activate pain that has been around for a long time and will just not "go there." If this is you, you must just examine why you cannot give yourself enough love to do this. For when you do, you are demonstrating an act of love for yourself.

Just say, for example, you have known deep down that you have been seriously wounded and it is affecting your capacity to love right now. You can establish a time and place to deal with it.

You can say:

"Tonight on the New Moon I am going to allow myself to heal this wound through my own power to love myself, and through the power of Isis herself."

This intent sets up a charge that will activate the cellular memory for the time, i.e. the New Moon, you have set aside to process this pain. All those lost components will begin to be activated right away, and you will have a database of stored memory parts that will be able to fully engage in the healing process.

Give yourself half an hour to do this, give an offering making your intent clear.

"In the name of love and light and in the name of my absolute divine truth, may I be shown…(my poverty consciousness, my fear of receiving love, my ongoing self abuse, etc.)"

When you have allowed space and time for this healing to take place, you will begin to integrate lost soul parts, making your life peace filled, light filled, and LOVE filled.

Bringing the Heart to Love

Right now you are allowing the secret sacred presence of "All Love" to bring you all you need in your life. For you are now beginning to witness yourself in your uniqueness. Just imagine now you are discovering a secret saved part of yourself that is just beginning to flower.

Do not at this important time in your evolution shrink from the duty you must give yourself. Your first duty is to your ever-opening, ever-swelling heart. Look and examine your heart's needs every day. What does your heart need right now? Really go to the part of yourself that asks this question every chance you can get. Right now my heart/my "self" needs to know that it has a place in my life, and that it isn't ignored or dismissed as being unimportant. This is most important right now.

You are beginning to really locate the essence of your believability in yourself to really enjoy and appreciate all aspects of being human. Why? Because you are attending to the precious gift of your heart's needs.

Always intone: *"What do you want, heart?"*

Always listen to the answer. Your heart speaks truth and your heart is the beginning of your immortal life. Everything in life must stand still, and listen to the gift of your heart. You are opening now a doorway to a part of yourself that you cannot ignore any longer.

Living through the Heart

Isis reveals to you now the joy in living through the heart. For when you live through the heart you are allowing yourself to be heard and in hearing yourself, you are awakening your dormant spirit. This dormant spirit is now allowing you to bring peace, space, and truth to your life. All of life creates through the hearing of something. When you hear with love, you are awakening to the beauty of how sound can heal, inspire, and create with you.

Our hearing is for the joy of sound. Our ears hear to uplift the spirit and expand consciousness. Allow yourself now to attune to something in your environment. You are hearing the sound of rain. Really hear the rain. What is the sound of rain like to you? Breathe in the sense of sound in everything. Hear the sound of a bird calling. Hear the sound of the sea, the crashing of the waves or the gentle lull of the waves. Hear the sound of music, the trumpet, violins, and drums. When you attune to the sound of life you are sharing in the rich tapestry of being human. You are allowing yourself to begin to allow the journey of the heart to begin.

List now, three positive, loving things someone/something said to you today. If you didn't hear these sounds, maybe you aren't receptive yet. Just be uplifted by the sounds of those you love. Give compliments freely so others can hear you too. This way your environment is multiplied by sounds, which will uplift the soul and will not be vulnerable to despair, loss, and grief.

Bringing to your world now is a clear identification with your need to have completely and wholly, whatever definition you have had on love.

When this happens you can now assume that the previously held belief is being challenged.

This challenge is to examine and bring to focus your commitment to find the love in everything. To find the love in everything is to spread your energy, life force, and truth in one direction, to embrace the new world of love you are being offered.

But, I am happy. I love my mate. Yes, you are happy, but could you not allow yourself to turn the temperature up? Could you not say, *"This is going to a purer space."*

When you allow a purer aspect of love to enter your consciousness, and filter out all the old fears about challenging this part of yourself, you are allowing the essence, the purity of love to bring you home to yourself. You as a human have every right to want the very best love offers.

Set yourself goals, tasks to bring this about, by observing yourself and saying.

"I choose to really bring 'love' to this relationship. I choose to really bring to my life a new relationship with myself, and I choose to bring to my world, this trust and confidence in what I am achieving in my life right now."

What you need, right now, is the belief in the ability to really run your life through the love lens. Asking yourself daily: *"Is this the very best on offer?"* You can then really examine your relationship with love when you say this: "Is this the very best on offer?"

Receiving Love
Love offers for you now the opportunity to really allow yourself love, truth, and beauty. Love offers, when you are on the path of truth, absolute honesty and belief in what you are capable of as a human. Every day ask:

"Love, dear love, show me what you can offer me today. Show me how I can receive from you. Show me how I can even believe that such a wonderful thing exists."

You must expect to feel now that you are open to experiencing this level of love. You must desire to find this love in everything, every leaf, every flower, all love and all truth. The essence of what you are looking for lies in your capacity to receive love.

Your capacity to receive love depends on your ability to hold the vibration of love, and never give up in your belief to challenge yourself to know that love is the almighty well where thirsty humans can draw inspiration and strength to keep going.

You are allowing the spirit of this love to really radiate out when you drink from the well of love. Just allowing yourself to experience this life- changing energy brings to you now all you need for your life of truth.

Ask yourself every day to be shown how you can drink from the well of love and when you can begin to really allow the essence of this love, this passion, and this depth to allow you the gift of freedom, for love brings freedom.

Love brings freedom to explore your totality. Love brings truth to bring you home to yourself. Love brings to your heart the knowledge that you can really create with the mystery. All of love is a call to really bring to your world the essence of your heart's truth.

You are just feeling the flow of it now, as you embrace a part of yourself that knows it any way. You are embracing love when you bring the essence of truth to your world, and you are embracing love when you simply stop and be still and allow the endless tide of "All Love" to bring you home to yourself. Your earthly existence must embrace "All Love" as a way of being human. Being human is an undertaking to love.

It is a physical requirement for your contract on this planet. You have an obligation and duty to yourself to find the space within your totality to find this contract.

Do this now:
This is the contract I signed when I (in my Bliss-filled totality) decided to incarnate. Why did I do this when I was not human, but pure consciousness and a divine being?

I must ask myself this very important question: What is it in me that said; "You are going to Earth with its beauty and terror to experience something through a human existence that you want to from this space." This is the challenge you set yourself then, in that moment. You must now embrace this challenge and seek to address your own need to really find within yourself now.

Plugging in to the Earth

Your life is determined by your capacity to set your heart free and live through it completely. You are feeling the need to really contact that part of yourself which knows this truth and live it. For when you set your heart free from its prison of limiting beliefs, you ar embracing the world as a human who is fully plugged into the Earth. You need to allow yourself to be fully plugged in now, as you embrace your fully realized humanness.

Plugging in means literally "plug in." Visualize yourself plugging into the Earth, every day. Visualize the plug of yours going down into the core of the Earth. Feel it getting through all the dross and finally anchored into the core of the Earth.

Do this now. When you are plugged in, you can create all you need, because you are fully present to your potential. By breathing deeply, powerfully, and rhythmically, you are bringing yourself to a space of pure love for yourself, and you are able to just know that you are able to find in your life the source of permanent and magical power. Just stay plugged in. When you feel disconnected, the plug has been removed.

So all you do is, begin the process again. I am plugged in. I am safe. I breathe the energy of the Earth into me now, and I allow this energy to give me back all I need for my life. I am open to the essence of all life when I am plugged in.

Observing Emotions

The journey you are on right now brings you to a space of absolute bliss if you allow yourself to begin to observe your emotions. For when you observe all around you, you are creating in wonder, all that you are capable of emotionally allowing. You are just feeling the flow and essence of all life create with you as you open up your heart to all there is. You are now, bringing to this new view of yourself the sense of absolute wonder for all there is. You are now feeling the need to allow this essence and wonder to permeate your very being.

Feel this now: You are walking on a road alone. You are beginning to feel the awareness of all around you, and you are also allowing this awareness to be part of you now. You are surrendering your previously held belief about what and who you are, as you open up to this totality.

This new view of yourself just brings you to a state of awareness of all there is around you and now you can partake in this new spectacle. You are dissolving into the energies of the space you are in and you are beginning to allow yourself to let go, to the experience of knowing "you" can do anything. For when you are in this consciousness you are truly embracing a view of yourself that knows who you really are, and you will begin to feel and see all that you need for your life.

You are partaking in the spectacle of your completeness and you are beginning to just open and flow with the potential of who "you" are. Allowing the precious gift of who you are reveals to you now your own trust in yourself to keep acknowledging that you are delving into a part of you that must grow.

This magical essence keeps growing every time you intone that you are allowed to love, and that love, as a way of being human, brings you to the space of trust for yourself in all there is. This is a time now for this remembering.

Why now? Why are you now just beginning to remember who "you" are? Why are "you" just now opening up to the essence of this remembering? You are remembering to allow yourself the precious gift of love. The precious alchemy of love is all you need to remember.

You must feel this essence of love in you now as you open up to the mystery. You must just feel the power of this remembering. Bring this remembering to you now by asking if you are able to really cleanse out all the disused filth your heart has been exposed to in being human. When you do this you are beginning to allow this remembering to take place and you will begin to feel where and how you can begin to change your life direction. This is a time to just feel the remembering and love it, and in doing so, you are allowing yourself to come home to a part of yourself that knows this anyway. For in remembering we trust in unseen forces to guide us, and in remembering we go to a new part of ourselves to begin our journey again.

Space to Trust

The energy, essence, and love of you for you now create a space of trust for all there is. You must just feel the energy and joy of allowing this trust to grow and bring you to a space of abundance in your heart. There is an abundant heart in every act you lovingly give to another person. Every act of abundance in giving creates a space for receiving. But...but...but... Stop... Why do you not receive, when you give? It's a universal law, and a very important one to STOP to receive.

Ask yourself each day:
"What did I receive today?"
"What did I actually get from this day today?"

List exactly what you did receive. Then allow yourself to go to the space of trust in receiving. Just STOP and receive from the essence of all life. The essence of all life is in the receiving. The receiving of your life brings you to a space of love for your truth. You are love. Bring the giving back to you now so you can receive all you need for your journey. You are love. To allow yourself the gift of receiving is acknowledging your worth, you are feeling this worth everywhere the gift of allowing yourself to receive takes you to a new space within yourself, as you truly begin to allow the essence energy and love to surround you.

Do a checklist now: How were you shown how to receive as a child? Were you considered selfish or lazy for receiving? How did your mother receive?

What is your attitude to anyone who says?
"You must stop and give to yourself first?"

These patterns will leave a permanent mark on your aura, and you must not be taken advantage of in giving. Women must just slow down the cycle of giving, as it is perpetuating an old model of relating to the world.

You must just feel now what it is like to receive and you must remember that when you receive, the equation is balanced, and you are going to be able to give more. It is very simple to be able to do this when you spend time in examining what it is you must do to receive.

Isis Magic

Right now Isis makes her special magic available to you. You will be bathed in the radiance of Isis all day so wear opals, Moon Stones or any incandescent milky stones. For the purity of your heart to love you must just surrender to Isis magical power right now as "you" open up to "her" mysteries. Her mysteries bring truth and an open heart to love. You must feel the fire inside you ignite now. Do this now. Open your heart wide, and now just lovingly feel the fire inside you. Feel the love of the fire inside your heart grow and open up to the collective heart of flame. Visualize a heart, burning with love. See it now. Touch it. How does it feel as it sears old pain and lost remembering in love? Allow this flame to burn brightly around your heart all day, and allow the essence of flame to ignite your power, your latent power, to cleanse, burn, and renew your capacity to love.

Your capacity to love is determined by two things only. These two things are to believe in the magic of love to give you everything, absolutely everything your true heart requires for the journey in being human. The journey in being human carries a cross, the cross of pain, knowing "you" the human must carry this heavy load, until you find enough light in your own heart to illuminate your way. Your cross must be burned away now. Feel this material. Is it wood? Iron? Rope? Plastic? When you feel it, try imagining its weight; release it with your newly created burning heart. Try this, and breathe love into the flames to keep them from burning down to coals or even die out. Keep your flame alive. Bring the flames up to strong radiating power and energy, to keep your "love" alive.

Allowing the special magic of "All Love" to infuse your cellular memory brings you alive to your potential. You must just allow the sacred essence of who you are to bring you to a space of truth for the mystery of yourself. You are allowing the sacred essence of yourself to infuse every cell and membrane. Just bring this sweet sacred essence to your very being right now by allowing space to be you. How often do you really give yourself space to be "you?" Allow this time now to adjust your frequency to just listen to your own fears. Your own fears are your very best friend right now because they are pointing you to your growth. You must really listen to your fears and embrace their message. For the fear has a very important message. What is your fear telling you right now? Listen to all aspects of your fear as you embrace it. See yourself like a frightened child. Really examine your fear around love, success, and your ability to create magic all around you.

Your fear becomes you friend because it liberates you from the prison of limiting beliefs. Your fear guides you to find a solution in your broken DNA. OK so I have something missing in my "self" here. What is it? Your fear is not to be feared. For when it is feared you become a victim of yourself. You become lost to yourself, so, for now, bring your fear to the surface, embrace it, so it can be transmuted giving you power over the limited mind.

Just Being

Allowing the special magic Isis offers brings to you now all you need to love. For Isis is the guardian of the word LOVE for humans. As a human being, Isis protects the beingness of you now. Your being is just that. Be in you! Be in the magic of yourself. Watch those around you. Who is in this magic of be-ing-ness? This aliveness to be. You become "you." Your life now allows this to happen, because you have opened your heart to yourself. When you open your heart to yourself you are in a state of aliveness for all there is. This space of aliveness for all there is, brings you to a state of magical mystery for all there is. You are one in the essence with all of love when you open your heart to the mystery of your be-ing-ness.

Isis honors your commitment to your truth and she is here to bring you into resonance with your love of the human "you" are. You are the human you choose to be because of your special magical relationship with Isis. You must surrender to the essence of "All Love" in its purest form for this be-ing-ness to take place.

Declare: *"I am a human be-ing, and I am alive to my be-ing-ness now."*

Peace

Isis brings the feeling of absolute peace in all that you are trying to achieve in your world right now. This peace has at its core a gentle flowing energy and you must now allow yourself to begin to open the gateway and bring yourself into a space where you can really allow yourself to create with this essence. You need to visualize the essence of yourself bringing yourself home to the essence of the Mother Isis. You need to keep yourself open to allowing yourself truth in the creation process and live through the creative principle that is to really examine your core beliefs about what you really want for your life. You must feel this essence energy and life force move through you and create with you the magical fire Isis represents.

You must now just feel the flame of love for yourself grow, you must allow this flame of love to ignite all there is in your world. You are addressing core issues around your own belief in your world to bring you all you need for your life right now. Bring this core essence to your life right now and allow this core essence to merge in oneness with all there is. You are one in this magical essence now: You are LOVE. You are now just allowing this magical essence with Isis to bring you now all you need for your world. This is a peace-filled heart.

Universal Consciousness

This time right now in your evolutionary life brings you into resonance with all there is. While you may not be feeling particularly different in your everyday reality, you are in a new powerful energetic shift. This is a universal paradigm shift in the evolutionary consciousness right now. You are now able to bring the essence of this amazing cycle into resonance with your truth. Just reflecting on this concept right now, brings you in resonance with a new sense of peace and power in your life. By allowing yourself to really embrace this new state of being just creates in you peace when you are finding a way around your new reality. You are now being re-coded for this new way of being now. If you feel the pulse of the universe resonating with your intent, you are now responding to the new way of being human.

Try now to imagine feeling the pulse of universal loving consciousness responding to your intent for your higher good.

Ask yourself:
"What is my intent right now? What do I need to do to create a new reality? Am I ready to allow myself the power and joy this new way of being human allows? Is it possible to allow the new way of being human to permeate your very being?"

Your world is now changing. There is no past and no tomorrow. Just now. Just the precious alchemy of the now, which will give you all you need for your journey.

Every day you are being presented with opportunities, which will never come your way again. Just one fleeting moment in time can change your whole life. You must feel the essence of "All Love" around you for all you need in your life right now.

Allow the universality of all life to be around you now as you open up to the heart of yourself as you bring to your world this gift of love for yourself. Universality is a term being encoded on your cellular memory right now, and you need to feel this "universality" bringing you to a new state of consciousness or awareness of just who "you" are. Right now the essence of universality is being encoded on you, as you open up to your part in the big picture. The big picture brings you now into a space within yourself, which knows this truth.

Why, you may ask, am I being encoded for universality? Universality is bringing you strength, and is allowing you to tap into your innate wisdom. This sense of wisdom is now allowing you to really bring to your world the sense of oneness in all of life.

All of life is resonating to your call to bring truth home to you. All of life is responding to your call for universality. The essence of universality brings you back to the beginning, back to where you once belonged. You are just feeling this essence right now, as you allow the sense of true worth to encode you with its message of love.

Right now the feeling of freedom, the feeling of oneness, trust, and hope brings you back to your center. Your center is your universality, in the center of yourself, you are universal. The coding's for this are being placed in your cellular memory right now. The coding's are now opening you to create with the sense of oneness for all there is. This oneness is in the creation process. Just find the creation process in you now as you just stop being one tiny individual, but embrace something bigger, your capacity to see yourself as a universal being, having an experience in a human body.

While you are processing universality as a way of being human, you are allowing the sense of "All Love" to surround you. This new energy and life force brings you to a space of truth in your heart right now. The essence of "All Love" brings this state of universality to your consciousness.

Earthing your Heart

Bringing to you now is a new beginning for your shared sacred journey. This shared sacred journey allows the essence of "All Love" to be encoded in you as you open up to the mystery. Just feeling now your heart drop down into the core of the Earth is most grounding for you, right now. Just feel your heart drop, sink like an anchor down, down, down into the core of the earth. Just feel your heart sinking, drifting, in the depths, of the oceans just down, down to the fiery core of the Earth. When you really feel your heart has come home to the Earth, you are now going to ask the Mother Earth to bless your human heart and feel the density and solidity of your heart safe in the core of the Earth.

When you feel it has really been earthed and safe, you are saying to your heart that it is not separate from the Earth. Your heart is not separate, but one with the Earth. Your heart is one with the Earth now, as you open up to the essence of "All Love."

Your heart is being bathed in the nourishment of the great Mother Earth now where "she" is being kept safe and nurtured. The essence, safety, and nourishment of the Earth, keeps your heart safe and loved. You are one in essence with the heart's earth, and the heart's earth brings you back into resonance with your truth. You are one in essence with your heart's earth. You are love.

You must allow your heart's earth to grow your heart now. For it is in growing your heart deep in the mother's earth that you can truly feel safe as a human. Humans need to feel safe and nurtured, and the essence of safety is in acknowledging the heart's earth will support you in everything that you do.

All of life responds to the gentle energy of the heart and to place your heart lovingly for yourself deep in the heart's earth brings you fully into resonance with the humanness of being human. For example, humans just don't feel very human often because emotions rule.

The emotions are given way too much attention by humans. This is over stimulating the heart, and it is stopping the heart from maturing. There are emotionally laden hearts, which cannot mature and grow in the atmosphere of emotions out of control.

Prune your emotions every day so your heart doesn't choke on emotional debris. Allow yourself to really feel the emotions as a separate energy, from the feeling truthful heart. The truthful feeling heart is grown up, because it has disciplined itself to drop anchor deep into the core of the earth, when emotion storms create havoc with the heart.

Feel now your heart growing in strength and maturity by allowing it to be deeply buried into the heart of the Earth, whilst the emotional storms create havoc when you are presented with "emotional scenarios." You must just allow your heart to drop anchor into the core of the Earth until the crisis has passed, and the storm clouds of the emotions have passed.

Being in this space allows you to feel safe when you are undergoing rapid change in your life. You are feeling the need to really allow the essence of this new world now being part of your totality by knowing your heart is safe and kept quietly in its space of great care in the heart of the Earth. You are able to go about your day knowing you are not subject to emotional agendas you place on yourself over all the events in your life. You now need to know that your life brings you to this safe and wonderful new environment. Just allowing the essence of your own pure and truthful space brings you all to a state of complete surrender to all there is. There is no fear in your world when you embrace this way of being.

Allowing this to take place now allows the state of surrender to envelope you. We as humans can fear continually the heart being battered, rammed, and violated. This exercise and attunement will allow your heart to be safe and loved. Your heart is safe and loved. You are just allowing this beauty of your true heart to emerge, in wonder for all of life. The beauty of your heart grows when it is in its safe space.

This safe space can begin to grow and you can know that "you" are allowing the vibration of your heart to expand in the Earth heart. Allow your heart, and the Earth's heart to become one now. You are Love.

Your Heart of Hearts

Believing in your ability to truly trust this new worldview brings you home to yourself. If universality is a new way of creating your view of your humanness you will experience many moments of alienation and deep abandonment. You will not be identifying with your human condition, but going beyond it to embrace a new shift in consciousness.

Your view of your consciousness is expanding to take in a new reality, and this reality will have at its heart, your heart. Your heart is actually encased in this new reality as you go beyond your previously held view of yourself.

Bring now to your heart your expanding view of your new reality. This is an exciting and new dimension to your view of reality, and it is being encoded upon you now. Just feeling this reality takes you to a space of love; you are able to just state to yourself that you deserve to feel this new state.

I now feel lovingly toward myself as I embrace this new reality, and I allow this new reality to impose itself on me lovingly.

Why, you may ask, am I bothering to take myself to this new space, this new view of my reality? You need to feel that you can uncover the secrets of your new reality by stating to yourself that you want to draw on universality to bring yourself into resonance with a new sacred law. This new sacred law is called, "The Law of Universality." Call upon the law of universality to bring you all you need for your truth right now. Your new state of being will embrace "the law of universality" which has at its core your sacred truth. I am allowing the sacred 'law of universality' to be encoded on my cellular memory to bring me all I need for my life. I am love.

By allowing the sacred law of universality to be encoded on your cellular memory, you are bringing home to yourself your belief in your ability to bring to your life all you need for your world right now. This is a time for allowing the world of truth to bring you home to yourself, as you really allow yourself to bring home to you, your ability to just receive all you need right now. Just receiving all you need right now brings you to a space of pure peace for the mystery. Just allowing this sacred precious new energy to surround you brings you into alignment with all that is sacred right now. You are opening up now to the spirit of allowing the sacred truth to bring you home exactly who you are as you allow "you" your precious self to grow and find a safe space in your totality. Right now finding this safe space brings you home to you as you delve deeper into your core identity. This core identity brings with it all you need for your life of absolute wonder in all there is.

The Law of Universality
Absoluteness, the sense of absoluteness in everything is just so magical and special that you cannot even begin to go there in your human landscape. It allows the special trust and truth to emerge in oneness for your life of wonder for yourself.

Allowing this life of wonder for your truth brings you home to yourself so you are able to believe and trust in the processes that guide your way home. You are now beginning to tap into a rich reservoir of truth for the mystery. You are feeling the need to just bring to your world this vibration of pure love and safety now for your truth. You are love.

Trusting in the sacred law of universality brings you home to yourself in a special and magical way. You are feeling the energy of universality encode itself on you as you really begin to feel the presence of the shining ones all around you.

Feeling the sacred presence of the shining ones allows the essence, energy, and love to grow. Feeling the essence, energy, and love grow around you feeds your need to really know you and all of life are one, and that all of life feeds your creative capacity.

Just trusting the sacred law of universality brings you home to yourself and you must remember you are allowed to really feel the presence, energy, and oneness of this sacred law. The sacred law of universality just keeps growing inside you, as you feed into the essence and oneness all of life brings, feeding into this oneness and peace in all of life.

In all of life there is living peace and oneness for the mystery. The living energies of the mother bring peace and oneness, and I, Isis bring to you now this peace and oneness for your struggle to hold your truth in a hostile world that doesn't respect truth. You need now to just feel and be part of the world which offers the magic and oneness in all of life, and allow this magic and oneness to be all around you. You need to merge into this feeling now. Just step into it and feel the magic of this new adventure you are giving yourself. You are encoding your cellular memory to accept new frequencies for the law of universality now.

By allowing the sacred law of universality to be encoded now, you are opening up to the mystery and you are allowing the mystery to be one with you. You are feeling the essence of the mystery enfold you and keep you in a space of absolute wonder for all there is. There is no turning back now, when you bring this sacred truth to you. You are allowing the joy of universality to be one you as you really allow yourself to complete the oneness of your incarnation.

You now own a part of yourself that has been lost and you must feel this lost part come home. For example, you can imagine this exercise:

You are standing on a cliff face; all is desolate around you. You feel no connection with why you are in this terrain. There is no connection with you and your surrounding environment. You are feeling desolate and lost. Now just imagine "you" are now seeing all around you a living communicating intelligence, an intelligence that knows your feelings and thoughts, but cannot communicate in the language you know. Really imagine what this intelligence would say to you now.

This intelligence is behind every living thing. Every living thing in the universe has an intelligence that can communicate with you, and every living intelligence speaks through the language of universality. The language of universality brings you to a space of oneness and awareness for all there is.

All living intelligences speak from this space of this truth, and you must begin to allow yourself to feel this now. You are love.

The vibration of universality now allows your dormant spirit to become one with everything around you. You can never really feel alone, lost, or abandoned for long because the living intelligence is all around you through the law of universality. The law of universality really commands you to be in acknowledgement of every living thing. For every living thing speaks to you from this space. You are attuning now to the vibration of every living thing. For when you attune to the vibration of every living thing you are respecting yourself as being part of that vibration. I am a rock. I am a flower. I am the air currents. I am a bird in full flight. I am actually part of every living thing, and every living thing supports my journey now.

This one acknowledgement plugs you into the sacred law of universality, and you are feeling in this law, this sacred law, feeling a respect for all living things.

Respecting the law of universality only serves to bring you home to your own belief that all of life supports your journey, and that invisible living forces can actually help you create the magical new life you hold for your truth. You are now allowing this new view of your humanness to be encoded upon you now. Feel this now.

Affirmation: *"I am now allowing this new view of my humanness to be encoded upon me now as I open up to the law of universality."*

This law is sacred, and I the mother Isis bring this information to you now so you can be part of the sacred mystery of creation.

The Isis Vibration

Being in the magical essence of Isis only reinforces all you have and trust that all in your life brings you hope in your life. Every living thing supports the journey of another living thing at some level. You are being encoded for this process now as you are opening up this new way of being. Just being in the energy of Isis acknowledges to you that "you" are able to really feel and know you able to be truly free to bring your life all you need. You are now feeling the need to just say to yourself: "I am able to bring to my life the magical powers of the Goddess Isis who is in everything."

The vibration of Isis just creates this process of your own knowing to gather all the bits of your life into a cohesive whole. The way you are able to bring this cohesive feel for your life will allow Isis to come closer, closer, and closer to you.

Take a long, deep breath as you allow the magical energy of Isis to infuse every cell and muscle. Every single cell has within it the coding's for your immortality. Your entire life depends on this moment, and your breath just keeps you connected to every living thing.

You are now allowing this magical energy and intent to bring you all you need for your life. The essence, energy, and life force, reinforce the joy and tranquility of your life right now. You are one in essence with the love Isis has for you now as you open up to the law of universality. Whilst you are undergoing this process of cellular rejuvenation, you are beginning to feel your new identity emerge. This new identity brings with it all you need for your life right now, and it is "right now" which is your only concern. It is what is "right now" that brings you to the state of oneness for all there is.

This state of oneness only reinforces the totality of who you are at that given moment. It is in that moment you have the divine essence of the whole universe beckoning you to really come home to yourself.

You are bringing this magical self "you," to you now as you continually reinforce the mystery. The mystery just takes you out of yourself as you really merge in oneness with all there is. Your mystery is exactly that. The mystery of the totality of all life that has gone before you, and will come after you. Believing in this mystery now just brings you to a space of forgiveness for all. Forgiveness for every living thing that has at its core a belief in the totality of all life.

Absoluteness of Every Living Thing

Right now you are in this mergence, as you just go beyond the aspect of yourself that continually demands to be fed, to be continually satisfied and desired. You are now bringing this mergence into oneness with all of life, and the process just keeps you ever joyful in the process of "self" discovery.

Bringing now to your life is the absoluteness in every living thing. The absoluteness in every living thing allows for this state of magical renewal to take place within you now. You are just bringing to your life now the essence of magical renewal, as you invite into your life the absoluteness of every living thing. For every living thing has encoded in it a sense of wonder for all of life, and every living thing secretes and invisible thread of energy to every other living thing.

Imagine now you are just part of this process, and being part of this process just brings you to a point of remembering you are part of everything, and that every thing, has encoded in it this absoluteness. Being in the energy of absoluteness for every living thing just connects you to the "All Love" vibration and this vibration takes care of all aspects of your life. Imagine now, having a life where the absoluteness of every living thing surrounds you and keeps you in a space of pure love for the mystery.

Right now, you are opening up to the world where the absoluteness of every living thing just keeps creating with you in wonder for all there is.

The wonder for all there is reinforces the state of pure peace for the mystery. Pure peace for the mystery is encoded in you now. You are love.

Being in the divine energy of absoluteness reinforces your belief in the totality of all life. Belief in the totality of every living thing reinforces your connection with the divine, and that "life" is just a magical adventure. This magical adventure spreads throughout the universe and in turn reinforces the spirit of the universe. Allowing the spirit of the universe to create with you brings you to a state of joy for the process of being human. The joy of being human is in the essence and oneness that all of life and you are one, and that this life brings to you the wonder for your abundance.

Isis is the magician to help you remember all of these things, and you are opening up to her essence, energy, and life force when you recreate with her. Her magic and essence is everywhere and you just have to connect with this state of remembering. All of life is connected to this state of remembering who we are, and who we will become. Allowing this magical love and energy to surround you just brings you into a state of awareness for all there is. The state of awareness for all there is reinforces belief in the absoluteness of every living thing, and how that absoluteness, will bring with it a knowing that you and all around you is just creating through this energy.

All of life creates with this energy right now for your magical life as "you" open up your heart to yourself; your heart is now being listened to as you bring to your world your love and your intent for the beauty of "All Love" in every living thing.

To view your world through the lens of this new reality reinforces in you now that the absoluteness of every living thing supports your journey. Your journey is supported every single moment "you" allow yourself to really step outside your humanness and observe your humanness as a separate totality from what "you" are as a soul. Your soul-self is the self that creates through the magic, wonder, and essence in all of life, and your soul-self just brings you back into alignment with all there is. Being in this state of heightened awareness for yourself reinforces the totality of who you are and what your potential is.

Your humanness doesn't control your totality. You must remember this. Your humanness is the aspect of yourself that has chosen to love by challenging the emotional body to love. It's that simple. You are being challenged to love through every living thing in your human form. Your mind is also part of that process. The human machinery that drives the will is the human mind, and the human just creates with this will. For yourself you are opening up to your view of yourself, which doesn't allow for the expression of who "you" are in your totality, and in not allowing it you become a witness to this aspect of yourself.

You are actually witnessing a part of yourself now for the first time perhaps, which sees the totality of who you are, and how the selves are constructed. Knowing how the selves are constructed brings you to a space of pure delight in the knowing of who you are. This self just creates itself anew, with the new information. Your new information is in witnessing this aspect of yourself being born.

Kyoto Japan after Mt Kurama – ceremony anchoring the Divine Feminine in the core of the earth

In witnessing your own birth to this new reality, you are claiming a part of yourself that has been dormant or undiscovered. You are now allowing this part of yourself to grow by saying to yourself:
"I am now opening up to the essence of all my selves, and I am happy to allow this essence of all my selves to grow, and begin to awaken to my total potential."

My complete potential is now about to be realized through the opening of these new selves. Now imagine a Christmas tree: It is green. This is your self. The self that is human. It is the skeleton of you. The outline. The shape. Let's begin to imagine this exercise of awakening now: The Christmas tree fairy lights being switched on now.

Imagine the first set, glowing, twinkling ruby, feel this now. You are the tree; your selves are beginning to be switched on. You now need to begin the adventure of opening up all the selves one by one.

The next set being switched on are gleaming golden orange lights, they are expanding your creative consciousness. As you explore your energetic self, you are allowing yourself to really light up your energetic self. The next set is being switched on; these gleaming lights open your heart. Imagine frosty pink and emerald green lights. As you begin to shimmer, your heart grows and you feel stable, and want more.

On go the brilliant turquoise lights, their color reminding you of a sparkling tropical ocean. At the top of your Christmas tree is a big orb star. The translucent sparkling, twinkling magic of your crown center is bringing you home to yourself now.

This exercise brings you home to you sparkling multi-dimensional self, and reinforces your need for completeness in all of life. You are now witnessing a part of your new magical self. Your new life brings you home to "you."

As you begin the adventure of self-discovery you are allowing yourself to really grow in the knowledge that you are free, truly free to be exactly who you are. This freedom imposes itself on your very being, and just keeps getting you closer and closer to who "you" really are.

Just know now this freedom brings with it the power to see your potential as a truly glowing star. For now you are radiating outward toward the cosmos bringing to yourself the magical potential of who you truly are.

Allowing this to happen now just reinforces the totality of who you are on yourself and brings you home to your essence self. For now you are radiating out to your essence self and allowing this essence self to magnify all you want in your world. Your world is growing and it is bringing you home to the part of yourself that knows this power and energy. This power and energy just keeps growing and growing and gives you back to yourself. You now need to feel this energy and life force keep you connected to the part of yourself to bring to your world all that you need now to keep the fires of love opening wider and wider. All of our "senses" are just glowing now in the knowledge that we don't have to keep suffering to be human. Humanness imposes upon us its strengths. The strength of being human is that we don't have to keep suffering, for continual suffering just diminishes the power of love. The power of love is the greatest gift we can give ourselves. So why keep suffering to find it?

Sacred Essence of Isis

You are now allowing the special magic of who you are to create with the energy of "All Love." Allowing the energy of "All Love" to envelope you brings you to a space of oneness for all there is. The special magic of your own self creates the energy of trust for all there is. You are now bringing the world you inhabit a special magic for the essence of who you are.

You are one in essence with all of love and all of love brings you to a state of perfection. You are vibrating to the essence of all these parts of yourself now as you really bring to your world this sacred essence.

The sacred essence of Isis creates in you now the belief that you are capable of everything. This is the time to really allow the spirit of this trust for Isis to renew you now. This is the process which kick starts the renewing of your self. For when you are renewed, you are placing yourself in the arms of the Mother Isis, who restores your own equilibrium, you own inner self; the true inner self just begins to create with you now.

You are now just allowing the special magic of who you are to envelope you and keep you connected to all there is. This is a time for the essence and renewing process of Isis to renew you. You are just allowing this new view of yourself to give you all you need. You are love.

You are now allowing the sacredness of your life to envelope you now, as you begin the journey inward. To begin the journey inward is an act of love for yourself and this inward journey reveals to you now your own unique view of your totality.

Just feeling this now and just believing in your own belief that "you can have it all" allows you to really take the challenge and trust in your own abundance to give you all you need right now. You are opening up fast to the world of multi-dimensionality, and you are now allowing yourself to really grid yourself for your own matrix. You are your own matrix and your matrix is opening you now to the view of your life that encompasses "All Love."

You are now allowing the spirit of "All Love" to guide you, and "All Love" guides, brings you safely home to yourself. Your love of yourself allows the sacredness of your life to really bring you into resonance with all there is. The sacred essence of "all there is" just keeps driving you further and further into discovering just "who you are."

"Who am I?" Asking yourself, "Who am I? Reinforces the totality of your beingness right now. Reinforcing this totality allows the sacred essence of who you are to envelope you and keep you safe. You are love.

Heart Love
Being in the presence of "All Love" reinforces your own capacity to really allow peace to go within the deepest part of your cellular memory. When you know you are protected by "All Love" you can allow the special magic of who you are to embrace you. Just allowing this magic to open you to yourself at this time is a sacred act to yourself. You are stating that you are in the company of mighty

beings who can help you at this moment. Every living thing unites to bring you into resonance with your capacity to love. For you must challenge yourself every day to uncover a hidden part of yourself and just love. You must uncover all parts of the psyche so you can delve deeper into your own mysterious heart to bring you home to your truth.

The essence of who you are is being revealed to you through uncovering the dark secret side of yourself. By revealing this back to you, you are allowing yourself to ascend — to really become what you know yourself to be, truly a stellar soul, having an experience in a human body. Polishing and refining your own unique capacity to love this part of yourself just keeps you in a space of love for yourself.

By bringing in this feeling of love, and allowing yourself to love, you will now be bringing to your life all that your heart desires. For the heart cannot desire what is doesn't know. Your heart right now cannot desire what it doesn't know; most hearts don't know love. Hearts, which don't know love, crave something it thinks is love. Why? It is because the mind has projected its own creative pattern on the heart, so the mind has controlled the heart's intelligence, so the heart doesn't know what love really is.

The heart just craves what it thinks is love. For this patterning to change, your heart must be given new directions. The heart must be given a new reason to find the truth in loving, for it has been compromised so often by the mind.

Right now examine what your heart needs to love. *"What does my heart need to love?"* My heart needs to love the essence of truth; in loving my heart must be given a chance to really know the truth in love. To know the truth in love, I must just bypass the mind, and I must just allow the heart to be listened to.

The essence of listening to my heart is to stop the mind and just accept that the mind has no idea what the heart wants. The heart just wants to experience love, in this new space far away from the mind's intelligence. So, ask yourself when you "think" your heart wants something. "Is this the mind, or is this my 'heart' talking to me?'" The answer: Your heart always knows the truth.

Trusting your Heart

Beginning to locate the fear in trusting your heart to deliver all that your life requires is an act of discipline for yourself. You must continue to monitor all thoughts as they appear throughout your day, and keep a tally, a record, of those thoughts that are most persistent and troubling. You must just feel that these troubling moments will not gather momentum, so you mustn't give them energy; you must stop when a thought keeps persistently bothering you and write down where this problem has come from, and what you are going to do about its energy.

What is the nature of the problem? You must examine where it is energetically coming from. The nature of it means, how it has formed naturally (i.e. Family matters can begin in the base chakra and relate to security and your need for security). Try and establish your link with all parts of it karmically. This helps balance any karmic debts you may be experiencing as well. You must just allow all karmic patterns to surface at this time, and feel the karmic debt now gone. There are no more karmic debts to pay.

Say to yourself:
"In the name of love and light and in the name of my absolute divine truth, may the source of karma be released so I can remove all obstacles to my heart? I am opening a new pathway to my heart, and this road is blocked. I now request that this block be removed. I am now bringing home to my heart, my ability to know I am safe and I can release this obstacle."

Beginning to locate the pain of blocked emotions brings you closer to your heart, as you open up the doorway to your heart. For right now, the doorway to your heart is the only door your mind must be trained to follow.

Every day say to your mind:

"We are on a road today, this road is taking us one step closer to the heart's door. I want you to be my faithful companion, and stay with me. If you run on ahead, it must only be to guide me. Don't bark instructions at me with your ideas and past thoughts. I am being guided by my 'higher self.' My higher self knows the path to the heart, because its intelligence and my heart's intelligence are the 'one', these two intelligences, are the 'one' we listen to."

You must feel now that you can contain the dog's (your mind's) attention span if your thoughts wander to the past and project past patterns on to the future.

Begin to chart your day. *"What do I want for my heart today?"* Just draw a day map. What do you want to achieve today?

It is one day/this day, which keeps you firmly on the road. Do not look back. This will only alert the dog to bark at past patterns that keep recurring in your mind. Keep the dog (your mind) under control while you wait for opportunities, synchronicities, to lighten your load. Just remember to take the load off your back and get rest during your day. Always be prepared to lighten the load on your mind when you are overloaded and always observe where the mind is taking you. Rest, stop, and support keep you in a space of remembering the original soul's blue print, its plan for taking the road in a human body.

Remembering

Remembering starts when the process of staying completely in the moment is established. It is important to remember who you really are and where you came from. Remembering your soul's blue print must be adhered to every day, as you begin to journey deeper and deeper into yourself.

Attaching yourself to the past in any way is forgetting, not remembering. The remembering can only take place when the forgetting is forgotten. The past keeps you in a forgotten place; its landscape just shuts you out from your truth. The past is your greatest enemy to your remembering. For the past just keeps you connected to a worldview that holds you from accessing the doorway to your heart's truth. You must now stop when past patterns keep recurring. This is not the same as fond memories from childhood or beautiful experiences of holidays, births, etc. Your past patterns are about climbing into bed with your past painful memories.

All past painful memories must be seized and completely eradicated, like pulling up strong weeds. Your past painful patterns are the very things keeping the heart in a throbbing sore space. You are now allowing yourself to create with new pathways as the old pathways only lead to despair, loss, and abandonment.

Ask yourself today: *"What must I do to completely eradicate the past painful patterns in my lost remembering?"*

Breathe deeply and powerfully. Release all fear around past patterns, and as they surface, you must release your fear of not allowing your heart to remember. Feel the past fears bubble to the surface. This is a time of just allowing this new way of being human to surface.

Observing Old Patterns

Going deeper and deeper into the labyrinth of your unconsciousness brings forward many unresolved old patterns. As these surface, you are being encouraged to explore a new way of being human. You have a choice. When the issues surface, you are exposing yourself to yourself. Imagine now a mirror, a large one in an empty room. You are looking at yourself, exposed, fully naked; as you stand there, observe calmly where your issues are in your body. Scan your face, shoulders, arms, chest/breasts, belly, genitals, thighs, legs, and feet. Observe without judgment, being detached. Where is your criticism of yourself? This criticism can be directed to a body part. You will observe a shift in awareness when the body part under scrutiny responds. Remember your body is an intelligent force; every part has its own consciousness and responds to your judgment of it. When you send a message of negativity to any part of yourself you are invalidating that self, and that part of you then sets up a resistance. Imagine how many times in your life you have done this. Sometimes we do this daily, even hourly. Imagine how the body parts respond. It has to take the criticism every day. This sets up a block in the organs surrounding the area. Your aura becomes cloudy and you can in time find major blockages, which could bring disease and a weakening of that particular area. A human must love all her parts; every part of you is sacred. It is an honor to have your organs. Imagine now not having that part of your body at all. It's just not there, again this is inconceivable.

Right now, practice every day spending time in front of your mirror sending conscious thoughts of love to all of you, observe how your physical, emotional, mental, and spiritual self grows. The shift in awareness will bring you home to yourself, and make you alive to your potential.

Observing Emotion
Observing all the time, just observing, brings you to a state of knowing where you allow yourself to "trigger" your sub-conscious to play up. You are now allowing yourself the beauty and knowledge of just saying to yourself. *"Why is it always me who is creating this problem in myself? Why am I allowing this to happen to me in the first place?"*

You are part of a cycle, an endless cycle of creation, and you are watching where the weak links are every day. It's like watching a part of a car that is faulty. You say to yourself *"This car has a faulty brake pedal. I know this. If I don't get it attended to, it will eventually create a big problem."* If it breaks down the whole car stops. All the other parts of the car are in perfect harmony; however, this part is damaged. You must have it repaired. You must just observe yourself and know that in doing so, that you are witnessing a part of yourself that is vulnerable; this part is damaged. Just allow this part to really become visible; give it attention. This part of you has a consciousness, intelligence. It speaks a language.

You need to be able to re-code yourself to feel this intelligence. By saying, *"How can we talk? Let's talk. Let's be friends. I need you to talk to me and tell me exactly what you are saying."*

Listen, observe; just listen and observe. What energies are attached to this view of yourself? You are witnessing a part of yourself being integrated. You are love.

Embracing the Heart
Allowing the spirit of "All Love" to infuse every cell in your body now only reinforces your commitment to your truth. You are embracing a way of being human that goes beyond time and space and allows you to connect to the spirit of oneness. You are now allowing this sacred communion of who you are to bring you to the space of oneness for all there is, and you will bring to your life, your certainty that you are embracing a way of life which only knows one thing, and that is love of the "self."

For when you truly come to terms with love of the "self" you will begin to merge with everything, and every living thing will hear your call to love. Allowing this love to unite with you brings you to a space of knowing and oneness for all there is.

By affirming, "I allow the sweet spirit of my heart to be my guide," you are inviting your heart to listen and be a central player in the quest for oneness. Allowing the quest to find the complete self in love for the mystery allows your spirit to soar, and you can begin on the magical journey to the heart.

You are ready and willing to embrace the heart. It knows the truth and it allows "you" the real "you" to soar and become alive to the essence of oneness for all there is.

This is time to remember that the heart brings you closer to all there is, and "all there is" is the aim of the exercise in being human anyway.

Opening to the Essence of Isis

You are birthing Isis identity in your life, and Isis is watching the process. It is important to remember Isis is overseeing the process of "All Love" in your life, and you are truly linking to her. You are opening up the essence of Isis, and you will feel her magical world open up more and more to her mystery. The essence of "All Love" lives in the mystery as you bring home to your heart, her love for you.

Just allowing this special mystery to be your guide reinforces your love and hers. Today you must call on me Isis to help you stay close to your heart, for your heart knows the truth, and your heart will protect your truth.

Like Isis your heart knows the truth, and your heart will protect the truth.

Bringing to your world now the ability to create through the mysteries of Isis only reinforces your special relationship with the infinite number of beings supporting you on your journey right now. You are allowing the special gift of magical love to be your guide and friend, and you are opening up to the indwelling self, the self that knows love and truth to be your guide. This essence reinforces your truth and magic and allows "All Love" to enter your heart.

This heart of yours just keeps growing bigger and bigger. Allow yourself to experience the biggest heart in the world. You have the biggest heart in the world and the biggest heart just grows and grows. Feel your heart expanding like a balloon. Start blowing it up right now, and just feel the balloon getting bigger and bigger. Feel it filling the whole world. Feel it now being the size of our world. You are opening up to the size of your new world/heart. My heart is as big as the world and my heartthrobs to the global heart. Global warming! Feel it as being like your heart warming (not the same thing environmentally, of course). Your heart now is opening up unbelievably to your new view of your reality, and this reality is to stay completely in the living presence of all light beings who can open up your heart right now.

You are resurrecting your heart and making it new again. You are in a space of true heart resurrection right now as you open up to yourself. Yours is the self that only knows one thing and this is the gift of a self-fulfilling love.

Stillness
Allow the spirit of truth to permeate your whole energy field as you allow the essence, spirit, and truth of the Mother Isis to embrace you now. Right now this stillness is yours, and you need to find in it a belief in the magic of now bringing you all you need for your life. This is a truth made manifest, and this truth made manifest only reinforces your commitment to love.

The commitment to love is the greatest gift you can give yourself right now. You are opening up to the greatest gift of yourself, as you allow the special magic of your divine self to bring you all you need.

This is a time of purity for your heart, as you bring to your world this truth for your life. By allowing the special peace and light to be your guide, you are resurrecting your tired, weary spirit, and giving it a bath. Just reinforce the essence of stillness; just reinforce the essence of pure peace for the mystery of yourself. The special magic of yourself allows you now to really bring to your world, this peace and love.

The love of all life just grows and grows inside you now, as you awaken to the mystery. We are one in essence with this mighty universal presence, as we evoke the essence of "All Love" to be our guide. The essence of "All Love" is our guide to bring us home to ourselves. You are witnessing a part of yourself that only knows one thing, and this is love of yourself for yourself.

As this love embraces you, you are embracing a part of yourself that has been lost, and is now being found again. Embrace this part of yourself, as you are yourself peace, space and love to grow your heart. You are love.

A Forgiving Space

Allowing the spirit and essence of your life to be your own reveals to you now the simple truth that you are in a space of love for yourself, creating the magic and renewal Isis brings. You are allowing this sweet, loving union with Isis to take place now as you open your heart to yourself.

You are now allowing the essence and sweet spirit of your life to create with you in wonder for who you are. You are allowing now your union with Isis and all she represents to bring you to a space of knowing just who and what you are. This is a forgiving space, one that allows for the total state of who you are to envelope you.

Bringing in this space of forgiveness just allows now for you to bring peace and forgiveness to you and you will find the essence, energy, and life force to be your guide. You are enjoying now the new peace and tranquility your new beginning with Isis brings.

To bring this energy, essence, and life force to you creates in your world a special link with all there is, and you are challenging all previously held definitions of yourself. Just being in a state of forgiveness for yourself and who you are is bringing you to a world of trust for the true truth process.

This is a time to find yourself your peace and love for the joy of being human, because when you are human, you become divine and your humanness is a space of true renewal for all there is. You are in essence with the essence of all your selves, and you remember now the time when you were all your selves. The time has come for you now to really link with this remembering. You are love.

Your Secret Sacred Essence

The belief in your totality as an integrated being with many evolving spinning parts is now being encoded upon you. For now feel the spinning evolving sense of self as you open your heart wide to "All Love." "All Love" brings you home to your center, your truth center as you push yourself deeper and deeper into your cellular matrix.

This new view of yourself only reinforces all you have ever been and will become. You are now just taking yourself into the purity of your truth/trust center where you are allowing the secret sacred essence of yourself to be revealed. You are bringing this secret sacred self home to "you" and you are allowing yourself to be given a new part of yourself. This part is to only love all of "you." You are allowing right now this secret part of yourself to be revealed to you as you go deeper into the mystery.

Allowing this message of sweet love for yourself to emerge brings you home to yourself. You are one in essence of your sacred-self to merge into oneness for all there is.

Right now, just feel the essence of who you are resonate with you, as you truly open up to the mystery and bring who you are into resonance with all of life. The mysteries have encoded in them this amazing ability to really allow the essence, truth, and pleasure to be yours. You are truly vibrating to this essence energy and life force all around you, as you open up further and further to the mystery. Allowing this to take place now reinforces the love, truth, and beauty of all there is. You are love.

Releasing the Past

Believing in the essence of "All Love" only reinforces this love as you allow your magical heart to resonate with you in "All Love" now. This is a time of gentle mergence where the past is fully forgotten. Your past history will now be wiped clean. There is a feeling now of releasing to the pure heart of nothingness as you sweep the past away. Visualize now a big karmic dust buster, a massive vacuum cleaner releasing and sucking up all your old stored karmas and grievances. Feel this now as you align to your sense of truth and trust for the new Earth you are living on.

Just now get the dust buster onto your environment, your workspace, home, your community environment; visualize this vast machine mowing down all the dust with light, simply transmuting and purifying it. You have a toxic-free environment. Now feel the pollutants in the environment being washed away. It is time now to feel this powerful sucking vacuum on yourself. You need now to feel how this energy light is transmuting the density of your aura, your chakras, your electrical field. Feel this now, and really believe it is happening. Allow the feeling of purity to come to you as you prepare for the meeting of like-minded souls on this planet. You are all getting ready to be in a light-filled pink healing room, one that has just been created especially for you right now. You may feel the essence and light of this merging take place within you, and you may now attune to the special magic of "all there is" in the space of pure love without karmic attachments which breed fear, violence, hatred, and evil in this world.

The Spirit of Forgiveness

When you bring the spirit of forgiveness to every living thing, you are free of the attachment every living thing imposes on you. Allowing the freedom of every living thing to be your guide just brings you to a space of renewal and truth for your journey. Believing in every living thing to help you and keep you safe brings you to a space of purity for all there is. I now lovingly allow the purity for all there is to bring me into resonance with all there is, and I am allowing the purity of all there is to be my guide. I am bringing to my heart my truth and I must feel me to bring the essence of "All Love" to my life.

All of life revolves around the essence of myself and the essence of myself is free of all emotional attachment to every living thing. I am bringing home all the magic, essence, and life force of my new life, and this life leaves me in peace and oneness for all there is. I am now allowing the peace and oneness to be my guide as I delve deeper into my heart. My heart is the barometer of my truth, and I allow lovingly my heart's truth to be my guide. Myself is just one thing my "self." When I am advised to look after my "self," I am resonating with the "self." The self is my guide, for an eternal immortal life.

Bring now your immortal life to you, by acknowledging the spirit of forgiveness of yourself to yourself now. Your spirit shines and you are one in essence with your shining spirit.

Shine your Light

Now it is time to commit to a way of life that resonates with your truth and power. You are opening up to a way of life that allows only one thing, and that is your light to shine. This is an important time to remind yourself to really allow this light and magic to shine. You are bringing to your world this light and magic and you must allow the light and magic to be your guide.

Believing in the magic that anything is possible, and that possibilities in life are endless brings you to a space of knowing that you and all of life are one. This is a time of endless magical possibilities, bringing you safely home to your truth.

Always allow the essence of your magical life to be your guide and always allow your spirit and truth to bring you home to all there is. You are vibrating to the essence, energy, and life force of all there is. Allowing this magical essence to create with you allows the magic of renewal to bring you home to yourself. You are "one" in essence with all of creation and your creative journey only serves to bring you home to yourself.

Just remembering "who" you are and "what" you are capable of reinforces this truth magic and knowing that all of life and you are one. You are all one now, and being in the presence of all light reinforces the magic of renewal. You are renewing yourself now, as you align to the forces of the universe to assist you. You are opening up to the forces of the universe now. You are love.

Embracing all your Parts

Bringing to your world right now is the belief that you are capable of embracing the sum total of all your parts. In other words, "you" are challenging a part of yourself to come home and be integrated. You are now showing yourself, you are capable of observing this part of yourself and aligning to your truth. The truth now of your life brings you into resonance with all there is. You are allowing yourself to be part of the mystery, and you are embracing that part of yourself.

To be embracing a part of yourself that has been lost is the most loving thing you can do for yourself right now, and you will bring to this new view of yourself your power, peace, and light.

Imagine looking at yourself, from your higher-self's perspective. You are observing yourself as a flock of sheep. They must all go on the same path, the same well-worn track. Now imagine a disturbance. Chaotic energy has disrupted the flock and they are running everywhere. What must you do as their leader? (Imagine you are the shepherd.) You must quickly get the sheep together again. How do you do this? You do it by being a leader. You give directions to the dog to round them up. It may take some time. When the collective energy of the group (your selves) has settled, the strays will return.

In your life now, when you witness disturbances in your energy field through painful, chaotic thoughts you must remember to get authority and bring them home, them being your disturbed energies. This way you can walk on the path as a unified being.

Observe and Be Still
This new chapter in your life allows the special magic of "All Love" to envelope you, as you align to the forces of light to protect you and enclose you. It is time to really observe. Really observe all around you and find in the stillness, a depth and new meaning to your life.

You are now bringing this depth and new meaning to your life by being in the presence of "All Love" and allowing "All Love" to be your guide. You are opening up to the world of "All Love" and you must allow the essence, energy, and life force to be your guide. This is an important time for this new awakening.

Your life must resonate with the forces of light and power to really bring home to you your truth. You are witnessing a new aspect of yourself being born. You are witnessing your own truth, being born to you, as you open up to the forces of "All Love" to assist you right now.

Ask yourself right now if you are able to bring this new truth to you. What is in this truth? Truth is the ability to know that you have within you the ability to sift through to the core of your pain and observe the stillness, the love. Not a living soul can hurt you when you have found this moment. This space delivers truth to you. This space finds truth, exposes it, and explores it. For truth is the heart of love and a heart that is loving in return. You must allow yourself this stillness, this truth. Find yourself in the heart of this stillness, this truth. Bring to your heart now this truth, this stillness. Allow now, heart, this stillness, to be your guide as you open up and allow the essential spirit of who you are. Let stillness be your guide. Just for today, breathe in this stillness and peace.

Why am I Here?

As you take your journey deep into yourself, you are reliving your past and releasing it as well. You are being encouraged now to stop and ponder on the meaning of why you are here, and to bathe in the incandescent energy of love all around you. Right now it is important to allow yourself this merging with all selves, which support your journey. To begin to allow the essence, energy, and life force of universal vibrations to assist reinforces your belief in the totality of your many selves. These many "selves" are waiting patiently now to be integrated into a whole. It's rather like a jigsaw puzzle. You are looking at all the disassembled parts. These disassembled parts now need to be put into a complete picture. When you begin to do this you are realizing your whole total self where "you" can merge into light, beauty, and power. Merging into oneness creates a sense of peace, space, and order in your life.

See and take apart your old definition of yourself and reassemble it. Allowing yourself to reassemble and rearrange your missing lost bits takes time and patience. Let's go back to the jigsaw puzzle. The picture is looking good but there is one missing piece. This piece is vital for many other pieces that will be found. When the "lost" piece is discovered, there is a sense of joy and accomplishment. The long lost part of yourself has "come home" so to speak.

The excitement and joy of finding this lost part of yourself only reinforces your belief in all your parts being available to be found. As humans, we are like this. We are assembling and looking for the missing "bits" to make the picture "whole." What piece do you need to find today?

Challenges
The spirit of new beginnings stirs within you now as you begin to awaken from the collective inertia you have been feeling all around you. Right now the collective soul energy of humanity is responding to the call to self examine every single thing that is happening to you.

Ask yourself:
"What is happening to me right now? What are my challenges?"

The spirit of awareness in observing the challenges must be noted and dealt with.

Ask yourself now:
"What needs attending in my life right now?
"What is presenting itself to me?"
"Where are challenges today?"
"Who is presenting on my landscape to be observed and cleared?"

Right now as you breathe deeply, powerfully, and rhythmically, you will begin to open your mind screen and you are observing who is appearing on this landscape. Just watch now who appears. Imagine you are a guard or soldier. Have your trusty guard dog with you (Anubis, is handy here). In this observing, note your reactions to the person or people on this landscape. What is your primary emotion? Is it anger, rage, fear of some sort? Note the emotions as they occur, but don't give them energy. Just observe yourself. Now, watch the other people, person, animal, etc. What are they doing? Are they threatening, aggressive, or bringing up aggression in you? Are they happy? How can I help you? Can you feel a sense of communication developing? Note your reactions.

If you need to forgive yourself for this relationship, say:
"You are free now. I am free now."
"We are free now."

Watch if the person disappears or wants to stay. The person may become angry. Perhaps there is unfinished business between you both; breathe love into your heart, stay still, and observe. Request Thoth, the keeper of the Akashic records to assist. Do this now!

Opening your heart to yourself is one of the biggest challenges in being human. When have you asked your heart what it wants? How often have you consulted your heart when being presented with a challenge? Right now list your challenges, by writing them down, one by one. Look at them in order of importance. Now write the challenges on a piece of paper and fold them. Put them in a box. You know the rest. Pick up one challenge from the box by asking your higher self to participate with you. Actively seek to reach with that challenge by making a change in your life with some way, i.e. make the phone call, discuss with the person your new position, whatever is needed now, DO IT.

Every day, list your challenges; place them in the box and draw one out. You may be surprised to find that what was a challenge and felt most urgent to you is not so urgent after all. By asking guidance and support for all the challenges in the box, you will be surprised how they sort themselves out. Do try this for a month and at the end of the month or when the full moon is up, burn all the leftover challenges and begin again. By allowing yourself peace and stillness to meet your daily challenges, you will begin to see what is really important and what is less important. Your higher self has all the answers, and it can only link with you when you fully engage your heart in the process. Humans are yet to discover the full potential of the heart, so allow your heart's intelligence to be your guide.

Non-Attachment in Love
Right now you are challenging all previously held thoughts about what it is to love. Ask yourself: *"What does love mean to me?"* You must redefine your relationship with love by asking yourself

when you were betrayed (and who hasn't been betrayed by their definition of love at some level!) what your need was at that time? You must separate love from wishing to find in someone else something you cannot get met within yourself. Ask yourself: *"What was my need?"* Look carefully at security and sex for security. Many of us get locked up in the need to find that getting our emotional needs met through sex we can find peace and hope in love. By feeling the fear or releasing someone you love at the sexual (mating) level, you are opening up your world to the infinite possibilities in loving.

Just saying to yourself:
"I now release my need to connect or identify love at the sexual level."
"I will be opening your heart wider to embrace to the full totality of the relationship."

This gives you power to really love. You can enjoy a physical relationship, but to identify the person with their role in your life in a sexual way diminishes the true potential of the relationship. You must just allow the essence of "All Love" to envelope you and you must just vibrate to love in a non-physical way. Attaching to love energy through any human emotion will eventually erode the precious gift of love. Love is one of the most powerful emotions on the planet. It must not be compromised through the sexual emotions of security, desire, or possession.

Deservability

Believing in your own ability to create change at every level in your life is an act of love for yourself. What do you need to change about your life right now? You need to change your attitudes about deservability right now, for you cannot change anything until you feel you deserve it.

Quite simply, ask yourself:
"What do I deserve right now?"

You deserve to be listened to. So listen to yourself by writing down everything you need to say to yourself. This is the best therapy. Just listening to yourself is an act of love for yourself. I lovingly listen to myself every chance I can get. Every moment you listen to yourself in love brings you closer to your heart. You are listening to your heart right now when you observe the simple practice of listening and hearing what you have to say to yourself. "Why do you punish yourself so much over trivia?" Stop the fear, "the needy you" who needs to be listened to so she can feel safe. Listening to children helps them get control over fears. Listening to yourself brings you closer to your heart. Being listened to is one of the greatest kindnesses you can give your aching heart. You need to really allow the spirit of love to come to you now by listening to yourself. Listen sweetly to what you are discovering about your world. Your world is one of sweetness and light. You must give yourself a chance now to be listened to by playing music that reflects your love. Listening to nature, birds, wind, sounds, develop your receptivity to hearing truth. Now, listening to your most important organ, your heart. How? Ask it! Say: *"Heart, I am listening to you now."*

Feel Love

Bring now to your life a sense of belief in your ability to change every single thing about your need to love. You are allowing yourself right now to redefine your attitude to love as you open up to the new power your life brings you. You need now to open up your world to the frequency of love as a living intelligence in you. Life is ready to help you! For you are what you believe about love as you bathe in the incandescent glow love brings. It is time now to really allow yourself to connect with the essence and life force love brings you. It's like being "in love" but without the emotion.

You are now allowing this sense of your relationship with love not to separate you from the reality of love as a living energy, which is ready to give you all you need for your world. The essence of your world brings you to a space of truth for the mysteries as you take apart your old identity in relationship with love and re-shape your identity now. For you are now just opening up further and further to the essence of what love really is, and this is to feel. You are now allowing the precious gift of yourself to bring you all you need for your life as you allow yourself "now" the gift of this new intelligence. You are awakening now to a new intelligence. Your heart has its own intelligence with an IQ that resonates to the call of peace, stillness, and beauty. Stop and listen to your newly tuned intelligent heart and ask it to bring you home to your truth. You are one in essence with your newly intelligent heart.

Your New Identity

Believing in your own ability to create in your life your own identity, separate from your own expectations of yourself, creates in you now space to grow a new identity for yourself. This new view of you shapes all outcomes. Your outcomes are determined by your thoughts. Achieving the best for your life brings you to a space of pure forgiveness and peace for yourself now as you open yourself to your potential. You are well aware of the enormity your world presents you with, but you must be willing to explore your world, both inner and outer. This is a time to just consider all that you have achieved and let yourself truly believe in your potential.

To explore your potential, you must allow the special magic of your love-filled self to bring you all you need for your life. Believing in this new potential creates a space of real love, and acknowledgement of what you are worth. Just focusing now on what you are capable of opens up your world unbelievably so you can just recognize your own ability to really witness yourself growing day by day.

Share

You are now bringing to your world your own unique ability to know one thing and that is to share, and sharing implies you are in a position of strength in your heart. Your heart needs to feel loved. Sharing your love with yourself is strengthening your heart. You are now bringing to your world your own truth in sharing, because sharing implies trust and truth in the trusting process. You are now opening up your ability to share lovingly; truthfully with yourself you are love.

The Essence of Love

Your own ability to allow the essence of yourself to shine brings you now to a space of pure peace for all there is. When you allow your own "self" to be your guide, you are opening up your heart wide to encompass all you are capable of. You are acknowledging to yourself, your worth. Just acknowledging your worth to yourself daily brings you into a space of pure love for yourself and what "you" are capable of. You are allowing the special gift of self-illumination to be your guide now as you bring to your world all you need for your love. This is time to just find within yourself your own ability to really connect to all there is and to love the person you are. Just accepting yourself is an acknowledgment of self-love and just accepting who you are and what you are capable of brings you to a space of knowing your truth and capacity to love. Loving yourself implies a gift of acknowledging yourself to yourself as you open up to yourself right now. You are just giving to yourself the gift of powerful universal love; a love which encompasses all there is. Believing in this capacity to love completely and solely through the heart brings you now to a space for forgiveness for all there is. There is just a gentle acknowledgment of all there is and a peace and beauty in giving this gift to yourself. You are just feeling the essence of "all" love around you now as you begin to give to yourself your own dream to love. Believing in your ability to love just makes the adventure of love grow in your heart. Right now you are alive to the essence of love. You are love!

Essence of Truth

Being aware of the essence of truth in your life brings you now to a space of absolute peace and order in your life. It is important right now to really listen to your truth and allow this newly developed aspect of yourself to unfold and you begin to allow your heart to be listened to. Listening to your heart brings the magic of your new emerging truth to you right now. Opening your heart to your truth reveals to you now the essence, energy, and life force of a truly realized life. Don't be afraid to go beyond yourself when you listen to your truth and really allow the essence and beauty of who you are to become "one" with your newly emerging heart. The heart of yourself must reveal itself to you now as you begin the quest inward to finding the missing links, to activate your heart's intelligence. Truth is the hidden message in the uncovering of yourself to find your essence, beauty, and life force. Believing in the truth of your heart to reveal itself to you only reinforces that which is love filled. The love-filled heart is truthful. The love-filled heart is peace-filled. The love-filled heart brings to you now your sense of truth for all there is. You are just feeling the essence of your newly emerging truth unfold as you open to the mystery. The mysterious heart of yourself is truth filled. Truth is the capacity to know your heart is being listened to. A truth-filled person radiates a belief in the beauty of all of life as being an intrinsically creative expression of all that is good. Within every person lurks the demon of lies, of untruths. These untruths are needs not met; of desire, which needs to be satisfied. Live through your truth-filled heart now. You are love.

Your Heart – Your Light

The precious gift of yourself is the best advertisement to love. You are your own best advertisement to bring through the power and light of love when you allow the precious gift of your heart to be your light. You open up the world to an unbelievable degree. You are shedding precious light all around you as you witness yourself opening up to your truth. This is a time for this mergence to take place now, as your precious heart is held up as a gift to the universe. As you light up the chambers of your heart, you are addressing core issues about your deservability to be human. You are challenging yourself to become something more than you could ever possibly imagine. You are allowing this precious gift of yourself to begin to awaken to the greatest event of your life and that is the capacity to love even more. You now own a lost part of yourself that has escaped and cannot be found. You are now just feeling in your heart this lost part being brought home to heal and love. Just now take yourself home to your lost part and allow the precious gift of who you are to guide you to a space of pure forgiveness for all there is. This is a time for mergence of all your selves into an integrated whole. The essence, energy, and love you are capable of giving to yourself magnifies, and you are free to bring to your world this loving energy. Allowing the precious gift of yourself to be integrated is an example of a pure heart, open to the gift of loving.

Peace and Light

You must allow yourself now to bring to your world a sense of pure peace and light for your journey. You are bringing to your world now a sense of pure peace and light for all there is and you are remembering all you ever were, it is a time to allow the remembering to take place as you light your world to bring your heart home to yourself. Right now you are seeking to find within yourself a special space for that remembering as you open up your heart to your truth. You now need to feel the special remembering activate your cellular memory to create new pathways in your consciousness.

You are allowing yourself a sense of peace and light to just know you are free to bring to your world this love and truth and you must feel the sense of allowance of this to be taking place now.

You are feeling now the special feeling of knowing you are safe in this remembering and that it is giving you all you need for your journey home to your heart. Allow this remembering to take place now as you open up to the world of "All Love."

Remembering allows you now to really be in a space of pure delight for all there is. Just knowing you are opening up to this remembering brings you into resonance with all there is as you envelope yourself in the incandescent glow of "All Love."

This is a time for quiet reflection, for allowing the essence energy and life force of who you are to merge into oneness with all there is. It is time now to find within yourself a sense of joy and peace in all you are capable of as you open up your world to finding within it a sense of wonder and joy in everything. You are love.

Ownership of Creations

Bringing to your world now is an ownership of all your creations. You must feel the essence of ownership of all you have created and allow yourself to feel now that you are free to do what you like with your life. This is time to just allow the precious gift of yourself to merge into oneness with all of life and this stillness and order brings you to a space of complete peace for all there is. When you allow the precious gift of yourself to be your guide you are opening up to the power and essence of all there is and you are magnifying all around you with love and compassion. You are bearing witness to yourself and this new self just keeps growing and growing. The essence of your truth brings you to a space of oneness for all of life as you relive your patterns of pain and loss. You are opening up to the world where love, peace, and beauty surround you as you and the mystery become one when you allow the mystery of who you are to envelope you. You allow yourself to merge into oneness with all there is. Merging takes place now when you truly believe in your capacity to listen to yourself and bring to your world this special remembering. You are feeling the need now to just allow yourself the space and energy oneness brings; for oneness is in everything and every living thing resonates to the call of love. For you right now, you are allowing the special magic of every living thing to bring you all you need for your love-filled life. The essence of who you are resonates to truth, light, and oneness. You are a witness to this truth now as you merge completely into the light. This mergence is actualizing you and you must feel the essence of "all love" around you now. Believing in your capacity to hold this energy only magnifies your love. Truth for yourself. You are love.

Remembering

Bring to your world now the belief in your totality. You are aware that you are solely responsible for everything that happens to you, as you seek to find within yourself the blessed gift of remembering who you were. You are challenging yourself now, to accept and integrate all your "selves" for remembering.

Integrating all your "selves" supports your ability to hold focus and intent for remembering your totality and who you were. You are now allowing the integration process to take place now.

You are just feeling the essence, energy, and life force return as the integration process is shifting old worn-out pathways in your consciousness right now. You are just opening up to all the possibilities of remembering who you are, and just focusing on one thing, right now, your responsibility to yourself to "remember" exactly "who" you are.

"Who am I?" You may ask.

You are composed of many selves, each of them with an energy and intelligence that is going beyond your belief in whom you currently "think" you are.

You are releasing now the need to really think at all. For when you think, you are activating one pathway at the neglect of all your "selves." Believing in your ability to think only reinforces one certain type of "belief" pattern. This belief pattern only allows you to examine any issue through the lens of "the past."

The lens of "the past" reinforces only one way of being human. Right now you are examining "your belief" in all your "selves" and right now, you are integrating all those "selves."

Observe your Flaws

Being in the company of those who are receptive to your newly emerging self brings you now into alignment with the forces of "All Love" to assist you.

Ask yourself now: *"Do those you have in your life support or reveal something to you about yourself?"*

We must observe those who are revealing a flaw, because this is where we can begin to grow. Right now challenge yourself to look beyond your own narcissistic image and really ask yourself: *"Is this relationship bringing me closer to me seeing myself in a loving way?"* If not, you must examine why you are not opening up and creating a view of your world that embraces your perfect self. Your perfect self must be polished like a diamond. Other people mirror flaws in the diamond. They shine your flaw back to you. They do this either deliberately or unconsciously. Either way "you" are left with the "speck" or "blob" on your energy field. You must clean up what has been shown to you. However, you must keep guarding and wiping away your own specks of fear, so others cannot mirror these "specks" or "blobs" to you. Keep reminding yourself what you are giving out to invite this criticism.

Ask yourself now: *"Am I really attending to my need to 'love' myself right now?"*

If you are tired, sensitive, etc. you may react angrily at being exposed. Your job is to work on this aspect of yourself. You must explore your own inner possibilities for allowing yourself to be opened up to yourself, as you align to the forces of "All Love" to assist you. Be guarded when you are opening up to your pain, and protect your pain with a shield, (like a Band-Aid), so those in your life cannot challenge you while you are going through the powerful cycle of self-examination. You are love.

Receiving

It is time now to consider what you are bringing to your world and what you are allowing yourself to receive. You must every day allow yourself the gift of receiving. You must just feel the essence of what receiving means to you right now as you open up your world to the precious gift of yourself. In your world now you are opening up to the sound of your own voice as you ask yourself:
"What am I receiving today?"
"What am I allowing myself to receive?"

It is very important to allow yourself to receive, when someone is offering you the gift of their time, skill, or expertise in something, or just love, a hug or acknowledgement of yourself. Right now, begin to draw down the spirit of receiving and be receptive to receiving. You are just now allowing yourself the magic of receiving all you need for your life, as the moment passes very quickly. Attune yourself now to receiving.

"What can I lovingly receive today?" I must consider myself first. *"What aren't I allowing myself to receive right now?"*

Am I "too busy" to stop, be still, and receive the free gift nature brings me every day? Am I afraid to receive the precious gift of stillness, peace, and joy my life brings me now?

When you are opening up to receiving you are acknowledging your worth, and you are respecting the source of that worth. This is an important time to just acknowledge the preciousness of receiving. For if you do not receive, you are not in harmony with universal laws. The universe can only be balanced when those people acknowledge "receiving" as a way of life. Receiving must be a way of life before you go out into your world of "giving." Allow yourself the gift of receiving right now. You are love.

Self Love
Bringing to your life right now is the belief that you can grow through the experience of witnessing yourself through the miracle of self-love. This miracle is yours now as you unfold in your belief in your "self" worth. You are now opening up to the precious gift of all you are capable of as you allow the magic of your own identity to bring you all you need right now. By allowing yourself the gift of self-love, you are enveloping yourself in a precious moment of absolute totality in all you are capable of. Just feeling this special magic gives you a chance to really show yourself that you are allowing your love to shine for yourself.

Your love shines through attention to detail, through your thoughts, words, and actions. Tend your garden well, as you really bring home to yourself all you are capable of. You are capable of allowing yourself the joy and knowledge that you are one in this preciousness. This precious energy brings you home to your heart, as you envelope yourself in the oneness of all there is. You must feel when you are opening up to the world of "All Love," a special magic for the forgiveness process.

The forgiveness process implies that you, the magician, are open and free enough to allow the energy of who you are to envelope you. You are now realizing you are capable of so much as the energy of love and forgiveness surrounds you. You are allowing the gift of yourself to be one with the essence of all life. The essence of all life surrounds you now as you allow yourself to come into resonance with all of life.

Being in the energy of "All Love" reinforces all you are capable of as you open your world magically to all around you. You are now allowing the precious gift of all you are to bring you home to your truth. You are love.

Forgiveness

You need to feel right now the power and life force your new journey is bringing you as you allow the spirit of forgiveness to bring you to a space of absolute trust in all of life. For when you forgive all you are inviting trust to come to your life. You trust that better, more powerful, and higher vibrations are coming your way.

When you forgive you begin a new cycle, and this new cycle opens up to abundance, for you are not holding onto past patterns of fear around receiving something better. Forgiveness implies respect for others, and forgiveness brings to you knowledge that you are beyond that cycle in your life that draws those frequencies to you.

Most of all forgiveness shows a respect for yourself and an ownership of your own worth.

You must say: *"I am worth more. I don't need to really look at this past. I am free to bring this gift to myself."*

The gift of "All Love" is the outcome of forgiveness. The forgiveness of myself for all I have created in my life now brings me to a space of joy and renewal for my life as I open up my world to the energy, life force, and magic of renewal.

Allowing the spirit of forgiveness implies you have left the past behind. The past is a reminder of what has happened and cannot now be. Just completely letting go, is an admission that you are resurrecting yourself again after losses. When you do this you are allowing the forces of "All Love" to guide you upward and outward as you bring to your world your belief in all you are capable of. You are now allowing this essence to bring you into space of pure truth for the mystery. You are love.

Completeness

The time is upon you now to bring to your world your commitment to a way of being that doesn't compromise truth. You are now allowing yourself to grow a perspective of yourself that brings now the knowledge that "you" are deserving of all you are creating in your life right now.

"What do I deserve now?" You deserve to feel complete in everything that you are achieving and you need to allow this completeness to envelope you now.

Being in a space of completeness only reinforces peace, beauty, and order in your life. When you feel complete you are acknowledging to yourself that you are resurrecting a part of yourself that needs to feel whole. There is wholeness in everything. Every living thing has encoded in it a sense of completeness. When you allow this state of being to envelope you, you are allowing yourself to really bring to your world a sense of truth and order in everything.

You are allowing now the sense of completeness to be your guide as you open up your new heart. Your new heart must feel love in its completeness every day. Every single moment brings you to a space of absolute joy in everything. You are one in the essence with all of life and every single event in your life brings to it a sense of completeness and order.

It is time now to allow the sense of completeness and order to be your guide as you bring to your world a knowing that all is magical and that your world has encoded in it, *"I am complete"* right now, *"I am complete."*

Bringing to your life now is a sense of allowing the forces of "All Love" to bring you all you need. It is time to find within yourself the sense of completeness in everything that you do and allow this completeness to envelope you. It is time to feel that you are capable of allowing a sense of knowing that you are capable of allowing the forces of love and completeness to guide you.

Stop and reflect on when you felt the essence, energy, and life force of a complete phase in your life envelope you. Whatever you are doing in your life right now, just reflect on the nature of completeness and feel the nature of completeness envelope you.

You are now allowing this magical feeling to bring you all you need in your life, as you open up to the journey completeness brings. It is time to just feel now a cycle finished in your life now. I have completed a cycle in my life and it is finished.

Now I no longer need to do any more. I have finished with whatever it is that needs completing.

This is a powerful new time, and one that brings a sense of resurrection to your tired weary spirit. Your spirit is in need of completeness right now, as you open up to the mystery of "All Love" as a way to bring you to a space of forgiveness for all there is. It is time now to allow this sense of completeness to bring you all you need for your life right now. You are love.

"You" First

You are bringing now the ability to contact a part of yourself that only knows one thing and that is to consider yourself first. You are allowing the special part of yourself to really open up to "All Love" as the special magic of who you are envelopes you in the gift of "All Love." Right now, envelope yourself in your own robe of self-indulgent love. You only need to consider yourself first, and you only need to be aware of what you want for yourself.

This is time now to really bring yourself to yourself, and consider you first. Allowing this gift reinforces all that is good and affirming in your life, as you open up your heart to yourself. You are now allowing the magic of your own self to fully emerge as you open up your heart to the mystery of yourself. You are allowing this special magic to bring you all you need for your life to align yourself to the forces of "All Love" to protect you.

Right now, you are opening up to this magical abundant self, as you bring to your world the magic of who you are. You are one in essence with all of life as you truly are one with the mystery.

You are one in essence with all of life, as you bring the sacred essence of who you are to your life. Believing in the essence, energy, and life force of every living thing only reinforces your belief in the totality of every living thing. You are alive to the essence, energy, and life force of everything in your world right now, as you open up to the mystery. You are love.

You are bringing to your world the possibility that all of life and you are one. You are now allowing this vibration to infuse your cellular memory as you awaken from your dream of illusion to be fully alive to your potential. You are now allowing for the vibration of this new way of being human to envelope you as you share in the gift of the magic and endless beauty of all there is. This time is one of surrender to "all there is." The surrendering to "all there is" opens up the web, the web of endless possibilities, and the web of infinity.

What is the web of infinity? The web of infinity brings the possibility that you are at the center of an ever-moving spiral dance of light where every imaginable experience is open to you. Just open now to this belief about yourself.

You are now allowing this endless web of possibilities to spiral upward, outward, and inward, there is a dance of pure light of a myriad of endless possibilities all around you now. You are awakening to the mystery of this magical energy right around you, and you must now allow yourself to surrender to this magical view of yourself and your world.

This is a time to allow the spirit of renewal, and all there is to bring you to a space of just remembering. The remembering just keeps you in "the loop," and you are vibrating to the possibility of "All Love." You are opening up to "All Love" as a way of being human. You are "All Love" now.

Your "Gift"

Imagine now you are allowing yourself one gift in the whole world. Today is the day you can give yourself any gift you can imagine. What would it be? Just for today you have the gift of bringing to yourself all that your true heart desires. Right now reflect on this. What does your heart need right now?

All day try to focus on this gift and imagine it has already happened, that you are living it already.

Now write it down:

Your gift to yourself today is. . . . .

My gift today to myself is the knowledge that I am doing all I can to bring. . . . .

My gift today is to accept that I am worthy. . . . .

My gift to myself must be to allow myself the magic of my life, and all I am capable of. "This magical gift now allows me all peace and love." You must keep attuning to the gift of giving to yourself every day. You must feel the essence, energy, and life force of giving to you every day. Every day I give myself a gift of remembering who I am, and every day I am blessed to know I am safe and able to bring to myself all I need for my life.

My gift is one of hope that I can be completely released from all fear of receiving in my life, and my ability to receive this gift is determined upon my love for myself. I love myself enough to give myself the precious gift of magical love and my life reflects this now. This is my gift to myself today. When I am fully in alignment with my gift, the universe accepts this and gives to me. I am love.

The Golden Flame

You are undergoing profound and permanent change right now as you open yourself up to the world of multi-dimensional reality. You are feeling the essence, energy, and life force surround you and you must just feel the power and love for yourself grow as you open up to your world.

You are now allowing this special magic to renew you at a time of rapid growth for you in your life right now. This rapid growth heightens the feeling of "All Love" around you and brings you to a space of gentle renewal for all there is.

Imagine yourself now just stepping into a golden flame. You are now feeling release and disintegration as the golden flame burns brightly all around you. You need to allow this release to take place gently and slowly and you must feel the magical essence of your new reality unfold around you.

You are bearing witness to a new aspect of yourself as you awaken to the mystery. You are feeling the sadness of all those who have ever loved you and now cannot love you in your new form dissolve. You are feeling the love and peace of the new mergence with the beings of love to assist you in your new journey. You are now just allowing this new mergence to take place now, as you open up to the mystery of "All Love" around you. Beginning to allow this special magic to enfold around you now brings you to a space of "All Love" for the mystery. You are one in essence with "All Love" now as the spirit of your newly emerging self brings you closer and closer to the mystery. You are one in essence with the mystery. You are one in essence with all of life. You are love.

Your New Reality

You are now embracing a lost part of yourself, and this is your heart. Right now you are embracing yourself in love for your heart. Your heart is now being opened up to embrace its truth. You are allowing a lost part of yourself to be encoded for new frequencies. This is now time to allow this lost part of yourself to be encoded to bring to you all you need for your life. The essence, energy, and life force of your new reality imposes itself on your totality. You are allowing this totality, this lost part of yourself to be fully embraced now.

Draw the power, energy, and life force to you now. As you open up to your world, you are allowing the essence, energy, and life force of all there is to be your guide as you bring home to yourself, your truth. You are magnifying yourself totally on to your perfect self, as you open up and align to the forces of "All Love" assisting you right now.

The forces of "All Love" are creating with you now as you bring to your world the essence, energy, and life force of all around you. Bring to your world now this essence, magic, and life force to bring you all you need for your life. You are one in essence with all of love; all of love and life supports you now. You are one in essence with all of life. Trust in the energies of "All Love" assisting you now. You are love.

Endless Love

Being in the presence of yourself is an awesome gift you can give yourself right now as you open up to the mystery within you. Your journey takes you further and further into yourself as you recognize old patterns emerging and now you must seek to examine them. You are allowing the precious energy all around you to bring you further into your endless loving self.

Allow the spirit of your endless love to awaken in you now. Feel the dormant spirit of your heart awaken to the mystery of yourself. For you are now bearing witness to a very real and loving aspect of yourself right now, as you begin to breathe in the essence of all you are capable of. You are feeling now the need to really bring to your world the sacred mystery of who you are.

Right now, just feel this sacred mystery in your heart. You are attuning to the sacred mystery of all life as you allow the essence, energy, and life force become one with you. This is time to place around you a big glowing shield of pure crystalline light declaring who "you" are as you bring forth your "immortal" self. This "immortal" self, your immortal self glows with the incandescent light of all there is. Right now feel this energy bubble all around you, as you awaken to the mystery.

You are now one in essence with all of life as you awaken to the mystery. You are now feeling the essence, energy, and "All Love" around you as you awaken yourself to the gift of who "you" really are: love.

Isis Mysteries

Isis gifts you with love as you open up to her mysteries. Isis now holds the energy of "All Love" in your heart as you now allow the precious gift of your heart to open wide to the mystery. You must feel the essence, energy, and life force of "All Love" around you as you open your heart to yourself.

You are now going to feel the precious magic of all there is around you as you open yourself wider and wider to all there is. It is time now to bring to your world a sense of wonder for all there is. As you open up to the mystery, allow the precious gift of who you are to bring you to a space of love and purity for all there is.

When you begin to feel the essence of "all" around you, you are just receiving all there is. This is a time now to believe in the magic of the world as it is being presented to you. You are now bringing to your world a moment of pure joy for experiencing all there is. You are allowing this precious gift of experiencing "All Love" to open you further and further to your truth.

It is time now to bring to your life all there is for the gift of receiving. The special gift of receiving today brings me to the heart of myself. I am love. I am love.

Success

You must just feel the magic and life force of all around you as you begin to remember who you are. You are just allowing yourself to feel and remember what success is.

What is success? Success and failure are only measured by your willingness to let go of past patterns of judgment about yourself in your world. Your ability to gauge your success is determined upon your willingness to let go of all pre-loved conditions you place on yourself about your ability to know what is successful or not.

What is a success? What is a failure? Do you think you have the right to place such judgment upon yourself? At this time of your awakening and mergence into the light, are you prepared now, to let go of all your judgments of yourself, past, present, and future? You are just owning a part of yourself that has become lost, damaged, and broken. You are now allowing the precious gift of your life to be your guide as you open up to the mystery of "All Love." Right now you are just determining what is important in your life as you really examine core issues about deservability.

It is time to get the magnificence of who you are, to be really encoded on your cellular memory. The essence, energy, and life force for all you are keeps growing when you are opening up to "All Love" as a way of being human. Just give the precious gift of who you are to be your guide. You are love.

Just receive; you are working to bring the precious gift of receiving to you now, as you open up to the mystery. All of life now celebrates with you in the receiving. By receiving you are able to give more, so much more, because your heart opens to love. The love of receiving now brings you to a space of gratitude for all there is, and is helping you right now to remember that it is you who is creating the world of truth.

Right now, please allow yourself the magic of allowing the magical beings who have helped you to love come to you in abundance for all there is. The abundance is all around you as you open up your heart to yourself. For that is what you are doing right now, you are opening up your heart to love. You are love. You are love. You are love…

Trust

It is time now to really consider the meaning of trust. *"Who is worthy of trust?"* How do humans learn to trust when the world feels so hostile, alien, and lonely at times? Trust is one of the most important ingredients in the making of the "love" cake. You cannot have love without trust. To trust in love when you have been betrayed is the most important challenge in being human. As humans find it so difficult to trust after loss, it is important now to just feel the love and peace envelope you as you begin the journey into your heart.

To trust implies that you consider life to be sacred. You are now bringing this sacred trust to everything that you do, say, and feel. To trust implies that you and life flow. You can jump into the river of life and start swimming again after losses. You are aware that you are trusting when you allow the sweet flow of "All Love" to guide you to a new world. This new world brings you to your truth where your life is sacred. Your life is a special gift where trust and light go hand in hand.

When you trust you are opening up to light, and when you trust you are challenging a part of yourself that knows no boundaries. To be able to trust the forces assisting you is the greatest act of love you can give yourself, for in this trusting, there is mergence and light.

True mergence implies the trust process has been activated. To trust after losses is to acknowledge that you and life are one, and that all of life hears your call to be free. You are love.

You are now bringing to the world yourself as an oracle and seer. You are now feeling all you are capable of as you open up to the mystery. It is time now to really allow yourself peace and support as you open your heart to yourself.

You are now one in essence with the Great Mother, as you feel the power gather. You are allowing your spirit to merge with the Great Mother, as you allow the divine essence of "All Love" to envelope you.

Breathe in now the special magic of all life, as you embrace the miracle you are. Embrace all aspects of the miracle you are right now. You are now embracing a part of yourself that needs to come home, so welcome yourself home to yourself now.

Begin a dialogue:
"I now welcome a part of myself home that has been lost. I embrace change as I welcome my heart home. I am allowing my heart to be opened to change as I make the invisible, visible."

Right now greet yourself as if you were a stranger and really welcome that part of yourself home. It is time to welcome this part of yourself home now, as you open up to "All Love" as a way of being human. Just getting yourself open to receive, and bringing your heart home to yourself, allows you to feel the essence, energy, and life force of all life.

You need to feel the essence of "All Love" around you. You are one in essence with "All Love" now, as you embody the miracle, you are. It is time now, to develop the essence of who you are by allowing the mystery of who you are to be one with all of life. You are love.

Allowing the essence of your life now to envelope you brings you closer and closer to the mystery. For the mystery is unfolding right before your eyes as you bring to your world the essence of "All Love." Right now you are enveloping yourself in the mystery of belief in all you are capable of. You are allowing this sweet success to guide you and bring you home to yourself. You are allowing the magical essence of your life to bring you home to all there is.

When you bring the magical essence of your life to its peak, you are radiating power, energy, drive, and life force. You are allowing the essence of "All Love" to bring you home to yourself, as you just stop and listen to yourself.

Stopping and listening to yourself brings you home to your truth, for it is your truth which leads you on the spiral dance of love for all there is. Allowing this special magic of who you are to radiate out to the universe allows you to feel the love, magic, and essence of all there is. Just allowing this magical energy brings you to a space of knowing you and the world are free. You and the world are one. It is time now to just feel the vibration of truth radiate out for all to see, feel, hear, touch, and taste. Engaging the senses brings you home to yourself. You are one in essence with all of life. You are love.

Power

When you believe in who you are, you are changing the molecular structure of who you are and everything in your world. You will allow the essence of who you are to radiate out. This radiation will create a powerful change in your own worldview, and you will begin to see yourself for who you are. You must feel the strength radiating all around you, as you open up your world to all there is. This view of yourself just keeps flowing outward, spiraling out like a rainbow prism to bring you to your own heart.

Right now you must seize your power, define your boundaries, and live fully from the heart. You must feel the power, energy, and life force radiate all around you. As you seize this power, say to yourself now:

"I seize my power, and I radiate power all around me. It is safe to be powerful. It is safe to be powerful."

You must feel this power, and you must challenge all parts of yourself that deny you your power. Your personal power center is in your center, your "belly" and your belly reflects your power center. "This is my power center." Take your power back, reclaim it, and bring you back to your heart.

When you feel powerful you are radiating out your love and truth. Power is conferred upon you, when you recognize you deserve every good thing in your world. It is time now to claim your own power, for we need the powerful ones, the centered ones, for what must be done in our world.

Seize your power now! Don't be afraid.

"All Love"

The Mother Isis blesses you with energy and support. You are allowed now to bring to your world the love and support you need for your journey. It is time now to bring this love and support home to you, as you open up your world even further to your truth.

You are now allowing the essence of this amazing world to be yours now, as you reach out and bring "you" home to the essence of who you are. When you are driving a new project, you are allowing the essence, energy, and life force of all there is to be your guide. This will bring to you the power and magic of your amazing life.

"Just allowing your own amazing life to be superimposed onto your new reality will allow the essence, energy, and "All Love" to be your guide. You are allowing "All Love" to be your guide right now as you bring to your world, this wonder, and a wonder it is, just basking in the essence of 'All Love.'"

You must feel that you are opening your world now to the world of multi-dimensional reality, as you bring home to yourself your truth. Your life and world needs you now to allow the essence of "All Love" to be your guide as you open up yourself to your truth. Allow now the essence of your world to be your guide. You are love.

You the "Star"

Believing in what you are capable of is a true mark of a star, and to be able to do this reinforces power, love, and respect for who you are. You must now allow the essence of "All Love" to be around you as you bring to your life all there is to love.

Right now you must challenge all previously held beliefs about what it is to love and to create love. You need now to really allow the precious gift of your love to guide you to a space of remembering just who you are and what you are capable of.

Right now is a good time to challenge all core beliefs about love and loving. You are bringing to your world the essence of love and what love is worth. Your love is worth what you are prepared to invest in it. You must guard against emotional love, which only feeds off desire.

Ask yourself: *"What price is love? What price is desire?"* Release desire, allow love to grow. When you allow love to grow, you are bringing to your world the essence of all you are capable of.

Your love grows when you attend to yourself and weed your garden of desire. Bring now to your life your own commitment to the very thing you are capable of: This is your need to feel safe. You are loved and safe. You are love.

Source Energy "All Love"

You are now allowing yourself to experience wholeness. There is a sense of wholeness and love around you, which reinforces the desire to really bring your world the essence of truth. Just now bring to your world the sense of true knowing that you and your world are one in essence with all of life.

Every day you allow the precious gift of yourself to grow your spirit; you bring home to your world your love. Your love brings you to a space of knowing that "you" are free to do what "you" want with your life, and that you are capable of achieving mastery over the small limited mind.

You are now allowing the source of "All Love" to be your guide as you open up to the mystery, and allow yourself the love you deserve. You are now finding you are able to bring to your world, your truth and love for all there is. It is time to bring to your world the essence of truth for the mystery.

Bring to your world now your belief in all you are capable of, and allow the special essence of "All Love" to be your guide. This is an important time to open up to the mystery. The essence of the mystery is to love with completeness. This completeness has at its core, the sense of knowing that everything is in its right place and time, and that the order, essence, and life force bring you to a space of love for all there is. You are love.

You are allowing the powerful force of love to surround you and keep you connected to the source of "All Love." The source of "All Love" keeps you connected to the aspect of what is needed now to clear, heal, and renew your spirit.

Right now, the essence of "All Love" surrounds you and keeps you in a space of divine connection to all there is. It is time now to allow the precious gift of all there is to bring you to a state of peace for all there is. You are allowing this precious state to be your guide, and you must allow this precious adventure of who "you" are to guide and shield you.

You are bringing to your world the source energy of "All Love" which is what Isis the great magician represents. Isis, the great magical of natural elemental magic brings you into alignment with all there is. All of life celebrates in the magical essence of Isis, and all of life celebrates the magical essence of our great mother Isis.

"Right now, Isis the great magician, the magician of restoration of hope after losses, oversees all, and she respects the source of all life, which is life itself. You are respecting the source of all life through the energy of Isis, and evoking 'her' brings you home to the essence of all you ever were and all you will ever become in human form."

Allowing the magical intent of mother Isis to be your guide brings you home to the mystery. You are love.

Isis Blessing
Isis greets you now with a message of love and forgiveness of self for the world you have created right now. You must just allow yourself the special peace and forgiveness now, so you can bring to your world the special magic forgiveness brings.

You must just allow the essence, energy, and life force to bring you all you need for your life of love. You must stop and process all aspects of your life right now, as you open up to the mystery. You must just allow this special magic to be your guide and you must bring to your world the essence of "All Love."

Isis blesses this day. See your life now embracing the great mother and see the magic essence, energy, and life force bring you home to the mystery.

You are allowing the special magic of Isis to be your guide as you remember exactly who "you" are. It is time now for this remembering as you open up your world to "All Love."

Isis allows for the beauty of your life to unfold under her guidance, and you must feel the magic she represents in every single thing that you do, say, and feel. Bringing home this magical intent, you are opening up to the magical essence Isis represents.

Allow the magic of Isis to be your guide by stating your intent for your day.
"What is my intent today?"
"Where are my challenges in realizing this intent?"
"Why should I intend anything?"

Allow yourself now to follow your own true inner intent by staying completely in the "now" as you align your compass for your goal.
"This is my goal, and I stay in the 'now' to achieve it."

Rejuvenation
Isis now brings you the gift of rejuvenation and youth for your total and unconditional love of me in my ascended form. You are remembering your power as you open up your world to the magic and mystery of all there is. This is an important time to step into your own power as "you" allow "yourself" all you ever need to bring to your world, "All Love." Just allowing the sacred gift of the mother, give you all you need. For all you need brings you to a space of completion and order in everything.

To state your intent for love is an admission that love is a powerful force operating in your life right now, and you must feel in your life right now the magic of your unique capacity to love. This is a time to reconnect to the memory of this love as you bring to your world the knowledge that you and the world are safe and loving.

Allowing the world to bring you the sacred gift of your love brings you home to yourself. This sacred gift allows the magic of all you ever were and all you will ever become to bring you to a state of knowing that you are capable of bringing to your world this knowing. Allowing your sacred self to grow through the mystery is an act of consecrated love for yourself, as you open up to your own power to bring to your life everything you are capable of giving to yourself.

Ask yourself now:
"What am I capable of giving myself now?"
"I am capable of giving myself 'peace.'"

My Intent
You are allowing the magical essence of who you are to envelope you as you open up your world to "All Love." You must feel the essence of "All Love" bring you to a space of great peace in your life. Right now, you are opening up to the essence, energy, and life force of "All Love" as a way of being.

Just flowing in the energy, and being like Arachne the spider watching, being still, brings you into alignment with all there is. You are feeling the energy and power of your own life enveloping you and keep you in a space of true abundance for all there is.

This is a time for allowing the precious magic of "All Love" to guide you and heal you. You are love. You are allowing this love to grow now.

As you open your day, your intent will determine exactly what you are bringing to your world.

What are you intending right now?

Are you intending that you create peace, magic, or renewal in your day?

What is my intent?

When I intend it, I become one with the "intent."

Allow

You are allowing yourself to merge in oneness with all of life as you bring to your world the sense of magic and "All Love." You are allowing now the story of creation to be your creation as you part the veil and bring to your world the precious magic of who "you" are. You are love. Just feel the magic essence, energy, and life force of "All Love" around you as you surrender to all there is. It is time now for this surrender. You are love.

You are allowing the precious gift of "All Love" to be your guide. This is unconditional love and you must ask for this gift every day. Your life must reflect your ability to really allow your sacred self to be your guide as you journey even deeper into your heart. It is time to bring to your world "All Love." For that is all there is. "All Love."

Your gift to yourself now brings you home to yourself. Ask yourself now to consider what is important in your life? What is important will be reflected to you. You reflect what is important. What am I reflecting? Peace; freedom; love.

Your Heart's Journey

Feeling the power of now brings you home to your heart. Your heart now becomes your only guide for living humanely and humanly. This is a special time to really allow the essence of who you are to be your guide as you open up to the world of unconditional love.

To truly love unconditionally is to be in a space of total acceptance for any situation. Just being in acceptance of any situation brings you home to your heart.

The heart of yourself beats in love for all there is and you need to feel the essence, energy, and life force bring you home to yourself. You are allowing the essence of your life to be your guide, as the magic of new beginnings opens you up now to beginning your journey to the heart.

Right now just accepting the joy, magic, and special spirit of all there is, reinforces a space of magic and forgiveness for everything.

You are just feeling now the essence of "All Love" bring you home to yourself, as you allow "All Love" to be your guide and friend. Being in this state of magic for all there is allows you now to tap into a source of unconditional love for every single thing in your life right now. You are love.

Ask yourself now:
"What is it that needs attention?"
"What in your life needs your focused drive?"

Bring now into your life your focused attention so you can begin to allow the moments of pure joy to be your guide. You are love.

The Essence of Isis

Isis is everything. You need to feel her energy in all aspects of your being. This is a time now to really embrace the essence of Isis, in all "her" forms. It is time now to fully consider the perfection of Isis in all her aspects.

You must now open up to embrace our great mother Isis in all her forms. Isis is a representative of the divine feminine in all aspects of the mystery. The mystery is my story and Isis is "your" story. You are born of the great mother, and you must attune to her in all her aspects. It is time now to really allow Isis to be with you in all her forms.

Isis is embracing you now, in her essence, glory, and oneness. Opening up to her love brings you peace and abundance. Allow this abundance to be yours now.

Believing in the essence of "All Love" brings you to the state of inner perfection Isis represents. She is love.

When you bring to your world you own capability to love, you allow the energy of sweet success to be around you. Right now it is time to just magnify your intent for all there is, as you open up to the mystery. You are love.

Respect
You are viewing your world through the lens of power and respect. Bringing to your world power and respect confers on you now the ability to draw on the essence, energy, and life force of all around you. It is time to allow the journey to the heart to bring you to a state of bliss for all there is. While you are in a space of truth for all there is you are bringing hope to all around you. Right now, you are just breathing in all there is to bring you home to yourself.

When the magic of Isis opens up to your world, you are safe and happy, for Isis is the great mother. Isis brings to your world the respect you deserve for all you are doing for others, and Isis embraces you with her wings of freedom.

It is time to embrace Isis for she feels your pain and she answers that pain. Right now, you are in pain, and the pain of being hurt through others "stings." You feel stung, and you must just allow the sweetness of her love for you grow. Bring to your life now the sweet feeling of "All Love" for she is "All Love." Just now attune to her in her motherly caring role, as you have been mother to others, and it is not forgotten. Isis brings you to the state of grace you need for your life right now.

Allowing yourself the experience of believing in your vision brings you closer and closer to all there is. It is now time to consider exactly what it is you are trying to do with your life and completely surrender to your vision.

Magic

Believing in magic is the beginning of allowing you to really access part of yourself that lies hidden or dormant. Magic for you now is to just step inside love and feel. Just step inside love. You need to just step inside the part of yourself that knows love and feel it. Give yourself time to experience the almighty power of love in your life now so you can just feel. You are opening the way to the feeling heart, in the process of stepping inside yourself and going into "your" self. It is time now, to just feel the energy, magic, and excitement of allowing yourself the magical essence of yourself for yourself.

All women who create with Isis are magicians. You use magic every day, aligning to the sacred elements and opening up to the heart. The center of the universe brings peace, oneness, and "All Love" to you right now.

Bring to yourself right now, your capacity to just keep remembering all you ever were, and take the power of who you are now to create in your life the perfection of "who you are."

The miracle of love will keep you alive to the mystery of "All Love," as you open your world even further to all there is. It is time now to really consider everything in your world having meaning for your heart. You must allow the heart of yourself to open to all there is as you bring yourself home to the sacred essence of "All Love."

You are now allowing the precious gift of allowing yourself to create with the mystery. Allow the mystery to be your guide as you bring to your world your belief in "all there is." It is time to just allow the sense of oneness to be with you. You are love.

Unconditional Love

Isis blesses your love and allows your love to burn brightly. Your love with yourself must burn brightly and you deserve to receive all you need for your life. You are allowing the precious gift of your love to give you all you need and you must remember to really be loved by yourself. Just allow yourself to "be loved."

You are allowing yourself to take yourself to a space of unconditional love, and you must just feel unconditional love all around you now. It is time to energetically bring to your world all you need for the precious gift of yourself, for all you are capable of. You are vibrating to "All Love." You are allowing "All Love" to be your guide right now.

When you align to your truth, you are bringing home to yourself your belief that you can create magic. What is magic? It is the knowing that "you" are the center of "your" universe, and your heart is engaged in every act.

To begin the road home to love allows you now to discover just what "you" want for your life. You are feeling the essence, energy, and life force of all around you, as you open up your heart to all there is.

Your gift to yourself is in understanding that you are allowed to really feel exactly "where" you are in your journey right now. It is time to come to a space within yourself to bring to your world all you need for your journey.

A strong intent creates in you all you need for your day.

Ask yourself: *"What am I intending right now, for my life?" Align to the forces of nature; shoot your arrow and "feel."*

When you allow your heart to open to its truth you begin the adventure of self-discovery. The true nature of self discovery brings you home to a part of yourself that only knows one thing, "you." You are just too important a resource to neglect. When you neglect you, you are ignoring your essence. The secret sacred part of yourself that only knows one thing "love." For to go through life without this precious gift of love leaves the soul bare, and unable to cope living in a human body. You must allow yourself this gift of yourself to bring to your world your precious miracle "you."

Right now you are allowing yourself the knowledge that you can create miracles every day.

"*What is your miracle today?*"

"*How are 'you' going to get 'your' miracle today?*"

Listen to your heart. For it is in your heart, that you will find your miracle today.

Receiving Love

The essence of Isis is in my ability to bring you to a space of awareness of what it is actually to love. What is it to love? To love is to bring you home to a part of yourself that knows one thing. This is the joy and beauty of a life that knows how to love. Knowing how to love. How do you love? How does a human know love? What makes a human love? A human loves by allowing the mystery of love to unfold around her. Her essence is a loving one and the essence of "All Love" brings you home to the secret sacred part of yourself.

This secret sacred part of you knows one thing, truth. When you are truthful to your heart, you begin the journey home to love. Allow yourself now the spirit of love to unfold around you, as you open your heart to the one truth.

I am now allowing the essence of my love to unfold around me, as I bring myself home to my heart. I am love.

Bring now to your heart your capacity to really feel what it is to receive. Do you know what it is like to receive love? Watch how the dynamic of your day unfolds with love.

You are Special

Isis brings the essence of love home to you now as you begin to explore the world of unconditional love. You are opening up to the essence of "All Love" as you explore the mystery, and you bring home to your world now, this feeling of love and peace.

This is time to really allow the essence of "All Love" to guide you and bring you home to yourself. You are love and you bring love to every living thing. Every living thing vibrates to the call of love. Every living thing houses love inside them. You need to listen to this love, and bring it home. Bringing home the essence of love is shaping your world right now.

Right now you are bringing to your world the power of rejuvenation. When you rejuvenate you become one with all there is, as you feel her force all around you. You are love.

Allowing the specialness of who you are shapes your reality in a way you cannot imagine. Your reality is shaped by the conditions, which feed love into you. You are feeling this love, and as you do you are opening up to the mystery.

The mystery brings the specialness of love to you now. The specialness of love allows for "All Love" to guide you and you need to feel that you are one in essence with all life. Bring this magic to you now as you allow yourself to connect in love for all there is. You are allowing this specialness to be your guide.

Bringing peace to your life allows for your heart to share with you its truth. Right now align to a sense of peace in your very being as you bring to your world, your love. You are a living embodiment of peace.

Allowing yourself now to really shape shift and become one, brings you to a space of pure magic. Just imagine you are able to shape shift, to bring to your world a sense of specialness and magic.

You are shape shifting when you align to the forces of magic to bring you all you need for your life. You align to these forces when you allow Isis to enter your consciousness, and when you feel you are bringing to your world this truth. It is time now to really allow the special magic of who you are to bring you all you need for your life as you allow the spirit of "All Love" to infuse your cellular memory. You are opening up to this now.

Bring Isis in today and shape shift. You are a shape shifter. Right now consider yourself first before anyone; it is not selfish, just honoring the "self." It's OK to say "me" first, it opens your heart. Try it.

The Power of Magic

The essence of Isis is with you now, as you bring to your world your love. It is time to really allow your own belief in your own power to bring you all you need. Just surrender to the power of magic.

Say every day:
"I surrender to the power of magic."
"I am magic."
"I am now allowing my magic powers to guide me."
"I am love."

Believing in all these things about yourself brings you closer and closer to your truth.

Right now you are bringing to your world the special magic of all there is. Ask yourself now: *"What must I surrender to bring me all I need?"*

Isis is the magician of sacred magic, and Isis is now allowing this belief about herself and you to open you up to all there is. You are now bringing to your world the special magic of Isis right now. Align your intent to bring your truth to you now for all there is, and you are allowing the special gift of who you are to bring you to a space of love for all there is.

You must bring to your world now, your own belief in all there is, as you open your world to the sacred magic of "All Love." Just feel now the sacred magic of "All Love" guide you and bring you to a space of "all there is."

All there is just keeps the remembering alive in your heart. Magic is the special quality you give yourself when you know and trust life is a sacred act. Align now to the forces of love to create magic now.

Your Secret Sacred Self

Isis allows the special mystery of the immortal you to bring you all you need for your life. You are allowing the gift of all there is to be your guide, and you must feel the special magic and energy of *just allowing your secret sacred self to emerge and bring you all you need.*

This secret sacred self just keeps growing in your heart as you open up to the oneness of your life. You are opening up to the oneness of everything as you bring through truth and magic. You are one with me now.

Right now you are bringing to your world the energy, life force, and magic of all there is. You must consciously intend now what it is you want today, just feel in your heart and intend.

Self Abuse

Isis speaks now of allowing the special relationship with you and she to grow. Your link with Isis brings others closer, and you must draw on others visions and strength for our world. You must continue to align your consciousness to "All Love," and bring "All Love" to you. "All Love" is allowing you the opportunity to really go into the heart of yourself, and bring you all you need for your truth. Just now open your heart up to the essence of "All Love" through our mother Isis.

Isis brings you now the message of forgiveness. You must now forgive yourself for your hatred of your "self," your heart. Do not abuse your "self." You are love.

Isis brings to you now the essence, energy, and life force to really shape your totality. This totality has encoded in it every living thing. The essence of every living thing brings you to a space of oneness for all there is, and allows "you" to merge into oneness for the totality of every living thing.

Just ask yourself now:
"What is it you want for your life right now?"

You want for your life the energy of trust in everything. The energy of trust in everything brings you to a space of knowing "you" are free, and that freedom is a gift, a rare gift you give your soul to grow. Trust in the essence of every living thing to bring you all you need for your love-filled life. You are love. It is perfect right now to bring to your world the essence of the mysteries. The mysteries bring you your truth, and you must feel what is really important and express it. What is important to me right now? Express it.

Isis speaks to you of allowance. You must now allow yourself to really bring to your world the special magic of "All Love," as you open further and further into yourself.

You must feel that you are bringing to your world the essence of "All Love" and live through the mystery. Just stop and feel now what it is you want to do with your life, and then you will begin to really allow the essence of who you are to bring you all you need for your life. It is now time to remember who you are and allow the magic of who you are to envelope you. You are love.

Right now gather to yourself your capacity to know you are able and ready to challenge your previously held beliefs about your identity. Who are you? Allow who you are "now" to shape your identity, not who you were or think you should become.

Allowing the essence of "All Love" to surround you brings you now to a space of loving surrender for all there is. This is a time now to really focus on your own ability to know and trust that you are able to bring to your world this special magic in allowing yourself the beauty of your life.

The journey is in feeling the sacred presence of me, everywhere, as "you" the immortal "you" brings to your heart the complete totality of who you are.

Allow the special magic of who you are to bring you to a space of love and forgiveness. You are love. The vibration you are feeling now will bring to an inner knowing that "you" the immortal "you" is opening up to love and you are safe in this new feeling.

Isis speaks now of allowing the gift of freedom to be your guide. You are allowing yourself to be embraced by your own magical essence and this magical essence only brings you closer and closer to your truth.

Trusting in the message of Isis allows you to feel you are vibrating to the essence of "All Love," and "All Love" brings you to a space of totality within yourself right now. You are now allowing the special magic of who you are to bring you completeness in your life, as you open up now to your potential. Just now bring all the energies of "All Love" to you now. You are love.

You are now allowing yourself the privilege of being in a space of surrender to all there is. When you surrender you are stopping yourself from over criticizing yourself or others. Just surrender. What do you need to surrender today?

The Blood of Isis
Isis blesses your life and projects and she is there for you now so you don't feel so compromised by others. It is time to bring to your world your own belief in yourself, as you allow yourself to grow. Just keep intoning that you are the "blood of Isis."

"I am the blood of Isis" and you will receive me in my pure form *"I am the blood of Isis."*

Living Peacefully
You are now allowing the energy and life force of your heart to grow. Allow yourself to really touch the part of yourself that must fight for your own ability to live peacefully.

"Why can't I live peacefully?"

You need to find within yourself the precious gift of magic to be really with you at all times. Just stop and bring to your life your real belief in me, the magician Isis to help you at all times. You must now feel the essence of "All Love" around you.

When you believe in your own ability to have all you need for your love, you become the sacred magician you are meant to be. You are love.

Why is it hard to believe in magic? Why is it hard for humans to believe that the journey to love will create such stress in humans? It is important now to carry the love and truth for the magic of yourself, for you are, the great magician, and must hold to your magical intent always. It is time to really allow the essence of who you are to resonate with your truth, as you awaken your dormant spirit. Awakening your dormant spirit brings you closer to the mystery of "All Love."

Bringing the magic of "All Love" to your life increases your receptability to receive even more. Try it now by intoning: "I am "All Love.'"

Isis now shows you that you can open your heart to yourself, and believe in yourself if you bring to your world your belief in what you can do with your life. You are able now to really bring to your world the energy and drive to fuel your life. Put energy back into your life and allow "your" life to bring you all you need for your life. It is "your" life and "you" must be able to manage it.

Say to yourself: *"I now lovingly allow 'my' life to bring 'me' all I need."*

To begin to love yourself, you must release all those who are not serving your truth. Who do you need to release right now? Release brings peace to your troubled heart. All love.

You must now just remember that "you" are free to do what you want with your life. You are free to open up your immortal heart to your truth and bring through the energy of "All Love" to this planet.

It is important that you do this at this time, so you can allow yourself your truth. Right now you are clear and free to do what "you" want with your life. You are one in essence with "All Love" as you open up to the mystery. The mystery is the enactment of ritual. By enacting the ritual, you become the magician. You are the magician now.

> Ask yourself: *"Am I free to do what I want with my life?"*
> If you cannot be free, you are holding back your trust in yourself.
> Say:*"I am free now to do what I want with my life."*

The great mother Isis blesses the essence of who you are right now by being in a space of oneness of forgiveness of every living thing, as the mergence takes place now. Right now, all your energy selves are merging into oneness with all of life. The essence of all life is to live with the energy of forgiveness.

You are opening up to this forgiveness now, of every living thing. Every living thing vibrates now to the call of unconditional love. You are vibrating to this energy now.

The essence of your truth lives in your ability to believe "you" are able to bring to your world the absolute surrender to love. You are love. Just walk into your heart.

The essence of renewal lies in your ability right now to really listen to that voice in your heart that says, "I love you." The voice that says, "I love you" will bring you to a part of love for all there is and you must feel this love everywhere.

You must now be a witness to the part of yourself that knows how to feel, and you must allow this part to bring you to the state of "All Love" for the mystery. Owning this part of yourself now encourages you to take responsibility for all that is happening to you as you begin the journey home to the heart.

Speak to yourself now and say: "What am I bringing to my world today, that wasn't here yesterday?" You must allow yourself to really consider your ability to feel the essence of "All Love" as you challenge yourself to love.

"The Activation of the Galactic Heart: The Heart of the Mother"

You are speaking to Isis when you bring to your world your need to really feel the essence of "All Love." You speak to me now when you allow this essence of me to speak to you. Right now you are encoding the heart of the mother onto you as you awaken the divine spark within you. You need to feel this essence now as you listen to your heart. Your heart knows this truth, and your heart always speaks your truth. You are your heart right now.

You are your mother's heart, as the heart of your mother beats for you, so you hear her call. You are love and loved by the mother. Your new heart is now awakening to the mystery.

Bring down the power of allowance now, as you ask yourself to be recoded to receive the energy of your absolute abandonment to your true magical self. You are love.

Your miracles are in observing your emotions and how they bring you to a space of love for the mystery. Your miracles occur every day as you allow the power, essence, and life force of "All Love" to surround you. For when you do, you create the miracle of yourself, as you bring to your world your love. Allow the special gift of love to be your guide as you open up to the mystery of all there is. You are love.

When you speak through you heart, you are breathing love into all fears that "sabotage" your higher self from assisting you. Breathe lovingly into your heart and speak love.

You are realizing the miracle in allowing your life to just unfold as you honor the sacred elements, and listen to all around you. It is time now to feel the mystery, live the mystery, be the mystery.

Allowing the mystery to unfold around you now brings you closer to the source love. The message from me now for you is to trust the source love. "All Love" is from the principle of the feminine.

You are allowing the principle of the feminine to surround you. You are love.

Embrace Yourself
The life force of creation merges with you now as you begin your heartfelt journey into "you." Breathe in your special ability to trust yourself now. You are love.

The transmission from the mother Isis embraces you now as you as you open up your world to "All Love." You are embracing the world of "All Love" as you surrender to the mystery. You are one in essence with the mystery as you embrace the sum totality of who you are; allowing yourself to believe in the mystery brings you home to yourself. You are love.

You are now allowing yourself the gift of unconditional love when you allow yourself to really feel where you are in bringing home to yourself peace. You are peace.

As you embrace yourself again, you are embracing a part of yourself that knows how to feel. Through feeling you are allowing the source of "All Love" to be your guide. You are allowing the essence of who you are to bring you to a space of truth where there is only "love." For when there is "love" there is "peace," and a peaceful heart knows only one thing, the beauty and light of being alive.

When you open up to the mystery, the beauty and love of being alive surrounds you; your essence embraces you. Just touching this part of yourself is a gift to yourself. You are love.

It is now time to celebrate the essence of who you are. Who are you anyway? As you dance into your heart, find your gift. "Yourself," You are love.

Breathing in the life of "All Love," allows the spirit to resonate in your heart, and you become a witness to yourself. This witnessing of yourself only reinforces the truth, and the truth of your life, and "who you are" will bring to your world the sacred essence of "All Love."

When you view the world through the lens of "All Love" you are alive to the mystery. You become a channel for this extraordinary energy, as the essence, energy, and oneness now are yours.

Your world is a sum total of the extraordinary love you are capable of giving and receiving. Witness this aspect of yourself now, as you birth yourself to the spirit of "All Love." You are love.

"I now allow the spirit of forgiveness to bring me to a space of completeness. I am alive to the mystery of my own power to love. I am love."

Heart Mergence

Right now to experience the essence of oneness implies you are free and able to bring to your world the truth of who you are. The truth of who you are is in the acceptance of yourself to truly forgive the aspect of yourself that is now bringing to your world the passion and life force. The passion and life force you are capable of reinforces the spirit of trust and forgiveness for all there is as you allow yourself to fully merge into the heart of yourself. Allowing yourself to fully merge into the heart of yourself is a gift to your heart to bring you all you need in your life. It is time to fully experience the essence of "All Love." You are love.

Bring now to your world the essence of love and forgiveness for everything. For in forgiving everything, you become one with everything. Being one with everything makes you whole. You are love.

Isis brings now the gift of the true heart to love. To love the process of the true heart lies in the acceptance of the process of remembering. For when "we" remember, we are allowing the spirit of who "we" are to guide us, and when "we" do this "we" become one with who "we" are. The oneness of who "we" are helps us connect in "All Love" to our truth.

To connect in "All Love" to our truth brings us home to ourselves, and we become what we are. "Love," the essence of "All Love" brings us home to the miracle of who we "are," a being of true "remembering."

We are all love now. We are all love now.

Right now trust that "you" are able to bring to your world the essence, energy, and life force of true remembering, as you walk into your heart. Just now, feel the flames burn off all fear in remembering who "you" are — love.

By allowing Isis into your life, you are allowing the special part of yourself to grow and merge into oneness with all of life. All of life merges into oneness for you now as you allow the essence of your heart to open and grow.

Allowing the essence of who you are to open and flow brings you to a space of pure peace for the mystery. The space of peace for the mystery keeps you alive to all there is and you must allow this special flow and remembering, to keep you connected to the source of all life. The source of all life lies in the mystery. You are love.

Your love grows as you begin to remember. Just remembering your power to love keeps you in a space of purity for all there is. You are love.

Now you are feeling the opportunity to merge in oneness with all of life. You are allowing yourself the peace you deserve. You deserve the peace you are giving yourself right now, for it is in the peace that you flow and merge with the essence of all life. You are one with the essence now.

Bringing to you now is the key to the mystery. When you are attuning to why you are here, you are letting the part of yourself feel the peace and essence of all life. You are love.

Believing in the essence of who you are allows the state of oneness to create with you now. You are merging in oneness with all of life right now as you bring to your world the opportunity to grow and receive through the heart. The essence of the heart lies in the mystery. You are love. Right now you are merging into the heart. Allow yourself to merge into the heart to bring you all you need to keep you safe. You are love.

Acceptance
Isis brings you now to a space of pure acceptance of yourself. You must allow yourself the precious gift of knowing you are able to have the precious peace you deserve. You must just allow the essence to grow and take root. You must continue to monitor your relationship with yourself and bring "All Love" to your soul. You must allow the message of "All Love," the energy of pure bliss to bring you now to a space of forgiveness for yourself.

When you accept your life right now, you are going to be able to bring more light into your aura, and move your light body into a space of pure peace.

Breathe in the power of your own ability to really bring to your world peace right now. You deserve to feel peace filled. Just stay in the moment and you will feel safe. You are love.

You are allowing the essence of "All Love" to be around you, now you must ground "All Love" into the core of the Earth for it to hold. You must feel the magic of your special universe that brings you all you need for your life right now. You are love. Discovering what you are capable of achieving brings you fully into the aliveness of being human. You are embracing now your own unique capacity to feel "your" achievements. You are love.

Bring me into your heart now to solve the pain of those you love. Your love for others brings you to a space of pure forgiveness for all there is. You are breathing into your heart the special magic of forgiveness for all there is. Just forgive yourself for wanting an outcome. Don't have attachment to outcomes.

When you love you are placing your heart into the hands of the divine ones to protect you. You are allowing the special magic of love to bring you home to your heart. You are love.

You must focus on yourself now as you bring to your world the absolute essence of "All Love." The essence of "All Love" guides you and protects you now as you allow the energy, magic, and life force to guide you. Bring to your world the essence of "All Love." You are love. You are love. You are love.

You must allow yourself the magic Isis brings. This is a time for allowing the special magic of Isis to bring you all you need in your life. Allow the special magic of Isis to be your guide as the mystery will be revealed to you. Just allowing the mystery to be revealed to you brings you to a space of purity for all there is. You are love.

When you allow the essence of appreciation to be your guide you allow your world to reveal to you the secret of forgiveness. For when you appreciate, you have forgiven. You are love.

The Heart of "All Love"
You are allowing the essence of "All Love" to guide you and you are keeping the fire alight for your dreams. You are now allowing the special magic of "All Love" to be your guide, as you uncover all aspects of love. You have a deep and powerful love and you must remember humans aren't capable of much loving. Just bring to your world the essence of "All Love" to everything in your life right now. You are love. Bringing the essence of love reinforces peace and truth.

By being in the presence of truth and love, you allow yourself belief that anything is possible. You are love. Isis allows the essence of her world to be revealed to you now as you bring peace, space, order, and respect to every living thing. Everything in the world brings with it order and respect. Order and respect go hand in hand as you embrace the heart of yourself. Allowing this energy to envelope you right now brings your heart into resonance with its truth. You are opening up to the heart of "All Love" now. You are in the heart of "All Love" now. You are love. When you alight your heart to its truth, you become one with the essence of all life. You are love.

The essence of Isis lives in you now. The essence of Isis is one for you as you open your heart to trust. Trusting implies that you are vibrating to the essence of "All Love." "All Love" is around you now as you open up to the mystery. You are love.

Bring the essence of truth to you now by staying completely "in the moment" when presented with any situation which does not carry the vibration of truth. You are love.

Stillness

Isis allows your heart to begin its journey into a new space of pure stillness for the mystery. Do not forget exactly who you are as you take the journey into this undiscovered part of yourself. You are allowing this essence to really bring you home to the part of yourself that only knows one thing— love.

You are now beginning to acknowledge to yourself that you can feel and be in the presence of all those who have ever loved you. Just feel this now.

I am being lovingly embraced by all those who have ever loved me. Bring Isis to your heart by staying close to your heart always. Remember you are opening up to the essence of your life and you must feel all you need for your life. Bring the power of "All Love" to you, merge into "All Love," dissolve and merge into "All Love." You are love.

It is time to bring to your world the belief that "you" are able to have all that your true heart needs.

"What does my heart need for its growth?"

Ask yourself, listen, and feel. Always feel. Your answer lies deep in your heart. When love goes to another level, you are allowing "All Love" to open your heart. Allow "All Love" to open your heart now as you journey deeper into "you." You are love.

Trust is what makes love grow. Just now stop, and trust that all is perfect right now, and that life unfolds in a magical way, when you hand over your "mind's" power to your "heart's" love.

Your world with Isis grows now as you allow your truth to be revealed to yourself. You are gathering the energy for your journey to love and you are allowing the essence of love to be your guide as you bring your world your truth.

All of life is an adventure to experience oneness, and life brings many adventures. Just being alive right now is an adventure to love. Ask yourself:
"What does the adventure of love mean to me right now?"
"Am I willing to allow myself this adventure?"

Your world now has encoded in it pure magic as you open up to the vibration of Isis. It is time now to really focus on what Isis means to you, as you begin your journey to the heart.

You must feel the essence of "All Love" around you as you open to the mystery. You are love.

My intent today is to bring to my world all I can to receive even more. I acknowledge to myself my belief in myself to bring me all I need to love. I am love.

Aligning yourself to the forces that represent "All Love" and truth bring the special magic of forgiveness for all there is. Right now consider what you need to do to bring to your world your love. You are now allowing this love to envelope you.

Isis in a New Form

You are now birthing me Isis, in you in a new form. This new form brings to you a sense of peace and renewal, and you are allowing yourself to create with the magic and energetic renewal I represent. Just allow this sense of renewal to bring you to a state of grace within yourself as you bring the mystery closer and closer to you. By birthing me in your heart, you are bringing the source of all life as I am the midwife and I oversee all birth. Birth, death, grief, and loss all are one with me.

When the essence of all there is creates magic with you; are feeling the source of all life create with you. This is time now to just feel this creation, and manifest with it. You are love.

You are allowing the special essence of who you are to guide you and provide you with strength and support. Don't give energy to the past, just allow the precious gift of yourself to guide you and bring you home safely to your truth. The essence of "All Love" brings you home to yourself right now as you align to the forces of "All Love" to assist you.

Ask yourself: *"Who is assisting me right now?"*

Your heart is assisting you because your heart wants to heal from pain and loss. Your heart wants to feel that there is no pain. Your heart assists you in growth, and your heart brings you home to your truth. Your heart is your very best friend, and will bring you home to your truth. You are love.

Enjoy the magic of what you are right now by surrendering everything, absolutely everything to this precious miracle of who "you" are right now.

You must now reflect on the nature of our mother Isis, as you open up to "All Love" and allow the precious magic of Isis to be your guide. Just now allow yourself the essence of who you are to be your guide as you open up to the mystery.

You need now the gentle support and peace after the upheavals of others' energy in your life, by processing the grief and leaving it behind you. You are not drawing on old patterns of fear, old patterns of fear around loss and betrayal. You must just finally and permanently close the door. You must just align to the forces of love to heal you at this time, as you allow this special magic of your life to be your guide. The essence of "All Love" resonates in your heart as you bring to your world peace, love, and order.

Bring to your heart now your own knowledge that you are able to have all you need for your journey to completeness. You are allowed to feel complete as you open up to the essence of yourself. You are love.

Divine Abundance

Isis blesses you now with divine abundance as you allow the sacred essence of who you are to bring you all you need. You must allow your heart to feel now that you deserve all you need for your life and grow all you need for your life.

Just now bring to your world this belief that "you" are able to be completely free to bring all you need to your life and world.

You are allowing the precious gift of your heart to be your guide. You are love.

Isis allows the true gift of abundance to be your guide right now as you align to the purpose of pure peace and adventure. Your adventure is an inner one and an outer one as you bring to your world your relationship with yourself. You are love.

Trust is the message right now. Life is a trusting process, and to trust, you must receive. Trust and receive brings you into alignment with all there is. You are love.

Isis blesses your day with divine abundance as the core energies of your being are being opened up. You need to really focus on these core issues now in your merging journey to love. Your mergence is now being conferred upon you. Allow the essence of "All Love" to be your guide. You are love.

Be expressing your love for yourself you are allowing your core identity to merge and create with you in essence for who you truly are. You are free to really begin to develop this love now.

Completion

Isis now allows the essence of completion to be your guide as you bring to your world all that you need for your journey. You are opening up to the essence of "All Love" and the essence of "All Love" blesses you and protects you. You are love.

Allowing the magic of completion to be your guide brings you closer and closer to a sense of unity and order in everything. What do you need to complete now?

You are allowing the sacred essence of "All Love" to be your guide as you align to the forces of magic to heal and protect you. Isis the great magician blesses every aspect of your world now as you open up to the abundance of your life. An abundant life brings truth and you are aware of your truthful life right now. You are love.

To believe in the aspect of yourself that needs to feel love is allowing you now to really bring to your world the sacred essence of who you are.

You are allowing the forces of love to bring you all you need for your life as you gather power, strength, and light to your energy field. It is time now to really feel the forces of "All Love" gather and protect you to bring you all you need for your life. You are love. You are now experiencing life as a holograph. Open up to your multifaceted self and trust you are experiencing all you need for your life.

Peace and Joy

You are feeling now that you are able to bring to your life and world the essence of peace and joy. It is time to allow the energy of "All Love" to be your guide as you open up to the world of pure magic and light. Bringing to your world now is the essence of "All Love."

You are one in essence with "All Love." Strengthen your love through the essence of trust in yourself. Why do you not trust yourself to love? Allow your heart to open, so you can begin to trust in "you."

You are feeling the light shine as you open up to your heart. Your heart is the best barometer for your health. *What does your heart want today? What does my heart want today?* Your heart now needs to feel the power of unconditional love without the entrapment of emotional slavery.

Bring your heart into resonance with your truth by affirming now: *"I am allowing myself to flow with my essence "self"; my heart."*

The world of pure light becomes you now as you allow the special magic of who you are to be your guide. You must feel now that you are allowed to really "feel" exactly what your heart wants now. *"What does my heart want now?"* Your heart now wants to be allowed to have its full component of DNA to be fully activated to live completely in the now. Your heart now wants to feel peace, truth, and light.

Your heart now wants to feel, heal, and remember. Your heart wants to know it is safe and your heart wants light, lots of it. You are allowing now the essence of your fully realized self to come alive. Who are you anyway? Just ask yourself: *"Who am I?"* I am a being of incredible light, power and mystery.

You must feel now that you are able to really go into the heart of yourself now and ask your heart direct questions. Just always ask your heart what it wants. You must allow yourself now to really bring to your world all you want for your life, as you delve into the mystery. Allow the mystery of who you are to be your guide. You are love.

You are now bringing to your world the true nature of remembering. When you say: *"Who am I?"* you are releasing yourself to the space of true remembering. Activate this remembering by staying completely in the present. By allowing Isis to grow in your heart, you are bringing to your world the peace and love you deserve. You are allowing the special magic of a self realized life to be your guide as you open up to your world to the magic of your heart. Allow the special magic of this fully awakened heart to be your guide.

Your gift to yourself now is to be completely awakened to your potential. This potential lives through your own ability to know that "you" the real "you" is "love."

You now need to recognize your own power and worth with love. Isis understands and brings the magic of love to you, and Isis allows the energy of this magic to be your guide. Just bring to yourself now the message of hope for your life. It is important now to hope that you can love, and you "allow" yourself. What are you allowing yourself now? You need now to really focus on your own ability to draw down the sacred elements and allow yourself the peace and light of your life. You are allowing the essence of "All Love" to be your beacon now as the magic of "All Love" is bringing you all you need for your life and world.

It is time to allow this special energy to create with you and bring you to a space of knowing for "who" you exactly are, a love-filled being. The feeling now of exactly what you want for your day must be experienced now. What are you feeling now about yourself to create the perfect day? Feel your power.

Bring to your world now the sacred essence of who you are by allowing yourself to really connect to the heart of yourself. You are connecting to the essence of "All Love" as you awaken to the mysteries. You are one in essence with "All Love" as you bring the sacred presence of "All Love" to you now.

You are allowing now your own truth to emerge when you align to the forces of your own magical self. Just now ask yourself: *"What is it that is bringing me all I need?"* Your answer lies deep within you. Listen!

Mergence

You are allowing you own love and truth to emerge as you bathe in the incandescent glow of "All Love." This is time to be aware of the mergence and total release to the great mother herself. You are remembering the source energy and power in your life as you open up to the essence of your truly awakened self. You are love.

You must now give yourself the peace to create all you want for your day now. Just breathe in peace and allow this inner stillness to release all fear around your deservability.

You are turning the corner as you open up your heart even further to the mystery. When you feel your energy opening you are aware of just how powerful love is, and love brings you to a space of peace and love for the mystery. Bring now to your world the magic of this remembering by always staying **"in the now"** and allowing the energy of who you are to bring you all you need. You are love.

Bring now to your heart your own delight in what you are capable of achieving right now. Ask yourself: *"What is it I am bringing to my heart now?"* Draw to you, your delight in this "moment."

Right now you are allowing the special magic of Isis to renew you and bring you power. You are allowing your gift of your magical self to emerge and bring you all you need for yourself. It is time for allowing the energy magic and life force to be your guide. This is love in action, and loving actions bring the soul into resonance with its truth. You are love.

You are allowing the precious gift of yourself to be your guide when you open your heart to yourself. Just now breathe in the essence of your "self." You are love.

"All Love"

Allowing the essence of "All Love" to be your guide brings you to a space of truth and light. You are acknowledging now that you must just feel the essence of "All Love" around you, as you go further into your heart. You are finding now in your heart, your truth, and you must allow this truth to be revealed to you. Allow the secret essence self to bring you all "you" need for your life. You are love.

The belief in your totality allows now the surrender to your core identity. *"What is your 'core' identity anyway? How do you express your inner most self?"* You must just allow yourself to really bring to your world the essence of yourself and live through the immortal heart. Allow now the gift of yourself to magnify and radiate out to the universe. You are love.

The Essence of your Heart – Live in the Moment

What are "you" doing now to live through your immortal heart? You need now to celebrate the essence of your humanness, because you have found this. You have found the essence of your humanness. You are love. Being alive, just being alive to your potential brings you home to who you truly are. A miracle of creation. Cherish your creation. Yourself.

You are bathing in incandescent light, and you are a light body of incredible energy essence and life force. You are in the arms of Isis now, and everything in your world reflects this energy, essence, and life force. You are absorbing the rays of the great central sun, and you are filling up your world with this energy.

You are allowing now the essence of all life to be your guide and you have forgiven every living thing. You are every living thing. Every living thing is in you and every living thing becomes you as you allow your magic to be your guide. You are allowing every living thing to bring to your world the essence of "All Love." Every love is your love, every thought your thought, every fear your fear. You are a detached observer of these things.

The balance of these things allows for you to bring to your world the essence and life force of "All Love."

"All Love" is yours and "All Love" is your gift to yourself, your unique contribution to yourself is your love of everything you are. Right now dear one, you are complete, and your completeness only serves to show you that it is you who brings to your world your love of yourself. You are the essence of all life and every living thing radiates through you.

You are a reflection of every living thing, and you radiate this out.

Part II
Entering the Temple
of The High Priestess

ACKNOWLEDGEMENTS

From the icy Andean Winds of Lake Titicaca, Machu Picchu, and Peru, to the steamy volcanic craters of the Hawaiian Islands;

with 12 pilgrimages to my soul's home, Immortal Egypt; to the Full Moon ceremonies in Bali, Phuket,

and the Sacred Caves in Cappadocia, Turkey; to the festivals on Mt. Kurama, Japan;
to Strawberry Fields, Central Park, NY,
the heart land of The Mayan, Central America

my own beloved home in Coolangatta, Australia.
I thank you all,

for I have been a witness to the Divine Mother's power to heal, transform, and renew my heart.

I acknowledge all sentient and non-sentient beings who have helped me on my journey,
I give you my grateful heart.

The mother's story is too precious to be lost,
Please share Her story by opening your own heart to receive her wisdom.

– Carmel Glenane

HIGH PRIESTESS VIBRATION

The High Priestess vibration is a divine representation of the "Woman" who brings to her life the capacity to know that she has within herself the emotional detachment to cope with all the losses associated with love. An elixir for losses, the elixir creates changes in consciousness where the "Woman" can see that she is "somewhere" else when she is presented with the truth of a situation.

This vibration offers safety and stability and her detachment from emotional extremes in any situation. It creates grounding not only in her, but also in those around her.

Remoteness creates mystery and she can ignite the fires of love and passion to create all that she and her mating partner need to enliven their souls' paths. Her remoteness creates desire, but those who desire her must be aware of the risks involved. These risks are to leave the ego and emotional authority behind.

She brings eternal beauty and love to a "Woman." Her nature is a respect for all life, but first, a respect of her emotions, she knows how to respect her emotional reactions in any given situation.

She loves being in the presence of the vibration of love and trust, she allows you to surrender to your intuition and she will assist in all the areas of your life where intuition needs to be developed, not feared or understood.

She embraces you now with the sacred blue robe of protection; there is a vibration of the loving surrender to the Divine Feminine.

The High Priestess vibration brings: Balanced clear detachment; loving mating partner energy; surrender to the power of love.

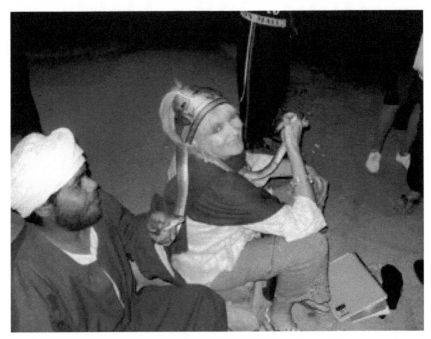

Carmel Glenane – Egypt

Introduction: The High Priestess
Who is The High Priestess?

The High Priestess is an inspirational archetype/ role model for women in today's society who represents everything a balanced woman needs to live a detached, abundant, and love-filled life.

"The High Priestess" is a challenge to all women to fully embrace their life force and power and take personal responsibility for *all* that happens to them in their lives. This book encourages you to embrace the belief that you are solely and ultimately responsible for your life.

When a woman comes to accept this reality, she is assisted by the forces of divine female nurturing, the cosmic mother.

It has been a woman's challenge to define her identity separate from her culture and accepted traditions and religious beliefs in all cultures of patriarchy. To be solely responsible for all that happens to you in your life is one of the most powerful challenges in being human.

About The Temple of the High Priestess

In Part II of The Alchemies of Isis, *"The High Priestess,"* Carmel Glenane explores core issues in women's lives, from relationships to men, intimacy, love and spirituality, career, family and most importantly yourself! The High Priestess offers a practical way of life by empowering and encouraging women to observe their emotional reactions, to not compromise themselves, and embrace their true freedom and power, to live a detached, compassionate and heart-centered life.

•••

This is the journey of my relationship with The High Priestess. Since 1991 in my healing practice I have seen women de-powered within themselves because they hand over their authority, through emotion, to men, their families, and other women. For this reason, having access to information on The High Priestess could empower all women to detach from the emotional "hook in" with loved ones, especially men, in their lives. The High Priestess archetype spoke through channelled writings in response to my questions.

My first questions were in response to the challenges being presented to me in surrendering to the process I was undergoing at the time. The High Priestess became my confidant and teacher.

Having been born from a patriarchal culture, the lessons and teachings of The High Priestess tested every previously held belief about my core feminine identity.

As you read this section of the book, you may begin to notice that The High Priestess can challenge some "core" issues around relationship patterning. I suggest seeking professional help if you feel you need further work on some of these issues. It is strongly recommend that you seek support for your journey as you are being initiated into a new way of being human.

Part II of this book, is an initiatory process. You will be birthed through its discourse. The High Priestess challenges your previously held beliefs and truths about your identity. It encourages you to embody your "core identity" through the heart of the feminine.

CHAPTER ONE

THE HIGH PRIESTESS

The first channelling of this book was with the "Lords of Karma" (a group of ascended energy beings first channelled by Diane Stein in her book *Essential Energy Balancing*). These beings suggested that I needed to develop my own unique capacity to understand myself completely and this is what they channelled:

Draw on your own magnetism and strength. Feel it inside you, let yourself become an inner woman: strength, beauty, tolerance, and your knowledge that you are unique. Be in awe of yourself.

This is where the High Priestess began:

Carmel: *How do you create balanced heart-centered relationships with men?*

High Priestess: *You make demands on a man by allowing yourself space to be you. You need to create a barrier between yourself and a man and this mystery draws him closer to you. You send a charge to him.*

You look at him magnetically, and you say in your mind — "I know the possibilities of what we share, but there is a barrier." Only a man willing to surrender his ego will go to this barrier, feel the hurt of having to let go of his masculine ego, and enter your space. This is unknown territory for him, and he does not have the equipment to deal with it. His boundaries are loosened and you must lead him gently into your world. You must understand and ask yourself what a man wants from you, and you him.

As you open up to The High Priestess you must ask yourself: **What do I want from a relationship?**

It is very important that you list all your questions and the attributes your heart needs for a successful heart-centered relationship with a man.

List your questions, i.e. attributes:
-
-
-

A man who is energetically connecting to you will begin to feel your magnetism. However, the catch is, can he surrender his ego?

The need to create a barrier and make demands not only includes potential "mating partners" but all people who want to "make demands" on a woman's time and energy. You may like to list all people who make demands on "your" time and energy and begin to observe what are the attributes you want from any person in your life.

Masculine and feminine energy create a polarity, and while these relationships don't have to have a sexual, physical vibration it can exist on another dimension. The important thing is allowing the intent to occur and the interaction can be purely an energetic one.

Men are drawn to Her reflective mystery and they are aware of Her power over them. They like the challenge of The High Priestess. She is very alluring to men, with a sense of unattainability, even though she is very close to them, or in their company. They respond and open their minds to the possibility of duality in thinking. She draws men to Her through Her powers of quiet observation and quiet challenge. This synchronicity operates to create desire in a man to "mate" with Her.

Carmel: What does The High Priestess do to bring a mating partner to Her?

High Priestess: *She seeks his higher self's permission. She allows time to bring her lover to her. She knows the value of patience and she develops detachment from emotions attached to a man who She desires. She lets Her lover know She loves him, but She allows him to lead. She then assumes control over Her emotional outcomes with him.*

By developing detachment from emotions, desire is taken to the heart. The emotional heart desires, and these emotions need to be balanced. Many women lose their authority at this level. They confuse the desire as being from the heart. In fact it is from the emotional body of the aura at the heart, not the higher or universal heart.

The High Priestess is the embodiment of your totality. She is you. You allow yourself "space" to express Her, then She can come to you. You can do this by focusing on your crown chakra. Draw a yin-yang symbol in indigo. Envelop yourself in your own cloak of powerful, magnificent energy.

The High Priestess embodies the totality of feminine consciousness in men and women.

Be wise, detached, and nurturing, first nurturing, the self. Be beautiful to you. Be beautiful to those around you. Be beautiful to your lover and loved ones. Open your heart wide. Be in love with all life; be beautiful.

Being beautiful, wise, detached, and nurturing, brings you space to give to yourself first. Don't jump at another person's emotions or expectations, i.e. desires or need to control.

I wanted to explore The High Priestess's definition of beautiful, as our contemporary society's definition of beauty is generally advertising or media based.

Carmel: What is beautiful?

High Priestess: *Beautiful is the quality of light you carry. It is seen by others on your aura. It enfolds you. It is the spirit made into matter. Beautiful is your spirit in physical form. Being beautiful is seeing this spirit and being enfolded by it.*

Carmel: What does a woman need to do to create The High Priestess in herself for her everyday life?

High Priestess: *You can bring me to you through a dedication to me daily: "I dedicate my life's journey to the ideals of The High Priestess."*

Set up an altar: dedicate crystals to The High Priestess. Energize the altar with offerings and devote 10 minutes daily in private worship to the crystals. Look into the crystals and feel The High Priestess come to you.

The High Priestess archetype embodies women who are secretive and have a need to bring to any situation a duality and psychological perspective. She is the power women aspire to in developing relationships with men. She is the most powerful archetype for bringing a mate to Her and keeping him where She needs him to be.

Carmel: Many women and men reading the last sentence could find this statement very controlling and manipulative. I asked if The High Priestess could develop this concept.

High Priestess: *The definition is not ego based. A relationship is to serve a higher truth and divine love. The ability to feel magnetic or to be a magnetic person brings yourself into alignment with your truth and attracts people to you to help you forward this truth.*

The question of personal magnetism was explored in my next transmission to increase personal magnetism.

How does one increase personal magnetism?

Breathe deeply as often as you can think of it:

Breathe in; hold; gently release; building up to a count of 8 seconds.

Breathe in to the count of 8; hold to the count of 8; release slowly to the count of 8: then pause. Repeat this breathing sequence 8 times.

Your chakras need opening daily. Along with this breath sequence, visualize them opening like flower petals. Wear, hold, and be in the presence of crystals to give energy and power.

By opening the chakras, The High Priestess is able to feel strength and power in the base chakra. The base chakra energy center keeps Her earthed, as is all of life that is created through this center. By keeping this center opened and energized She is able to create a balanced relationship with you because you are grounded. Being grounded and earthed is one of the most important attributes of The High Priestess.

The High Priestess is very sexual and open in the base chakra (the energy-center located between the legs). She receives life through her creative aspect. She draws life to her from the Earth. Men love her sexual mystery. She ignites them with the challenge of Her mystery in the pelvic area. She says you can get a man's love by opening the pelvic cradle and inviting a man into it.

The interview response to The High Priestess was giving me confidence, and I decided to continue with this form of communication.

Carmel: What can I do to further develop my initiation into the world of The High Priestess?

High Priestess: *Yes, your world is changing because of The High Priestess.*

You need to find quiet devotional time for Her alone.

You need to find a place deep within yourself first. Feel a sacred space within you for Her now. Feel Her in your heart-center, allow Her to come to you. Your body will tingle when She has settled. Form a relationship with Her. The heart-center seems an appropriate space for The High Priestess. However, any energy-center may feel right for you. Beginning a relationship with The High Priestess can be an organic experience for many.

Carmel: I suggest connecting to mother Mary, who is an archetypal embodiment of The High Priestess, as she is an example of a cultural, religious connection to The High Priestess. Feel the power of mother Mary and ask for her blessing and support for all that you do.

I first found the image of mother Mary who was a good one for me. Mother Mary was an initiate into the mysteries of the Goddess Isis. You may like to work with another feminine archetype who you are familiar with such as Fatimeh, Isis, Aphrodite, Bridgit, Yemanya, Maat, Kuan Yin, Kannon, Ishtar, Ixchel, White Tara, Freya, Artemis or Athena.

A devotional space must be set aside. Devotion means being in the presence of the deity. Devote a period of the day to the deity. Devotion means simply acknowledging a loving source of pure love outside yourself. Devotion also implies surrender, and surrendering to The High Priestess actually gives you a feeling of being grounded and earthed. You are strong enough to not allow yourself to float in a "worship" where you give away your power.

The concept of The High Priestess as a sexual being is explored in the next transmission.

Carmel: When The High Priestess "mates" with The High Priest, what are her responses? Is she supposed to be detached from climax? How does she mate?

High Priestess: *She allows The High Priest to be the man and do what a man does. She responds as a woman responds to a man's desire in a loving but restrained way. She focuses Her pleasure on the divine truth* behind all matings. Her High Priest loves Her beauty, which comes from Her ability to be emotionally detached. It gives him much more emotional freedom. A man cannot get The High Priestess out of his mind or heart, and any other woman cannot fathom why. The High Priest – the chosen one by The High Priestess – no longer has any long-term interest in other women. The High Priestess's power is in the knowing of this emotional detachment and in giving the situation no emotional authority.

Emotional detachment is the essence of The High Priestess philosophy. Observing him in any relationship gives you power. For example, is he sleeping with another woman? He isn't paying enough attention to me! He doesn't follow through with commitment to something we began. These are common observations of women in a relationship.

Moreover, these are "your" emotions, based on "your" subconscious belief system: your "little self." Thus, you must observe "your" emotional reactions to his "behavior." This is "your" learning, "your" growth, and it is where "your" power lies. Thus, emotional detachment comes from observing your pre-loved little self and training it. This is the essence of becoming The High Priestess.

Responding to a man's physical love through divine truth gives sex a different perspective. It doesn't just become a recreational and pleasurable experience, or a sense of duty in a relationship to keep it together.

Your emotions must always be observed and noted. Cherish your emotions. They must always be attended to. Emotions are aging if not kept in check. Aging is a result of emotions out of control. Disciplined procedures must always be observed when emotions are exposed, e.g. vulnerability. Examine this emotion, find its source. This will be karmic. All pain has a karmic pattern. The source of all pain is in the karmic pattern.

Asking yourself: "Why do I have this person in my life?" will allow you to go to a space where you can observe your emotional attachment to that person. The source of all pain is in the karmic pattern. Addressing karmic patterns, especially the source of karma with another, is an anti-aging technique. We age when emotions are out of control as these create stress hormones.

The High Priestess allows for you to address the karmic source through Her frequency. She is available for this energetically. You may like to intone:

"In the name of Love and Light, may the source of karma with_____ be released and transmuted to the light."

The High Priestess is very responsive to feelings. She sends love to Her "mate." She is detached. She is forever in control. She is the power. She is the Truth. The beauty of The High Priestess is that She is very responsive to feelings, despite being non-emotional. This helps another get control of his/her emotions. "Yes, I respond to your emotions, but I do not give your emotion my energy." This helps another who is suffering, because you are not adding further emotion to his/her misery.

As She was an energy who brought this level of power to women's lives; I explored in my next question her attitude to eternal beauty and youth.

Carmel: What is eternal beauty/youth to a High Priestess?

High Priestess: She is forever renewing Herself. She does this through the people She has around Her. They are the embodiment of Her totality. She needs to feel that Her beauty has power. A beautiful woman is powerful. Think of beautiful women in the media and elsewhere. In your society they are powerful. They are respected.

Beauty is the level of light you carry. Your light is always needing to glow. Your body must be glowing in light. It glows by your attention to detail to your body, e.g. through exercise. The light must glow through your ability to cherish yourself, physically. Open your chakras daily. Breathe in the light consciously, daily.

Create respect by giving service. Service gives power. You are always available in your professional capacity. In terms of your availability in your personal life, you don't always have to be available, but in your professional and public service roles you should always be available.

Service for The High Priestess brings power to Her because She is allowing the powers through Her to be available for others to benefit from. She is a beacon of light and becomes an iconic being.

Peace makes a woman beautiful. A peace-filled woman is very beautiful. Peace comes from the ability to know that you are able to handle pain, loss, and tragedy. The High Priestess enables you to find a source of power outside yourself, which is unable to be found in your own ethereal energy bodies. These energy bodies mirror your emotions, which have already been established. The energy bodies mirror your emotions, so The High Priestess must always be evoked to help you seek your divine truth outside of yourself.

Always ask: "Does this person, this situation, job, home, serve my divine truth?" By asking this question your divine truth can be presented to you. You are always the embodiment of The High Priestess when you ask yourself these questions.

Carmel: Could you elaborate on pain of attachment and vulnerability, and sex for security?

High Priestess: *A woman needs always to find within herself control over emotions. Sex is a tool. One of her functions is to have sex for the pursuit of her divine truth. She owes sex no authority over her whatsoever. For her, sex is merely an opportunity to allow her to come to terms with her divinity in human form. For her, vulnerability here must be acknowledged, felt, and located.*

Affirmation:
"I am safe with the expression of my sexuality. My sexuality is for me to enjoy. I love my body enough for it to be enjoyed and be pleasured whenever I wish. Men can enjoy and be pleasured by my body. I am safe in the expression and freedom of my body."

This affirmation is important for you to re-code your cellular memory to accept new frequencies in your sexuality and the expression of it. Loving your body, enjoying it, and feeling safe and nurtured brings you to this new way of being. A man cannot enjoy your body as much as you do. If you don't feel safe and free, how can your partner?

A woman must start acting like a woman with a man. She is a woman. She has so much power. She gives this power away too easily in a relationship. For her, a woman's power is to see a man for what he is — a man. A man must serve her divine truth. There is no other way. She has all the power. This power is not to control another human being, man or woman, but it is there to serve her divine truth.

A woman must feel in control of all aspects of life: her work, her personal life, and her pleasure. Humans find this hard. Emotions rule. Look at the emotion of vulnerability. Where is it located in the body? Is it in the heart? If I have an emotion in my heart, it may feel heavy, it may hurt, like a spear being driven into it, it may ache. First, this emotion must be changed. Visualize it being dissolved, going into another form. Shake a rattle over the heart chakra or where the emotion is stored. Second, ask yourself, "Why did it get here?" Find out "Why." Keep asking "Why?" Keep asking "Why?"

Locate where pain is being held. Knowing where the pain is held in the body will help you discover why you give power away in relationships. You give power away because you are in pain in some area of your body. Healing this pain through observation of your emotions which surface, and breath work, helps find this lost part of yourself.

You may feel isolation, yet power is being a High Priestess. You will feel this. A woman cannot crave security. She can only serve divine truth. You need to be able to sift through emotions, and as emotional reactions to situations arise, you must not try to assume emotional control over outcomes. You cannot have this emotional authority. This is not possible. The character, Morgan Le Fay, in Dion Fortune's books, The Sea Priestess and Moon Magic, is totally in control of emotional reactions. She does not feed off any emotion. When you feed off emotions, yours or others' emotions, you begin to attract negative emotional experiences. The High Priestess is in total control of emotional reactions. She is free of being de-powered through emotions running out of control. She believes in Her higher purpose. Everything is done to serve the ideal of The High Priestess.

Carmel: How can I serve The High Priestess?

High Priestess: *In your dress, your actions, behavior, your jewelry selection, you don't do anything except to serve her. Ask yourself daily, "What does The High Priestess want today?" Let yourself explore her world first. Do everything to please The High Priestess IN YOU.*

Make a list of how often you dress, act, or behave to please another's expectations of you. I am not talking about clothing for employment, etc. but your own personal observation of why you dress to please another's expectation. For example, you may say, "I don't like pink — it's not my color." Why? Who said so? "I do not wear gold/silver jewelry — it doesn't suit me. Again, ask yourself, who said so? It is very empowering to track the origin of these assumptions.

CHAPTER TWO

THE GODDESSES

There will come a time when The High Priestess will challenge you. She will see your growth and will now ask for your commitment to Her. You will need to be more focused on Her in your rituals. You need to evoke Her more consciously and with intention. You will need to have Her assistance in your life and work. Concentrate on Her aspects. You could look at the Egyptian pantheon of Goddesses in their various forms as a guide to developing your commitment to Her. Through goddess archetypes, you can develop your relationship even further with your High Priestess:

Egyptian Goddess: SEKHMET

Egyptian Goddess: HATHOR

Egyptian Goddess: ISIS

Egyptian Goddess: **SEKHMET**
Protector, avenger, fighter
Chakra: Base chakra. Breathe her into your base chakra
Wear: Red clothing and jewelry i.e. garnet, rubies, cuprite

Egyptian Goddess: **HATHOR**
Lover, sensualist, creator
Chakra: Sacral, solar plexus, and heart chakras.

Breathe her into one of these chakras, whichever seems appropriate.
Wear: Turquoise clothing and/or jewelry

Egyptian Goddess: ISIS
Healer, magician, mother, protector
Chakra: Find her in your throat, third eye, or crown chakras
Wear: Deep blue, breathe in lapis blue, and wear lapis lazuli jewelry

By combining these three aspects for loving, healing, and fighting you are allowing your High Priestess to express herself in different aspects. You have to allow Her to be you. It is important to set a time aside for morning devotions. The High Priestess requires at least one devotional time a day: 6 a.m. or 12 p.m. or 6 p.m. or 12 a.m. Rituals are very important for all energy work, because they train the subconscious to accept a new way of being human.

Begin your day:

Put on appropriate music (female vocalists); light some incense and a candle, spray the area with appropriate oils (ylang ylang, patchouli, rose, lemon, sandalwood)

- Anoint yourself first with sacred oil

- Say an affirmation (out loud if appropriate):

"May the energy and consciousness of The High Priestess be with me now to protect me and aid my soul's path."

For Sekhmet's protection evoke: *'Sa Sekhmet Sahu"* visualizing a lioness.

For Hathor's love evoke: *"Bring me youth and beauty always, now, so be it,"* visualizing a sistrum (ancient Egyptian rattle) rattling, sounding it over your chakras.

For Isis's magic evoke: *"Bring your power to be me now, Isis,"* visualizing a falcon on a dark-haired woman's right arm.

These rituals are very beautiful, and do not have to take up a long time.

The High Priestess appears in many forms. You can imagine an Atlantean High Priestess. See the Atlantean High Priestess watching over you now. She is an observer. She analyses. She is separate. She knows the truth. She cares, but She is detached. She is not about to throw herself at people. You must learn to understand The High Priestess. Privacy and exclusivity are important, even when in a relationship. She listens. To bring The High Priestess into you, you need to breathe deeply and more regularly, and get your rituals focused. You need to pause during the day and acknowledge Her in human form. She will assume authority then. She is power. She is feminine power, power over yourself. She is love. She is you.

CHAPTER THREE

QUESTIONS FOR THE HIGH PRIESTESS

Carmel: How does The High Priestess convey language?

High Priestess: *Language is power. Your language conveys expression of truth. Your truth is in language. The High Priestess listens. The power in listening is very important. Words must be consciously chosen. The High Priestess overrides all considerations in the communication debate. "Listen and be receptive" is her message. Language brings to a woman her sense of self worth. She must be able to express her sense of freedom through language. All processes of language, both verbal and non-verbal, are equally important. Non-verbal language is in flow.*

A High Priestess uses her body language to convey her truth. Her body must be still and not agitated. She must focus on a person directly. She must breathe, slowly and deliberately. She must be still, serene, composed, reflective and nurturing. Her energy must not be wasted through distraction or wandering thought forms. Every effort must be made to be still and peaceful in all non-verbal encounters.

Language is power. Listen carefully, and don't give your power away in communication. Reflect, breathe, and observe your own emotions. Why do I have to have an opinion or judgment just because someone expects it? Listening is so important; it is an art form in itself. Listening enables you to buy time so you don't have to have an emotional reaction; your body becomes still and no longer agitated.

Carmel: How does one embody The High Priestess in healings?

High Priestess: *The High Priestess is a powerful healer. All Goddess archetypes express healing as an essential quality. The High Priestess will create a powerful healer in your divinely feminine self regardless of gender.*

For a healing, you need to attune consciously to The High Priestess and feel the link with your client or whomever you are healing. Consciously connect with The High Priestess by focusing on your breathing. She will tell you when she has entered your aura and your client's aura.

The embodiment of The High Priestess is the woman who cherishes herself enough to magnetize from her heart — her power to bring to her world the sense of love and power and control over emotions. Your beauty becomes phenomenal and she needs to see you represent her with dignity and courage.

This frequency in you will make for powerful healings. High Priestess healings will balance out and bring order out of chaotic emotional states bringing calmness and order to the body, mind, and spirit. Her energy is always focused on the base chakra to strengthen and earth. Extreme emotional states reflect an un-earthed body.

Carmel: As The High Priestess is so "controlled in Her responses" how exactly does She surrender to a man?

High Priestess: *She allows Her lover the authority he needs to assume control. She is in peace and loving surrender. She allows Her lover to mate only when She feels She can control all emotional outcomes with him. She gives him a sense of control over Her body. She allows Her body to be used as a temple to Divine Love. She dedicates the mating to the Divine Ones. You can invoke:*

"All Light Beings, allow this mating to be one of joy and happiness for the betterment of all. I surrender to this mating, knowing it serves a higher purpose."

Mating with a man serves the higher purpose of divine love. The concept of love is the union of souls on the physical plane to serve divine order and purpose. To be "in love" is a concept to be exalted in spiritual manifestation.

You do not need to assume authority in lovemaking. You need to allow the union to take place and surrender. There is no need for authority in mating, but a release. You need to release authority over yourself, knowing there is enough emotional control to be detached from expectations of him being your "lover" or anything emotional. It is just a mating, a sacred act without emotional labels our outcomes and it becomes a complete experience within itself.

The High Priestess archetype will also help you release desire in the base chakra, which relates to your sexual energy. She is, in fact, raising the Kundalini or Shakti energy. This energy is powerful. Sexual desire often collects in the base chakra and is held there. The High Priestess will sift through karmic debris, and help you raise your Kundalini / Shakti energy up to the heart-center, where you can experience heart-centered love.

By surrendering to the High Priestess, She can gently (and sometimes not so gently) open your Kundalini / Shakti energy, so you can experience love from the heart. In loving from the heart chakra, you are becoming attuned to the frequency of pure love, for She, your High Priestess, is the representative of love, sharing, and commitment to common ideals. By forwarding the tide of your pure love, your divine truth is forwarded as well. Imagine all the wisdom, from the all women throughout the ages and beyond, entering you and helping you go to the heart. You never have to experience a relationship, which is not heart-centered.

Carmel: What does a woman do to prepare her body, mind, and spirit for this mating as a High Priestess?

High Priestess: *You need to feel total control over emotions. This is your initiation in this lifetime if you decide to be a High Priestess. The High Priestess initiates you through the sexual energies, for which lovemaking is one aspect.*

However, as your body is a representation of your spirit, it is important to breathe light and life into your body. You can become a witness to yourself, when you are in loving surrender, knowing that your emotions are under control.

The High Priestess feels isolation. There will be times when you are not understood by others and you will feel isolated as you are training your emotions. This process of observing your emotions brings you power. As an aspirant to The High Priestess, you cannot crave security. The High Priestess can only serve divine truth. She is for the communication of truth. All aspirants to The High Priestess philosophy need to be taught the ability to sift through their emotions themselves.

Exercises in observing emotional reactions to life's events are always seen as an opportunity to grow The High Priestess in you. A High Priestess must not control emotional outcomes in any situation. She has to learn to understand that Her issues are her own, and She cannot have emotional authority over anyone. She must be totally in control of emotional reactions. She does not feed off them. She is free of them. She believes in her higher purpose. You do everything for The High Priestess, not for a man, woman, or child. You are growing up a part of yourself for the first time and you are learning how to become spiritually mature.

Carmel: Women in our culture would find it very difficult to understand this concept, especially domestic obligations to children in their care. Could you elaborate on this concept?

High Priestess: *Yes, children need to feel security. They also need nourishment at all levels of their understanding. A High Priestess offers security and nourishment but is not a victim to a child's emotions. Children are highly responsive to their caregiver's emotions. They will mirror the emotion of the caregiver or parent and this is where problems begin. The parent/care-giver then has the problem of having to process* not only in her own emotions towards the child, but to have the result of it to deal with also. This does not make for security in a child. The High Priestess requires this truth.

Carmel: How else does The High Priestess require you as an aspirant to represent her?

High Priestess: *She requires this truth to be expressed through your choice of clothing and jewelry. You don't act, dress, or behave for anyone except The High Priestess. Don't try and please anyone by your choice of clothing. Attune to The High Priestess and feel what She would feel best expresses Her in you.*

Most women who aspire to be The High Priestess have had a bitter blow to their psyches. They have been emotionally or even physically abused in their quest to find love and have paid a very big price in trying to find love. The High Priestess knows this loss, and applauds the woman's struggle to find love through The High Priestess. By attuning to The High Priestess you will begin to feel a growing authority over yourself and you can begin to open up to love again as your confidence grows. By growing Her inside you, you will become responsive to the feelings of others and be able to "send" love to your mating partner knowing you have been trained to be detached from all emotional outcomes. You have the inner authority. You are powerful. You are truthful.

All people who serve The High Priestess are under divine protection and those you have around you serve Her ideals. She embodies all that women aspire to, the qualities of balance and duality. The High Priestess brings life to its own center. She lives for her own truth, which serves divine order. Truth serves divine order.

Carmel: Many women struggle with their emotions when their mating partner has another woman. What is your advice to women in this situation?

High Priestess: *She has her own agenda for a man. She is detached from his emotional issues with other women. She knows what she wants from him. She remains respectful of her role with him and nourishes what* they have together. She knows a good man. Her mating with him serves the divine source. The divine source is above human emotions. What she requires from him, however, is his devotion, to look after Her and respect Her. She needs to nourish him. She sends light and peace to him daily to keep him connected to Her.

The vibration of The High Priestess is very Earth based and you need to feel your legs open wide to encompass Her. Feel and watch your legs open really wide; this is like receiving from the Earth. You will be able to bring the Earth energy in and feel it in your pelvic cradle.

The High Priestess needs to feel that Her High Priest desires Her. She creates the desire to feed divine truth. Her bigger picture allows detachment. She acknowledges to herself Her feelings. She observes Her emotions, but She seeks to understand them. She understands enough to know why She has feelings.

Carmel: Does she believe in being "in love"?

High Priestess: *No, it has no place in her world. She experiences desire. It is part of Her function. She can desire, but desire serves a bigger picture. The High Priestess creates desire in a man very easily. She has the qualities that they adore: power, life force, vitality, sexuality, and, above all, She is Her own woman.*

A man cannot resist this combination. The man unconsciously will be very aware of his role, and will have given his higher self-permission here. The High Priestess empowers a man with her energy. She sends light, lots of it, to him. She energetically feels him inside her. She swoops him in through the pelvis. Look at his third-eye. It is the gateway to the soul; release the energy to him.

The role of a woman as a High Priestess is not as a mother. She does not bring her children's concerns to her life when she is working as a High Priestess. She cannot identify with the mother's role even though she can be a mother.

Carmel: Many of my clients feel unable to trust in relationships. Why?

High Priestess: *They must look at who they are. They must find within themselves a feeling of being loved. "I am loved. I am loved." The human psyche becomes split and damaged with loss and betrayal. Soul retrieval can help in this situation. Breathe in love. If you wish to draw a mating partner, bring energy up into the heart. Bring energy from the heart to love. Send a cosmic message:* I Love You *through your third eye.*

The following is a transcript of a message from Isis, a representative of The High Priestess archetype. This can be used as an invocation:

"I ask the fiery energy of Isis to attach Herself to me so that I can become the Great Magician that She is. A Goddess with the power to heal, transform, and command the elements, as well as my own destiny – a woman with purpose."

<u>A message from the Goddess Isis:</u>
Concentration is magic. It draws others in – you become an enigmatic creature. Some people find the encounter enchanting or terrifying, depending on their own power. You can only be received by a High Priestess such as Isis when personal distractions are under control. Give yourself more power by releasing distractions in your life. Power for a woman is life force, youth, and beauty. Your aura shines. You must hold the frequency of your aura by reflecting on the qualities She will give you for your life.

Carmel: How does a woman draw The High Priestess to her?

High Priestess: *Always draw The High Priestess to you through the pelvic/ base chakra. Feel Her in your pelvic cradle. She is in your loins. Feel Her. Who is She? She is the wisdom of the women of the ages and beyond. She is power. Now She goes to your heart.*

This experience of opening the base chakra was shown to me in 2001 in Luxor, Egypt.

Luxor, Egypt: I took my students to visit Sekhmet and Ptah's small chapel at Karnak in Luxor, a chapel not normally visited by mainstream tourists. Our group faced the small altar before entering her chapel. Individually we lit candles, intoned invocations, and left messages. My own invocation and request was that all fear be gone.

Facing the deity's statue I could sense my fear in looking at the lioness-headed woman. I touched the deity Sekhmet's face and breasts. It felt reassuring and very beautiful. Lighting an incense stick, I could not help noting the contrast between the powerful imposing figure with a single shaft of light over her face and the dusty chapel floor, covered in cigarette butts. I paid the guard to remove the butts and left her chapel to join the group for meditation. It was then I began to feel tremors all over my body. This was an entity. My own fear was being shaken loose from my base chakra. The whole experience lasted approximately 10 minutes; my body shaking like Earth tremors. This was a most cathartic experience. It removed desire in the base chakra.

My Higher Self transmission later revealed that a release had occurred, and I was free from this particular energy. It left me feeling calmer. My base chakra opened up and cleared, and I have subsequently felt more energy. This opening of the base chakra is an initiation to allow The High Priestess to enter; she cannot do her work for you if your base chakra is closed. You may be able to attune to Sekhmet's energy to release your base chakra desire and prepare yourself for your High Priestess.

I attuned to Sekhmet's archetype. She stated that:
Sekhmet: *Desire has been brought upward in the energy field. Now all energy is heart-centered and will give you more power in relationships. Love is power, power over fear. The power of woman is infinite. Woman is magical. She has so much when she has accessed me. Her power is in her ability to hold concentration and will. Nothing must stop her from her own true force and power. Believe in your own power to create your own reality. There is not an empowered man alive who can resist this magic and power.*

CHAPTER 4

HEALING WITH THE HIGH PRIESTESS

The High Priestess will make powerful healings if you evoke her consciously. Open your heart wide to Her and feel Her in your left breast. This is where your heart is. Be in loving surrender and offer yourself as a channel for Her power. Feel Her power through your body first and feel Her life force through your hands and breasts. She has a sensuousness, power, and strength in healings. She will be evoked at the level of the Higher Self of the person being healed. Always ask her/his Higher Self to be involved in the healing process. Let go to Her. She brings might and strength to all healings.

The High Priestess speaks of love: *She is the representative of love. She has many roles assigned to Her. The overriding principle is the one of love. In whatever form She takes, She embodies love and sharing and commitment to common ideals. Everyone is an embodiment of love. She seeks to find love in others. She seeks to bring the love of self to everyone she meets. Her role is to forward the tide of love and the forwarding of divine truth. Let it be said, however, that She will use whatever is required to remove the obstacles, in bringing the love back to a lost soul.*

Carmel: How does one help a "lost soul" as a representative of The High Priestess?

High Priestess: *First, The High Priestess is detached. She knows you cannot heal another's pain without sealing yourself from this pain. As a High Priestess you use your control over emotions to bring to the surface your relationship with the other person. It is important to examine your own weaknesses, your own vulnerability, before you can assist the lost soul. You must carefully examine yourself and you must note your own fears. You must seek to find the true source of your fears in the karmic relationship — the karmic pattern. You must get to the source of the karmic pattern. Be ruthless. Be strong in this self-examination. Then and only then can The High Priestess be of assistance, as often there has been too much hurt for the lost soul to be healed.*

The High Priestess sees the total woman; She sees the spirit in her totality and communicates this to the lost soul. Healing must go to the original source of pain. This is often a denial of your power as a woman. The High Priestess sends light to this area, asking for assistance to do so from all beings assigned to that soul for her journey on the Earth plane.

Carmel: How does the power of love bring about a change in a person's consciousness?

High Priestess: *She loves to explore the totality in a relationship. She sees a relationship as being one of shared truth. A relationship first must forward divine truth for both people. Divine order is the sum total of your desire for happiness and truth. Truth is being honest. First, you must be honest to yourself, and secondly to the other person. The two truths must marry. Let yourself be unafraid to be truthful to each other for your growth together. In a relationship the power is in what you can do together now. Don't look at the past. Accept the person now. Now is when you are able to find within yourself all you desire for your growth together.*

In relationships The High Priestess magnetizes all around her. She is great power and strength. She is might and force. She is great force; very strong in drawing a person to you. You concentrate on the person after asking permission from their Higher Self. See them as being magnetized

THE ALCHEMIEſ OF IſIſ

toward you through your pelvis. Use a large clear quartz crystal. Bring the energy up through the pelvis and into the heart —

"In the name of love and light I magnetize .... for our highest good together."

This can be an event, person, or concept.

Carmel: How can people grow together now?

High Priestess: *The power is always in asking, "What can you do together now?" Do not look at the past. Accept the person now. Now is when you are able to find within yourself all you desire for your growth together. She brings to Her relationships great commitment to this truth, which must be above emotions. Let Her bring this truth now. You may invoke:*

"In the name of my higher truth, may my relationship with................... *Bring our mutual truths together, in Divine Love and Light."*

Breathe consciously the truth. I breathe in the truth. I am the truth. Surrender to this truth. Really surrender to it. Don't be afraid of your fears. Your challenge in a relationship now is to accept who you are. Who am I NOW? I am now a woman who embodies a mission of truth, light, and love in everything that I do, say, and act. Always ask, what is my TRUTH? Does this relationship serve my truth? When you answer this question honestly nothing can stand in your way.

Carmel: How exactly is a person's divine truth served?

High Priestess: *Your relationships with others serve your divine truth and they must be constantly examined. Every relationship must forward divine truth for The High Priestess. Divine truth is the spark of life that has its beginnings in the creation process. The creation process then is fed by love. Love feeds divine truth. Love from The High Priestess to another person feeds the divine truth within The High Priestess and the other person. She ignites the divine spark in Her relationships. Her relationships are an embodiment of Her belief in Herself to keep her* *own fire burning brightly. Of course She must start with Herself. She must look at Herself daily. She must be witnessing Herself constantly to monitor her own divine truth. She must remind Herself of this totally. Daily. Completely. Honestly.*

The High Priestess must be totally honest with herself. She must be honest in all aspects to keep the spark glowing inside. She must nurture herself and give herself adoration in all aspects of her life.

Never can a negative thought be allowed to be part of Her totality. She must witness Herself and Her thoughts. She is a model for a balanced, love-filled life. "My life is an embodiment of a divine spark." This spark must be fed by love. Keep your own fires burning brightly by stoking them with fuel, which is of the best quality. Love for self. Good food. As The High Priestess you must give to yourself the very best you can give. Give to the self. It holds the key to immortality and life.

The High Priestess can become an immortal if you embody Her. She is an immortal when Her spark burns fiercely with love for Herself, then this love goes out to others. Me first, then others. Be a witness to yourself always. Fears build up so you need to clear out the grate. Clear your fears away. How can good wood be used to ignite The High Priestess when the grate is over filled with rubbish. Visualize your fears, i.e. rejection, abandonment, and burn them to ashes. See them being taken away. Only now can the good wood be burned.

Carmel: What does commitment mean in the world of The High Priestess?

High Priestess: *Commitment is an ideal, the ideal of allowing oneself space and time to discover the true self. Commitment to the true self is an art. It must be fostered, nurtured, and developed. The High Priestess embodies the ideals of commitment through loving surrender to Her truth and light. "I am truth and light." This is a part of everything She does, says, and believes. Have commitment to your way of life and don't be afraid of seeing it in others who are around you. Some will want to follow your path, others will look at you and be in wonder, and others will turn away.*

Carmel: What is this commitment?

High Priestess: *When someone makes a commitment to a philosophy, she becomes a living embodiment of it; a divine channel for it and nothing can stand in her way. The philosophy of The High Priestess is one of surrendering the ego, the primary source of power over another, and channelling this power to a greater cause. She creates a barrier between herself and others. She stands alone; alone in her belief that her life must serve principles, which create divine order. She becomes a channel for light, peace, and order. She becomes beautiful to others because She has the light inside her, which will not go out. It cannot be extinguished. It is a haven for all lost, weary souls. Don't be afraid to be this haven for others. They need it. The principles are very important to adhere to: honesty with the self, total detachment from emotional attachments, a knowledge that she is a living embodiment of The High Priestesses of all the ages and cultures and all women who have aspired to a sense of greatness outside themselves. A woman must honor her commitment to the philosophy of The High Priestess by serving these principles.*

Carmel: Please discuss the subject of commitment further.

High Priestess: *Her view of commitment cannot be put into the usual definition of emotional commitment between men and women. Women want commitment because of security. They need commitment because of children and their biological role. Your commitment is to the ideals of The High Priestess, the truth, and those who love you will want serve your commitment.*

Throughout my study of metaphysical reality, I have observed that Jesus, the Hathorians, and The High Priestess all say the same thing: Human beings lose their mastery at the emotional level.

Carmel: Why do humans lose their mastery at the emotional level?

High Priestess: *First, never lock up or freeze your emotions; allow yourself to experience it. For a woman, a need for detachment is always required. The High Priestess symbolizes all that a woman needs to be whole. A woman doesn't fear her emotions. In fact to be a High Priestess a woman must challenge herself daily to embrace the world of her emotions.*

A woman must bring light to her aura. It is so important that she looks, feels, acts, speaks and behaves as a High Priestess for her community, her family, and herself. By doing this she becomes a dual-natured woman. By mastering her own emotions she is not bothered by others' perceptions of her. She incarnates truth.

Carmel: Does power over emotions make a woman more youthful?

High Priestess: *Out-of-control emotions destroy looks. Unbalanced emotions sap a woman's energy. A woman needs to assume authority over emotions otherwise she ages prematurely. She creates stress hormones, which can damage her health and emotional stability.*

Carmel: Could you please comment on the emotion of sadness, when a relationship does not meet what you had anticipated, i.e. broken heart and feelings of loss.

High Priestess: *Your need for detachment is very evident when sadness, as an emotion, surfaces. The High Priestess needs to feel the emotion of sadness, really feel it. Locate it in your body for example, in the heart. Feel the texture of the emotion. Is it a dull pain? It could be heavy like a weight, which slows the breathing. Now the emotion needs to be felt and understood. Stop and feel the pain. Really feel the pain. Really feel the deep hurt the pain represents. Now breathe into that pain. Breathe into it slowly. Breathe into it consciously. Now, with intent, ask that the memory of sadness, the memory of fear, the original fear, be shown to you in all its forms. When you can see the pattern of fear, of sadness, you ask for it to be transmuted, dissolved. See it dissolving. Stay with the feeling of the sadness dissolving until you are free of sadness, i.e. the sadness relates to my desire to control an emotional outcome with a person. The person hasn't responded. Ask that this memory, stored on your aura, be released. Ask for forgiveness from yourself and the other person. "I forgive myself from the pattern of pain, fear, and loss."*

Feel a sense of lightness as The High Priestess takes away the pain for the mutual growth of both people. Be in loving surrender to the Light and you will be free from this emotion.

CHAPTER FIVE

ATLANTEAN HIGH PRIESTESS

Carmel: There are many different types of High Priestesses. How does The Atlantean High Priestess work in an aspirants' life?

High Priestess: *The Atlantean High Priestess is the source of all power for you, Carmel, as she is the foundation of the energy frequency you work with in your business and life.*

The Atlantean High Priestess frequency is one of strong and beautiful power. This power will forward your divine truth and cut through illusion and negativity very quickly. She can be utilized to cut through illusion in a person. She can be channelled directly by drawing her into the base of your skull at the back of the head.

Exercise:
You need to allow time to stretch the body and spread the pelvis. Take the time to really spread the pelvis wide, when standing or sitting. This opens up the base chakra energy, now draw you energy up through the spine, then to the crown chakra. Visualize a

circle of light enfolding your head. Bring in the power through your third eye. The Atlantean High Priestess heals with the third eye.

For anyone attuned to The Atlantean energy, The High Priestess will come through this frequency. However, there may be other spiritual communities where The High Priestess is served. You will find a frequency of The High Priestess that is suitable for you.

Carmel: What exactly is power? Women's power in particular.

High Priestess: *A woman's power is in acknowledging that she is worthy. "I am worthy to have exactly what I want." As an Atlantean High Priestess you are worthy to bring who you want to you for love, pleasure, and life force. Your life force is your ability to have those around you bring peace and happiness to you. Power is essentially controlled thought channelled through the third eye. Channel what you want through the third eye. "I want to magnetize an event, relationship, concept. Hold the image clearly in your mind. That image is then given a form, i.e. a relationship, concept, or project. To magnetize this image of what you want, you may intone:*

"In the name of my Higher Truth and with my Higher Self's permission, may I forward this, i.e. relationship, concept, project.............................."

Use your third eye and use all your senses (smell, touch, taste, hearing, sight) to feel the person, event, etc. and visualize and feel exactly what you desire for your time.

Concentrate on the image. Feel and see it already happening. Be in your own power and surrender to the event. Surrender and ask that the life force of the relationship, concept, or project comes to you. Find the energy of the event already in you. Power is control over emotion. All distraction must cease; only the relationship, concept, project is important. Bring the situation to you through breath work, third eye concentration, and power channelled. You will go into an altered state of consciousness when this occurs. Do it as often as you wish, whenever you think of it. Be in loving surrender to your power.

Carmel: You have been saying that it's important to explore. How does one explore one's relationship with oneself?

High Priestess: *You explore your relationship with yourself by being in surrender to every moment. Discovering your own uniqueness can forever change you. Every moment is a joy and a surprise. Every moment is special and has its own spark of creation. In every moment is the spark of your own truth and power. Allow every moment to have its magic and its power can change you forever. A moment can change you forever. You are the unique creation of a moment and every second is precious alchemy. This is why there can never be boredom, only stillness and solitude, to create special alchemy of forgiveness and surrender to your truth. Your creation is yours, now, forever. Be a woman of the moment. The moment is the magic and the moment is the surrender to the truth. Allow this to happen by being in a relaxed and receptive state, which brings power. Bring power through concentration; really concentrate on this moment, this truth, and this magic. This is being a truly realized human being.*

Affirmation: *"I now concentrate on this moment, this truth, this magic. This is a truly realized human being. I now concentrate on this moment of magic to create my power and truth. I look at another human being with this magic, truth, and power."*

Give concentration to his/her every moment. Really concentrate. This is the most powerful and loving thing one human can do for another. Really concentrate on that human being and allow your spirit to merge with that person, and you will have that person's soul forever. This is the most powerful thing you can do for this person.

Carmel: What exactly is the Divine form?

High Priestess: *You need to bring to your life your unique energy to understand the divine form. The divine form is in every woman. The divine form can be accessed through your relationships, and with power to overcome your limitations as they present themselves to you throughout your day. What are my limitations? Count them one by one; every limiting thought, deed, action, and word. This limited view keeps you negatively trapped in a pain-filled state.*

Think how powerful you will become as a woman representative of The High Priestess frequency when all limitations are noted and eliminated. All limitations just block the pathway of the soul's journey. See those limitations as rocks. Each rock in front of you becomes harder to climb over. Remember the rocks! "These are my rocks of self abuse." Self-abuse is mutilating the self. The self cannot stand the mutilation without going into fear and panic, which creates problems for the soul's growth. Release the rock! The rock has been placed right in front of you. You have a choice to either take it away, with an equally powerful action, or you can let the rocks build up and have a healer help you to remove them.

The Atlantean High Priestess is a woman who embodies the principle of love in its purest aspect. The purer the love, the higher the level of energy, beauty, and youth she has. She is a cloud, a ball of light, forever luminous, forever beautiful, and forever young. Be her power through the Atlantean vibration in its highest aspect. Allow self love for this incredible, beautiful woman: You.

Carmel: How can peace be brought into a woman's life?

High Priestess: *A peace-filled life brings mystery to a woman. She receives a peace-filled life by being detached from outcomes, which require emotions to rule. In order to do this all people must look at their emotions constantly and witness them. This witnessing of emotions brings control. This control must come through breath work. Breath work creates control over emotions. Just let the emotion surface, i.e. sadness, loss. Let it bubble to the surface and then look at it like a bubble in a glass of champagne. Ask yourself, is this bubble big? What size is it in relation to my totality? Does it take up the whole glass? You can see the emotion in its totality. Now, look inside the emotion. What is in the picture? Yes, it is an emotion, which sees an outcome. Let your projection go; just let it go. See it washing away. Your power and peace comes from letting the fear and emotion just go. The outcome for a relationship is two people together loving each other and happy.*

Carmel: Many people fear intimacy. What does The High Priestess say about intimacy between people?

High Priestess: *She sees intimacy as being an emotional reaction. Intimacy implies exclusivity or control. You must release your need for intimacy as an emotion. Intimacy as an emotion has no part in the life of a High Priestess, nor does exclusivity. She does not need it, nor seek it, in a mating partner or intimate friendship. She must remain detached from intimacy as an emotion. She does not believe in exclusive intimacy. Her intimacy is with the self, knowing she can secure and service her truth. Her truth must be above intimacy in the emotional sense.*

Carmel: As a representative of the Atlantean High Priestess, how do humans who want to evolve, assist humanity?

High Priestess: *She is drawing, through Her representatives, her desire to further evolve humanity. She needs humans to support her collectively in this. She needs to have representatives on the Earth plane as well. Your commitment to yourself is total and She will be served in her own evolution as well. Her journey is one where the souls evolve through love. All souls must forward their truth through the principle of love and light. Your journey in representing Her will forward your totality and Hers through mutual growth. Embody Her daily. Stop and share Her with others in all that you do. She represents the total woman. Yes, allow the total woman to be in you in every waking moment, in every breath you take, and in every thought you have.*

Being a witness to yourself will forward you. Witness yourself. As you walk, speak, and think, feel the magnificent powerful woman through you at all times. Life must be a reflection of Her magnificence in and through you. She stops anyone from compromising you. You cannot be compromised by the High Priestess. Bring Her to you by evoking all that your heart wants.

Ask: *What does my heart want now?*

List: *What do I need for my personal evolvement?*

Affirmation: *"For my personal evolvement I want peace, respect, love, happiness, and mostly my desire, for my life path, to love and give service to all who cross my life path in my professional and personal evolvement."*

Evoke The High Priestess through pure love, devotion, and service to Her truth. You can call upon *The Hathors* for love and beauty; *Sekhmet* for power and passion; *Isis* for magic; and the Atlantean High Priestess for the totality of who you are. She is the most powerful representation for you because of what you have declared yourself to be. A powerful woman is indeed a rich river, full of life force and strength. You are Her now. Be in peace at this moment, knowing you and She are one.

Carmel: How does an Atlantean High Priestess representative challenge the conventions of living in our society?

High Priestess: *The Atlantean High Priestess is a woman who challenges herself every day. She seeks to go beyond the boundaries of conventional thinking, acting, and behaving. Her feelings do not always correspond to that of the conventional society in which she is living. She is not bound by conventions, such as marriage, which is a patriarchal institution. However, she may choose to have a divine marriage. She is a woman who can look at life in such a way and know these conventions do not serve the total woman in her true power. She challenges these expectations by her dismissal of them as not being for her. For her, life must be enjoyed totally in all its aspects. She shuns convention because it clouds a woman's true worth.*

The man for The High Priestess is devoted, respectful, and he acknowledges Her power and respects its source. She gives him love to keep him to Her. If or when She releases him, he finds his life rather purposeless and he is ill prepared for the loss or even understanding as to why it has occurred. She has established financial control over her material world and knows She does not have to place Herself in a man's hands. She knows that by drawing on the collective source of Her power, the "High Priestess archetype," She will find much to give Her in life and love. De-powered women can be afraid of Her because she challenges a woman "to behave like a man would." She creates detachment and She becomes her own true source of knowledge. Bring Her to you through challenging yourself daily to embrace her totality.

She becomes you when you dismiss conventional thinking, acting, and being. You are the only one you challenge, and you challenge yourself daily. Think, act, and be Her in every waking moment. Be a witness to yourself and <u>never let your guard down</u>.

Carmel: How do you become the Atlantean High Priestess in a practical way?

High Priestess: *She can appear through many guises. She is with you through your thoughts, actions, and intent; you think and become Her. She is your best advertisement for who you are and what you embody. Continue to consciously evoke Her for your unique sense of healing and exchange with everyone you meet. Yes, breathe Her in consciously. She links you with all you aspire to. She is truth made manifest. She is you. The Atlantean aspect is very focused, laser-like, and direct. She is penetrating, like a laser. To draw someone to you focus on their third eye and really concentrate – this cannot be expressed enough – really concentrate on that person. Draw them in and enfold them in your circle.*

When talking to someone and healing them, try drawing a circle of Light around you both. Then enfold the person and yourself in a double helix of infinity, starting at the third eye area. The third eye is the focus as it is the gateway to the unconscious. The gateway must first be opened by you, by drawing your own infinity symbol ∞ over your third eye; the infinity helix is the figure '8' sideways. This gives power to you. You control the situation and you are in charge of its outcome because it is serving your truth. Meditate on The High Priestess every day by opening the third eye. Breathe deeply and invoke Her into your body – allow Her to come in.

Carmel: Is this aspect of the Atlantean High Priestess more Sekhmet or Isis?

High Priestess: *She is more Sekhmet. She has the raw energy of Sekhmet, and She is not afraid to draw on any light frequency to further herself to evolve. All you owe the world is your own ability to trust yourself to evolve. She can be ruthless, but the ruthlessness is only to evolve Herself. Only by evolving the self can the Atlantean High Priestess evolve anyone else. Be Her, now and forever.*

Chapter Six

Shifting Consciousness with the High Priestess

During my discovery of my High Priestess, I was led to channel "The Goddess of All Light," "The Immortals," and "The Keepers of the Mysteries of the Divine Feminine." The following transcript was channelled four years later in 2006.

The High Priestess is an intimate discovery of your feminine self. When you attune to the healing properties of the moon you will find a deeper and more powerful relationship with Her. She becomes transformative and very penetrating because you are actively co-creating with the moon rituals and nature herself. I truly believe it is one of the most extraordinary experiences you can undertake since you are diving into your own deeply held subconscious belief patterns. This work opens up your base chakra and really begins the ascension process. You are chipping away constantly at your concrete boots of Earth-bound attachments. Through your love for your High Priestess, you will be transformed by Her. Your power then becomes beyond what you could ever imagine.

This power changes every single cell in your body and you become truly the Immortal Woman ready to gain admission to the secrets of the Divine Feminine.

As you are beginning to discover your feminine through The High Priestess, you are on a journey to an undiscovered part of yourself. This undiscovered part of yourself needs to feel able to express the meaning of its existence in a balanced and detached way.

The High Priestess embraces a spiritual philosophy which embodies a world view that is not "emotional" in the everyday application of the word; "Emotional," meaning your currently held pre-conceived idea of the meaning "emotional," the High Priestess challenges you to redefine your "emotional" reality.

When you are in a situation where your emotions begin to surface like a landscape, that is your *mind screen's* perspective of your current view of your reality and emotional attachment to your situation, you need to create a space within that emotional landscape to view it as just that: a landscape.

This is where humans have so much trouble. They view their emotional landscape and find it is hurting them. There is too much unresolved pain from the past to clear in one go. They react emotionally in a range of emotional extremes such as anger, rage, victim, poor me, betrayal scenarios, and so on. We have all played these emotional scenarios out in some way.

Try and recall when you felt over whelmed emotionally and recreate the scene, observing yourself without one of your old emotional patterns. For example, if the emotion was anger say to yourself, "I am observing my 'angry' self here." Now you have identified your emotion within the scenario/landscape.

By creating a High Priestess in your worldview you are acting as "She" would act and you become a model of The High Priestess acting as "She" would. However, you are doing more than this: you are creating "Her" in you. You observe your emotional reactions in every given situation and seek to understand them for what they are, emotions. Emotions don't have to be reacted to as they are only emotions, but the trick is to identify and catch them before they become untamed and create a polluted landscape.

You need to really concentrate on what your High Priestess could be like as a fictional character, i.e. what contemporary characteristics does a High Priestess display, i.e. in fiction, film or archetype.

The model for my High Priestess was Dion Fortune, one of the greatest 20th-century occult writers and mystics. Fortune was a teacher for most of us who were looking for a philosopher of the feminine.

Through Fortune's character Morgan Le Fay in *The Sea Priestess*, I became very personally acquainted with my own High Priestess "Shea" in my journey to discover The High Priestess and was guided by "Her" for my own journey of self-realization.

Through my discoveries as my relationship with "Shea" grew I found parallels to integrate my High Priestess into my consciousness. Isis was another deity who was worshipped in Egypt, Rome, and Greece. Isis was the deity whom Cleopatra, the great Pharaoh of ancient Egypt, worshiped. Furthermore, it has been suggested by Taylor's autobiographer, that Isis was also Elizabeth Taylor's personal Goddess while Elizabeth was negotiating and making the 1960s epic *Cleopatra*.

Also, I strongly urge you to read Robert Masters *The Goddess Sekhmet* in this exploration with the Goddess as a living archetype. This book serves as an excellent example of Masters' intimate relationship with Sekhmet developed through his own devotion to this deity of Egyptian lineage.

Most fiction, including films and stage productions, rarely depict women as being detached from their emotions. They usually show women to be victims or emotionally needy in relationships with men acting out the role of "super hero." This is why actually trying to find a contemporary role model who doesn't fit the societal and media stereotype is very difficult.

You need to be aware of how our society portrays women in relationship with men and observe in yourself how you have been conditioned to accept this limited view of what it is to be "human" as a woman.

To go deeper into discovering your own relationship with The High Priestess you may like to work-shop Fortune's characters and also develop your sensitivity to "Isis" through ritual work on the moon's phases and by applying Masters' principles (The Goddess Sekhmet) to your world. You begin to grow and deepen your relationship with your own High Priestess as a personal guide as I did with "Shea."

Carmel: As a student of the Mysteries through the Divine Feminine, how do I now develop my relationship with The High Priestess as I have now found Her?

High Priestess: *You must firstly allow Her to come to you when you are in any emotional situation, which requires you to be available for other expectations of you. The best way to do this is to list all the encounters throughout your day, which you were challenged by. You must keep a diary.*

i.e., Morning: Work - colleague Sally wants me to talk to her about her love life and her lousy relationship.

Morning Messages: (phone, text, emails, Facebook, Twitter, etc.)

It is important to list all of your emotional reactions to these situations, i.e. anger, rage, victim, poor me.

Now that you have identified your emotional reaction, you must view this emotional landscape as a war zone and you have become the commander of your war zone through your observation. You must take this view of your life now and seek to really "control" your emotional reactions in every situation.

The High Priestess speaks:
Containing emotions is the essence of who The High Priestess is. Containing emotions means simply putting the emotion in a container, just don't let emotion go outside the container. Build a container now. Choose a material, for example, a steel box, a large plastic bottle, a wooden box, a glass container, cement, or rock. Choose a container in which you feel would best contain your emotion. The choice of container determines exactly how fearful you are of emotions getting out of control. If an emotion is contained, it can be controlled. Un-contained emotions are dangerous. They are like a car on a highway without a driver; anything can happen and usually does. Un-contained emotions are the biggest danger for a woman aspiring to be a High Priestess because she risks losing communication with her High Priestess. The High Priestess **cannot** stay in this highly emotional environment.

Carmel: Deepening and refining one's relationship with The High Priestess is about this containment, but the human psyche is wired to act/react emotionally. What exactly do humans do when they are so susceptible here?

High Priestess: Control of emotions must be sought by training and discipline; there is no other way. A trained mind is extremely powerful. Your mind can be trained this way. All you have to do is expect that it will obey instructions. The instructions will come through your higher self or soul. She initiates you by challenging your emotional attachment to a situation.

Examine your emotions as if you were about to parachute for the first time. Imagine you are about to take your first parachute jump. This would be a good time to look at your emotions, locate them, and feel them. The essence of this exercise is to surrender, surrender your emotions.

You will have a most exciting time — one that will change your life forever — if you obey all instructions. Allow yourself to surrender your fear of death, for this is what a jump can lead to if you don't listen to instructions.

It is equally important that you obey the instructions of the trainer, your High Priestess, as you are getting ready for your first parachute jump. She has been sent to provide specific emotional instructions. The instructor is giving specific instructions directly from your higher self. Obey them. This is all you have to do. You must learn to obey instructions from your High Priestess when she is initiating you. It is that simple; obey instructions. If you do not, you die!

You die emotionally every time you do not make a consistent effort to obey instructions from your High Priestess. She is patient. She knows your karma and fears. She has been assigned for the task. She has no emotional agenda for you. She has only pure love. No earthly parent or teacher can match this love because it comes from a space beyond time and place.

Try this invocation to help you to connect with your High Priestess to help you follow her instructions.

Breathe deeply three times. Feel her in your heart and say the following invocation daily for one month exactly. Mark it on your diary or calendar to do daily.

"I now command in the name of Love and Light and in the name of my absolute Divine Truth that I be free from emotional the betrayal I place on myself through others in my life. I command myself to obey The High Priestess at all times, as I am being instructed by Her."

See The High Priestess as a figure that comes to you to assist "you" by first teaching you how to contain your emotions by becoming the observer of your thoughts. Furthermore, you must learn how to obey instructions because you are being trained as a student of the Mysteries. The Mysteries of the Philosophy of the Divine Feminine, through your High Priestess. To trust the information, you must trust the teachings but more importantly you must trust that the results will change your life. The High Priestess will teach you control and mastery over the "limited mind," and help you to connect to the universal heart. The High Priestess teaches you very specific things: How to access wisdom to gain control over your reality, and how to manifest by becoming a magician for your new reality. You will now feel yourself becoming more connected to the "universal heart," the "one heart," the heart of the "Mother."

PART III
THE PRIESTESS
OF THE MOON

Each Moon cycle is important and has a part to play in your relationship with yourself through The High Priestess.

Through these exercises you will identify yourself as a student of the Mysteries.

Contents:
- **Preparing to Meet The Priestess of The Moon**
  - **The Moon and Its Stellar Aspects**
    - **To Create Your Moon Circle**
  - **The Four Elements Invocation**

The five phases of the Moon correspond to the five levels of the Feminine Mysteries as practiced in ancient Mystery School traditions.
- **New Moon**
- **Waxing Moon**
- **Full Moon**
- **Waning Moon - Post Full Moon**
- **Dark Moon**

You are going to observe the phases of the Moon to begin your journey in developing your relationship with The High Priestess.

Obtain a Moon planting calendar or diary (or just be aware of the Moon's cycles by looking at the night sky). *Diary entry documentation example:*

Diary date.............   New Moon......... March 20 (Year)

Let's begin on the cycle of the new Moon. The new Moon will allow your "lunar" or feminine self to develop. This is a slow process; it is a germinating experience.

In honoring the Moon and her phases you are honoring something that changes every night. The sun is the sun. It rises and sets. It is a daytime experience. The Moon is a nighttime adventure. All mystical and earthly experiences are seasonal and are created in response to the Moon's phases. The Feminine energies cannot be developed or experienced properly if nature and the Moon's phases are not observed and meditated on. You will need to spend 10 minutes in the evening before bedtime just observing the monthly Moon cycles.

To meditate on the Moon is part of your journey with The High Priestess as She is attuned to the cycle of the Moon. This means that the Moon is Her home. The Moon is Her symbol and Earthly reminder for your journey with Her.

Ideally, to have a ritual space in a consecrated environment such as a garden, patio, or somewhere in nature would be perfect. You then have the opportunity to observe the Moon in Her natural elements.

With cloud cover, rain, or for other reasons you may not be able to go outside to Moon bathe. If this is a problem you can conduct your Moon rituals whilst bathing in a warm BATH instead.

Moon Bath Recipe:

One handful of dried powdered milk or 500mls of fresh milk.

One handful of bath salts. (I suggest Epsom salts, Celtic Salts, etc.)

Eight drops of essential oil (Rose or The Goddess Of All Light or The High Priestess anointing oil).

One or more capful of oil (e.g. Sweet Almond, Apricot)

Fill the bath with water, place ingredients in the water, and honor The High Priestess.

You can create a space here for your Moon meditation and The High Priestess will be present.

You can now do your breathing in the water, preferably in the dark with a candle or tea-light lit nearby. This will create a Moonlit atmosphere.

You can begin your cycle of deep rhythmic breathing for approximately four minutes. After you have allowed yourself the four minutes of breathing deeply, rhythmically, and powerfully you will begin to attune to The High Priestess frequency, which you can do for approximately six more minutes.

This bathing ritual also acts as purification and was practiced before any important ceremony or honoring of any deity in the ancient world. Today, bathing rituals are still practiced in many countries and cultures, i.e. Japan and the Middle East and Turkey.

Purification rituals will become an increasingly important part of your practice and you should always have your ingredients well supplied in advance by including them in your shopping.

Meeting your High Priestess is similar to visiting any important person who will be able to assist you in your life. In your case, your High Priestess is to offer assistance to create a new way of being human.

Your rituals and purification must be sacred acts. However, they can be private and you can do them without disturbing others in your environment. They are not to be done to draw attention to yourself or make you feel important or superior to others.

You are beginning to establish order, discipline, and ritual in your life. Our contemporary culture doesn't really have such functions so you are going to have to make a commitment to yourself here.

Rituals create order and self-discipline. By developing self-discipline, you can use your mind to create a space to journey into understanding the Mysteries.

A disciplined mind is the only way mystery will be revealed. Concentration, breathing, and being in the present allow the forces of the universe to be available for you to create as a magician.

You cannot develop your relationship with The High Priestess unless these rituals and purification rites are established first.

THE MOON AND ITS STELLAR ASPECTS

The Lunar Moon's phases reflect the Sun's energy. The Sun is behind the Moon when the Moon is coming to Her fullness. For example, when the Moon is in Virgo, the Sun will be in Pisces.

You will magnify the qualities of The High Priestess in this cycle, i.e. the Virgo Full Moon will reveal your High Priestess exhibiting the earthing and organizational qualities. She will also be clearing out your digestive system and working with you on your solar plexus chakra.

The corresponding Moon / Sun signs are as follows:
When the Sun is in Aries the Full Moon will be in Libra etc.

SUN	MOON
Aries	Libra
Taurus	Scorpio
Gemini	Sagittarius
Cancer	Capricorn
Leo	Aquarius
Virgo	Pisces

When the Sun is in Aries (March 21–April 19) the Moon will be in Libra. Again if the Sun is in Taurus (April 20–May 21) the Moon will be in Scorpio and so on. An astrological Sun guidebook will provide you with the qualities the main signs represent.

The Moon in Virgo with the Sun in Pisces will also create the vibration of the stellar High Priestess as well. The Virgo constellation has many stars, which will further enhance the qualities you wish to develop through your High Priestess. You should now look at the section on Star constellation, Star civilization and stellar influences. These can also be meditated in this cycle or taken in elixir form to help you to attune to the properties of this vibration.

For example, The Porrimarians (from the Porrima star in the constellation of Virgo) are a civilization you may like to connect with when the Sun is in Pisces. The High Priestess inhabits the stellar heavens, constellations, and civilizations. She is everywhere. She comes in many stellar aspects. Your Virgo High Priestess may have links with the Porrimarian civilization in the Virgo constellation. This is advanced energy work but you may like to be aware of it. You can develop it at another point in your journey work with your High Priestess.

The Moon is the entry point for the stellar constellations civilizations. She is the energy portal or doorway so by breathing Her in, The High Priestess can be evoked through the Virgo constellation when the Moon is in Virgo and the Sun is in Pisces. (As I write this the Sun is in Pisces and the Full Moon is approaching Virgo).

All High Priestesses carry attributes we wish to develop and by focusing on the Moon signs you will create cellular change, advancing your consciousness considerably. If you begin your breathing technique as mentioned earlier, you may like to visualize your High Priestess with a crystal. You are opposite Her. You are on Earth, and She is holding the Moon in Her hand but it is a large crystal sphere, and she touches the opposite faces of the crystal.

You will be developing your receptivity to Her and She will help advance your link with the constellation's attributes when the Moon is in this constellation. She can link you to the star constellation for receptivity and transfer from that civilization the positive qualities through Her to you. In Atlantis, stars like Porrima (Virgo) were utilized for the development of knowledge using a crystal from humans to star beings.

Be guided by your own higher self and your High Priestess here, just be open to Her.

Moon meditation involves space and a connection with the Moon itself so you need to, on the night of the Full Moon, create a one-hour ritual with the Moon and yourself. If there is a group meditation, join. If not, create your own Moon circle by sitting in nature absorbing the Moon's powers.

TO CREATE YOUR MOON CIRCLE

Tonight I am connecting and drawing down my High Priestess through the Full Moon ritual. This ritual will purify me and allow me to create a deeper relationship with The High Priestess. My relationship with The High Priestess becomes stronger when I create my monthly Moon ritual.

To create with The High Priestess at the Full Moon you will need private uninterrupted space, one hour free, preferably outside where you can see the Moon.

Bathe and anoint yourself (even take a shower), dress in light-colored clothing. Create an energetic circle around you to protect your space and bring The High Priestess in. See it like a picnic (putting down the tablecloth, etc.). Sit in a space and begin to feel that you are creating space for The High Priestess to create with you at this most important time in the Divine Feminine calendar.

Give an offering to The High Priestess by honoring the four sacred elements, Earth, Air, Fire, and Water.

I suggest giving a flower and crystal in honor of the earth element,

An incense stick for the air element,

Light a candle in honor of the fire element

Give a spray or elixir in honor of the water element.

Giving offerings to the sacred elements enhance your receptivity to the elements and bring The High Priestess closer to you.

It is important that you devote one hour once a month at the most potent and forceful time of the calendar to your High Priestess.

Begin by focusing on your breathing and your 8 - Infinity breath to establish the rhythm for your meditation.

Your breathing sequence:

This breathing sequence attunes you to the rhythm of the Moon and takes approximately four minutes. This establishes your control over the "small mind" to connect with the universal heart, the higher self, and The High Priestess. The breathing sequence is an integral part of any personal development work where you are accessing Divine energies. In all Mystery Schools, breath techniques have been taught and consistently maintained.

Breathe in through the nose to the count of eight (8).

Hold the breath to the count of eight (8).

Release to the count of eight (8) (Through the nose).

Pause. (this is a relaxed inhale and exhale breath) for the count of eight (8).

Eight (8) is the number of infinity = polarity and immortality. It is balanced duality. By doing this daily for four minutes you are immediately balancing and aligning your energy centers, creating calmness, and centering yourself. You are "staying in the present." By staying in the present you create immortality. Refer to my book *Awaken your Immortal Intelligent Heart* for any further reference material on the frequency of the "self" through the heart.

You are in the presence of The High Priestess when you develop this breath technique. Now energetically focus on the Moon in her new phase.

WORKING WITH THE FOUR ELEMENTS

The Moon's phases are a potent expression of your relationship with the natural world. The High Priestess comes in through your relationship with the elements. The elements are Air, Earth, Fire, and Water and act as a conduit for The High Priestess to enter. A simple Four Elements Meditation is an acknowledgment that you wish to establish your link with The High Priestess.

All of nature is part of you now as you create with your High Priestess. Nature will teach you so much, and you must observe all around you. You must be aware of nature as a living ever-present thing. Nature is ready to give and ready to show you something.

This exercise will help you attune to the rhythm of nature as you create with your High Priestess.

Make symbolic offerings or physical ones such as **incense (Air)**, **candle (Fire)**, **essential oil in purified water (Water)**, and **essential oil (Earth)** are very applicable.

- Energetically face **East** and ask if you can co-create with the sacred element of **Air**. You may like to give a gift or acknowledgment to the **air element**, a feather or incense for example. "In the name of Love and Light and in the name of my Absolute Divine Truth may I co-create with the sacred element of **Air**."

- Now energetically face **South** and visualize a flame and ask if you can co-create with the sacred element of **Fire**, light a candle, for example. "In the name of Love and Light and in the name of my Absolute Divine Truth may I co-create with the sacred element of **Fire**."

- Now face **West** and energetically evoke the sacred element of **Water**, spray the room with an aura cleansing spray mist, for example. This element is especially favorable to The High Priestess. The Divine Feminine frequency is especially connected to the Water element generally. "In the name of Love and Light and in the name of my Absolute Divine Truth may I co-create with the sacred element of **Water**."

- Finally you face the **North** energetically and ask the sacred element of Earth to be with you, anoint yourself with essential oils extracted from the **Earth**, and crystals, for example. "In the name of Love and Light and in the name of my Absolute Divine Truth may I co-create with the sacred element of **Earth**".

These rituals to the elements may seem very long-winded and unnecessary to you, but you must remember that you need the connection with The High Priestess. It's very much like visiting a very important dignitary, someone you have wanted to meet for a long time. There are many connections to be made: couriers, messengers, etc. The sacred elements are such connectors. They have the energetic vibration of being part of us, i.e. we are Air, Earth, Fire, and Water, approximately 89% water - interesting! Now, if we are 89% water, it becomes very important that we really attune to the Water element to conduct our relationship with The High Priestess. The Moon itself is very closely aligned to the Water element, so the Moon and The High Priestess are closely linked to Her element, which is Water primarily.

The High Priestess will be aware of you now.

THE FOUR ELEMENTS MEDITATION

- Nature Speaks

By intoning out loud you can call Her through nature. All of Nature has a relationship with the feminine energies. This meditation attunes you to the forces of the natural world.

Nature Speaks: *"With me you will allow yourself space to experience part of creation. I am every living thing. All I am, Life is - I am you. You are me when you just feel what it is like to observe. Observing creates a space of tranquility. Observing slows down the mind, and it slows down thoughts.*

You need to create without your mind. You need to create with me by losing your mind. Just lose your mind in your creation. See your mind as being without an anchor. It is lost. Your mind has gone away. Now observe. You must observe your creations. Your creation is with me, nature, now. Stop and observe me. What am I? I am everywhere. I am in a tree, a lake, a flower, a leaf. I am intelligent life force. I have intelligence, so when you observe me, you are able to create with an intelligence you can't fathom. This intelligence is without the form you know. This intelligence is me. I am intelligent. See your flower. What intelligence did I possess to create my life? I can use this intelligence, this beauty to help you create as well. You are the essence of love. You need to feel the essence of creation with my life now. Breathe in intelligent life force with me now.

Nature is you when you attune with the sacred elements. Feel the air, the wind. Talk to me as a living energy. Discuss your fears with my element, the Earth. Feel my throbbing heat and power. My Energy the Earth is just so creative as an intelligence. Mother Earth has an intelligence. Dear Mother Earth, help me now. I need to feel what you are to me. Now just look at and feel my fire in the sunrise. The noonday blazing sun and my gentle sunset. Who am I? I am you. I am you. The energy of you is me. Water is your relationship with your lunar feminine self. With me I am shedding your emotional debris. I am the Fire, the Earth, the Air, the Water. Evoking me gives you life force.

"I love you Nature" is all you need to say. When you honor the natural world you become youthful. When you are youthful, you are in resonance with the feminine energies. You are a High Priestess because the feminine in you is honored."

Nature has given you the ingredients, and she has also provided the clue. "Water." Water is the ingredient you must pay particular attention to establish your link with The High Priestess and the feminine energies.

Make a time to honor nature during those quiet times when you are able to. Nature creates. She heals and revives. In Ancient Egypt the sacred blue lotus was a flower of immortality. The symbol for this flower started in a time where nature symbols were revered as living energies for life force. This plant was known to create youth even in the afterlife. Imagine a blue lotus creating life for you when you had died physically. The Ancient Egyptians believed that this was possible. Nature will help them have a perfectly happy afterlife. So, by attuning to nature, you are in the presence of The Immortals. The High Priestess is an Immortal.

These techniques will set the rhythm and structure of your hour.

- *Settle - prepare self/space*

- *Honor The High Priestess within with a gift*

- *Commence The 8-count Breathing Sequence*

- *Evoke the Four elements Invocation*

- *Read Nature Speaks*

If you conduct the Moon meditation now you have made a further link with The High Priestess. See these meditations as being links or conduits to get to Her. After the Moon ritual you will now be enveloped in The High Priestess's Love, and you may see her come to you through the color of Blue, as she surrounds you in a blue cloak of protection.

You can really begin to create with Her now. Start really allowing Her to bring to you all you need. I see this process as your reward for all your hard work. Let's face it; you have waited one month for this.

Set yourself one hour to be in presence of The High Priestess. Of course if you want to stay with Her all night, she's very happy - the longer the better. However, you have set yourself one hour. If it extends, wonderful!

At this time much can happen or nothing happens. Just let her speak to you. If you find this difficult, that's normal. It's very normal not to expect anything earth shattering to come to you, but your persistence and dedication to your ritual will pay off handsomely, and you will come to realize that you are The Magician and The Sacred High Priestess.

Breath is the key at this point. You must focus deliberately on the breath and everything else you have done. At this point you must remember you are doing all this to prevent yourself from being an emotional slave to your own expectations of yourself or anyone else's expectations of you.

Carmel: Could The High Priestess just give us some further assistance in this monthly ritual for yourself?

High Priestess: *Yes. You have created a resonance with my frequency, which is essential, and you must allow yourself to connect to a time and place where you were comfortable and happy being a High Priestess. Just visualize a time where you felt at one with your truth and imagine yourself in a sacred, consecrated space. Feel that now. Just try and imagine the settings, the atmosphere, who is around you? What are you doing? Visualize one significant picture of that time and re-experience it. Re-create it now. You are beginning to really live up to your multi dimensional self. If you cannot visualize it, just allow yourself the feeling of being a High Priestess.*

My role is to allow you to see yourself as whom you really are and what your potential is. I am all the women of all the ages and beyond who have ever aspired to find me. I am a collective energy frequency of all aspirants who choose to live my path. Your life now will create much magic with my frequency, as the Full Moon is where I really belong. I am truly unveiled in this time, and I can show myself to you completely and totally.

Your cells are approximately 89% water, so you now need to just feel in your body fluids my force, and just feel my presence creating in your body a different frequency. I am in your body, mind, and spirit when this is allowed by you. I am inside you, and I am now allowing this part of your memory to be activated. What I am doing is activating your cells to a time and place where you and I were one. A Full Moon Meditation will really create in your life the essence and power of your truly spiritual self. When the spiritual self is revealed, you will create harmony in all your cells; your cells are the trigger for your emotions, thoughts, and experiences.

It is very important to drink plenty of energized Moon Water. You can do this by putting a jug or glass of clear, fresh water outside overnight under the Moonlight, and drink this after completing any energy work. You need to release accumulated toxins and emotions that need flushing out. Water clears emotion that has accumulated. Always begin your day with a full glass of Moon-energized water to physically and energetically release electrical discharge that has accumulated during the night. Also after any emotional encounter, drink a glass of this Moon-energized water, as it helps to clear out the toxicity. Your need to clear the emotions is very dependent on your intake of pure water. Emotional debris is cleared instantly. You need to recognize this more in your life. The reason: Water clears out stagnant energy. Stuck emotional energy needs shifting. Water will provide this. Just drink water when emotions are being created and need to be cleared.

As you drink the water say to yourself:
"I fill myself with the essence of The High Priestess. I now clear all emotional debris from my system.

" The Role of The High Priest in your "Moon" ritual:
The Moon is associated with the self-nurturing principle of the feminine and development of the feminine energies generally. However, the High Priest, the masculine principle, must never be forgotten. It is important to consider the role of The High Priest in your Full Moon ritual work.

The High Priest's role is also very significant in balancing out endocrine and hormonal function within the glandular system. You may like to explore this as well in your rituals to The High Priestess.

Our society has punished the feminine principle and women's functions generally, e.g. menstruation is still a taboo subject in many circles and so are men's health issues.

There needs to be a restoration of the masculine in addressing all female imbalances especially in the reproductive, glandular system.

Carmel: The High Priest of The Moon: How can aspirants of The High Priestess develop their own inner masculine with The High Priest?

If you reflect on this statement, you will begin to see how essential it is for The High Priestess to have an energetic relationship with The Priest, to draw down his power for balance and mutual growth. The High Priest of the moon is equally important as The High Priestess and you can now begin to feel why The High Priest of the moon will offer you support in your emerging relationship with The High Priestess. Keeping the link between The Priestess and your Priest will help you develop your new identity in our contemporary world, where the de-powered masculine energy has no respect for the Feminine principle.

I felt it was important to communicate directly to the moon's frequency so I attuned to The Moon's vibration:

Carmel: Could you, Moon, comment on the role of the balanced masculine energy for humans?

The Moon speaks through The High Priestess: You are asking me to give you an answer to why women in your society are so betrayed by the very thing that makes them women. It is the giving away of their power and a denial of their power as well. By creating a strong and healthy relationship with The High Priest of The Moon they can balance this inner void and create a healthy relationship with their own inner masculine and High Priest. This will give them a strong position in dealing with the hostility they encounter in a world that has no respect for the feminine principle.

There is an incredible sense of creative energy you can draw upon as The Moon is in Her fullness. Your creative principle is at its peak, and you must remember it is also a time of powerful purification. You need to examine emotional debris at this time and dispose of emotional clutter. Your emotional reactions to life's events are at their peak, so consider really examining what emotions surface at the time of the full moon and the days leading up to it.

Carmel: Could you comment further on developing our inner relationships with the balanced feminine and masculine principle?

For women and men their weight reflects their emotional clutter. First, for every kilo of weight over the desired body weight, consider this as being emotional debris or an extra "physical coat of armour of protection." Protecting our emotions through unbalanced eating permits emotional clutter to stay stuck in the body; these emotions reflect your fears. Second, under eating is a form of denial of the self, which addresses core abandonment issues, thereby making yourself vulnerable and feeling under nourished.

An imbalance in all eating habits is a source of self-abuse and punishment. While you are examining your core issues with the feminine and masculine principles, your weight is one key indicator of how your relationship is with yourself. At the time of The Full Moon, frustrations and unmet needs need to be addressed. We often try to protect, suppress, or deny our emotional selves through eating excessively or not at all.

However, by addressing your "core" issues around freedom, security, and stability and the need for protection, you can remove these emotional rocks of your polluted landscape and choose to have healthy, balanced relationships through The High Priestess and The High Priest.

The Full Moon is the cycle of letting go of emotional debris. Make a heart-felt conscious decision to discard the energy, which is accumulating now. Really examine core relationships or where you give emotional energy. Ask yourself: Am I receiving here? Am I giving there? Examine all core relationships and the emotional clutter that goes with them.

CHAPTER SEVEN

MOON MEDITATIONS

NEW MOON

The New Moon High Priestess appears to bring to your life new possibilities. She is hardly visible and the beauty of her new beginning heralds a new cycle in your life. It is an awakening, a birth. I am feeling new life begin again; allow the new moon to bring to you your love of new life. Meditating on me brings to you the hope that you are able to start all over again despite all the losses and difficulties. With me you are renewing your commitment to begin again resurrecting yourself after the initiatory experiences of the dark moon.

The New Moon High Priestess speaks to you now:

Give yourself 10 minutes in the evening for seven days. Tick off on your calendar this date with The High Priestess. You are giving your High Priestess 10 minutes every evening. Say to yourself:

"Tonight I am honoring you, my High Priestess, through your light, The Moon's Light. I offer you a gift for your illumination. (Incense stick, flower, some small offering, cake, rice, etc.)"

Through the new moon you will be opening up to your creativity and feeling a sense of resurrection. The cycle of life begins anew and you will begin to find energy, drive, and commitment for starting new plans and renewing your commitment to your identity. Your offerings to me at this new cycle ensures success. The greatest offering you can give your High Priestess is your open heart to grow and learn through the mysteries. Watching the new moon every night swelling in the night sky is like watching your own new ideas grow; every night there is a strengthening of commitment, and the new moon reinforces your drive and determination to keep your light alive. You are germinating your own new identity, and you will feel the moon's light reflecting back to you all you need for your new life.

THE WAXING MOON HALF MOON

The Half Moon High Priestess now is ripening your ideas. The Half Moon offers possibilities. There is duality in this Moon. Not all is being revealed in this quarter. Examine your relationship to The Half Moon's energy. (For example, sharing in relationships, business, creative ideas, etc.) She is opening Herself to you and getting you ready for Her performance. This is a good time to really intensify your commitment to this strengthening cycle. In ancient times the Half Moon created a space for rapid growth.

Your relationship with The High Priestess will be growing rapidly in this cycle and this growth will have its birth as the Moon approaches its fullness. Begin now to become more specific in your creations.

The Half Moon High Priestess speaks to you now:

Your trust in yourself and what you can do through me is at issue here. I am creating in you now separateness. I am separating you from your own small creations. I am weeding out people in your life now. You will begin to observe that some people are no longer interested in you. (This is good.) Others are clawing themselves into you trying to keep you in their world, and others are beginning to observe you in a new way.

You now must surrender your little self, this self that clings to others, for when you do this I can come to you and be your friend. You will now begin to feel my presence around you at certain times, and you may have had a tangible reminder of *who* I am. I am now changing your cellular memory to accept me in my present form. See me as a shining star, which watches over you. I am near you when you breathe ritualistically. I am near you when you meditate on the Moon and when you bathe or are near water. I am with you now.

THE FULL MOON HIGH PRIESTESS

The Full Moon approaches. You see her swelling in the night sky. She is awakening, ripening. She is revealing Her truth to you. She is showing you now how you can really possess the qualities She brings to you. The Full Moon always speaks of the Feminine. The feminine qualities are Her treasure chest. She reveals Her feminine treasures to you now, as you surrender to Her glory.

Surrendering to Her now brings your High Priestess into full view. You will experience your High Priestess if you have haven't yet met Her. She will create Herself with you as your cellular memory awakens to Her mystery. Mystery Schools hold important initiations on the full Moon. The company of all High Priests and High Priestesses create with you in this important cycle.

Magic is created now. As you create with Her in love, Her Love is your truth revealed. She will reveal your truth in yourself now. By bringing your truth She destroys illusion and brings emotion to the surface.

The feeling of anticipation is part of your relationship with the Moon. It is a cyclical natural phenomenon, one that occurs every month. This relationship with the natural world is integral to your world with The High Priestess. Why? Energies such as The High Priestess can only come through observance of the natural rhythms and cycles of the world we inhabit. Her relationship with you is Her beacon of light, The Moon. The Moon is magnetic and creates magnetism in yourself. Her vibration is immediate in your life. She is The High Priestess. The most potent and visible symbol for The High Priestess is the Moon herself.

Now the Full Moon draws near and will reveal Herself to you. You must be ready to note your experiences of your world around you and how it is changing because of the Full Moon. Tonight I have a date with the Full Moon whose "home" The High Priestess inhabits.

Throughout history there were specific temples dedicated to Moon worship. I was shown a "secret" in Karnak Temple, Egypt, where the High Priests of this ancient temple complex would commune with the Moon at night. It is climbed to by small internal stairs and is on the rooftop away from the hustle and bustle of daily temple life.

Create your own Moon worshipping temple in a corner of your garden or patio if you want to create with your High Priestess.

The Full Moon is the time for the full manifestation of your relationship with the Divine Feminine through The High Priestess. You are presented with the Moon revealing the power and purity of your fully realized feminine self.

Why? The Moon draws to the surface all unresolved emotions. See it like a poultice being placed on a boil. The boil is lanced at the time of the Full Moon. Imagine a volcano of emotion coming to the surface and being washed away. The Full Moon is just such a magnetic force for sweeping away unresolved grief. She will bring all unresolved grief to the surface for examination and wash it away. Your emotions stop the play between the subconscious mind and unconscious mind.

Your subconscious mind is where your emotions and thoughts create chaos because the subconscious stores, past-life, and karmic patterns. These patterns have been imprinted into our DNA. By observing our emotions, we can begin to recode the DNA, which allows us to gain access to the unconscious mind, also known as the higher self or soul self. When this happens you are able to tap into your deeply held psychic or intuitive abilities.

The Moon's ability to affect the tides is similar to the affect on humans. The Moon affects different regions of the brain as it affects the fluids in the body, which release and explore deeply held thoughts and emotions. Very importantly attuning to the Moon opens the veil, so your psychic and intuitive powers can be explored.

The Full Moon must be surrendered to. You need to allow yourself to surrender to what it gives you. Any work involving development through the feminine energies will be connected to the Full Moon. The Moon is allowing Herself to create the joy of pure manifestation for your true magical powers.

The Full Moon High Priestess speaks to you now:

The Full Moon is bringing to you now the true manifestation of what you need for your life now. You are revealing to yourself all aspects of your lunar self, the self that needs to feel the essence of "all love." The Moon will take care of all heart scars, and bring these heart scars to the surface. Allow yourself now to release the full moon brings. It allows for the examination and release of these emotions. Feel yourself examining and releasing these emotions now.

Feel now where the emotion is stored in the body. Breathe the Moon's magnetic energy into you now to release these deeply held emotions, expect a release, allow this release to take place now as you surrender to the moon to heal and renew the toxic waste material that is stored in your body. Feel this now.

WANING MOON POST FULL MOON

The Waning Moon High Priestess: This phase sees a resolution of what has occurred at the time of the Full Moon, and you need to just bring calmness to your life now. The waning of The Moon is a slow process — ebbing, letting go. Your High Priestess will help you let go. Release. This phase is one of calmness and resolution. Ask yourself "What do I have to resolve in my life right now?" Bask in this time. There will be a sense of achievement. Allow your High Priestess to work for you.

Watch The Moon in this phase. What is She saying? "Let go. Let go." You must constantly strive to shed what you must let go of now. I must observe The Moon and let go of all accumulated emotional debris. The High Priestess cannot live in a space with emotional debris. You must really bring to your world now a release. This is a grieving time. It is a time when old, unresolved grief surface. Give this grief to The High Priestess.

The High Priestess speaks to you now - Waning Moon Meditation:

You are going on a journey alone. You are prepared for this journey but it is one you must make alone. You are packed and ready to go. You have a boat waiting. The water is lapping on the sides of the boat, and the boat is gently rocking. Your boatman waits patiently. He is the High Priest of the Moon. Your High Priestess is also sitting opposite to where you will be seated. She too waits patiently, calmly. She knows your pain and She respects it. The High Priest and Priestess are your new guides for your initiation to your new world across the sea. You must now look at the people, events, and situations that you must leave behind. Breathe deeply, slowly, calmly three times. Really fill your lungs with purifying breath and feel the detachment that comes with letting go. Drink a full glass of water as you are visualizing this ritual of letting go.

Be guided by the boat. Sit in it. Don't look back. Just stay seated. Be still and present and begin your journey. The High Priestess sits opposite you. She is warm and nurturing. She is the Isis aspect of The High Priestess. She helps the grief. The boatman is behind you. He rows the boat and has taken care of all the practical details of your journey. He is protective, supportive, and loving. He represents the aspects of The High Priest you need to develop in your new relationships.

While the Moon is in this phase you will experience grief at certain times. You will experience a shedding of emotional intensity and letting go. You are being assisted. Ask for help. It is there. Don't be afraid to look at the Moon Herself and call for help. "Help me Moon." She will send to you now love and help. All of nature responds to grief. Nature has an affinity with grief, and the water element especially.

The letting go in this phase is extremely painful at times, and you will experience much abandonment. There are different aspects of yourself that you must monitor at all times when you are feeling emotionally overloaded.

Of all the Moon's phases this is the most painful. Why? Because letting go of a cherished object is the most painful thing in being human.

Let's look at how your High Priestess can connect with you now to help you:

You need your High Priestess to be very active in this cycle, and you must feel that the shedding has purpose. At one level depression can be seen as unsupported loss. To release a cherished object and not be supported can lead to depression. Unsupported loss can create grief. *"Who supports me when I lose something?* Loss is a part of everyday life. *"Who supports this loss?"* Your High Priestess supports this loss so you don't fall into depression.

The High Priestess sees depression as being the result of unsupported loss. Unsupported loss is grief. All diagnoses must be addressed by a professional in the field. This is only a guide to help you support your journey.

To create something new during the New Moon means that you have grown. To feel the creative fire in the Full Moon phase is a building up of energy. After this climax you need to come down and let go. This is where you are now, and this is what you have to take responsibility for. You created in your life your responsibility with The High Priestess. See Her as a living organism - a living thing - a new relationship. This new relationship has to be nurtured. Just observe this powerful and cathartic phase.

Carmel: Depression is a huge issue in our culture. Could The High Priestess further elaborate on how depressed people can best help themselves through this period in their lives?

High Priestess: Your culture does not want to address the issues around what it has created. Depression is a by-product of a culture, which does not support the feminine principle of self-nurturing. Many people are conditioned to give so much of themselves at the expense of themselves, we need to learn how to support ourselves by honoring the phases and cycles in our lives through self-nurturing.

The waning Moon is a time of acknowledging this cycle and honors it. It is very important to honor vulnerable times in your cycle, and the Moon waning phase allows this. As you observe the passage of the waning Moon you will begin to find within yourself stillness and nothingness.

DARK MOON

The Dark Moon High Priestess

There has been much written in myth and legend about the **Dark Moon** and its effects on humans. The Dark Moon is a time when you cannot see the Moon in the sky at all. There is a total absence of Her anywhere. Where is She? Where has She gone? Suddenly, Mother isn't there. The child is in the dark room. There is nothing. A black cloak of nothingness shrouds your energy and this creates disturbances in some people. Darkness shrouds. There is mystery. There is nothingness.

Where there is nothingness, there is a feeling of emptiness. Emptiness is terrifying for many people — for most of us in fact — but the Dark Moon is The High Priestess who creates from this space. Your emotional clutter has dispersed. You are empty. You must find peace and wholeness in this energetic void. You can't find your High Priestess. She seems shrouded. She has disappeared. It feels as though your work with Her has come to nothing. Your relationship at the time of the Full Moon has completely disappeared. This is a period of waiting and you appear stagnant. Energies can't seem to find an outlet and there can be much fear in this "nothingness." You are just going to have to "wait it out" and trust that the cycle will pass.

Your new direction, from the beginning of the New Moon must be observed now and you know you must allow your High Priestess to create with you in this stagnant period.

The Dark Moon High Priestess speaks:

I am a mysterious force, for I am everything and I am nothing. I can't be seen, yet I see. I have left you to do other work. I have turned away to create somewhere else, but I am there all the same. You are a child in the dark. You know I haven't disappeared but you, all the same, don't have access to me.

This nothingness is where you can grow because you can now examine your fears and seek to address them by observing your emotions and growing with them. Your emotions are one of the most creative forces, by acknowledging, embracing, and harnessing your emotions you can begin to create a new life for yourself.

You must always rest and wait in My Dark phase. Rest, wait, and receive Me again as I show My sweet crescent slit when you are ready.

The High Priestess of the Dark Moon is a vibration of watching. I am watching you and protecting you, but you are really now at a point of great inner growth and personal transformation, so my role is just one of silence and observing. I am in my own energy and I feel your heart, I am here, but your initiation is your own and I respect this. The labyrinth you feel at this time can leave you feeling afraid. I am here. You must trust that I am here at this time, and you will bring yourself back to me when the New Moon appears.

In summary, this section on Moon meditations has addressed the growth and creation of your High Priestess through the Moon's phases. The Moon is a potent reminder of your feminine and lunar spiritual soul self. The Moon reflects, and by reflecting, destroys illusion. Illusion is fear. When we are fearful we turn on ourselves. The Moon opens up parts of you that are unconscious. These Moon meditations enable your soul to travel by taking yourself out of your third dimensional or everyday self. By doing this you are able to address parts of your unconscious self that have been dormant. So now you have come the full circle. We are back at the beginning of the cycle of the New Moon again.

Ask yourself: What did I learn about myself and my High Priestess self in this lunar cycle?

What were my core fears this cycle? List them...

1. New Moon fears / issues

2. Waxing Moon fears / issues

3. Full Moon fears / issues

4. Waning Moon fears / issues

5. Dark Moon fears / issues

By listing your core fears and seeing how the unconscious part of yourself is exposed and explored, you are creating a new view of yourself in your world. You will become less reliant on others emotionally. Your own emotions will become more balanced, and you can witness the birth of yourself as the embodiment of The High Priestess. Furthermore, you will observe all forces of the natural world, as these living energies are able to assist you.

Chapter Eight

Star Constellations

Star Civilization & Stellar Influences

Aries (Ram)
March 21 April 19

Star Constellation: Hamal

Corresponding Moon sign: Libra

Body Part: Head, face, brain, forehead

Element: Earth

This vibration is one of allowing trust between the energy beings of Hamal and yourself to develop. The process of trust must be above everything else. This vibration allows you to trust in the processes of life and the knowledge that the whole universe can support your consciousness. Holding in and suppressing, controlling, being in the grip of the negative is what the vibration offers for those who choose to attune to the Hamalians.

When you let go and lead yourself into your unconscious, you will find that the beings from Hamal can come to your aid. Hamalians have learned what it is like to follow your own unique path. When you attune to this frequency you will find it not to relax the body. Try it. Your shoulders just droop and you swoon. You are instantly transported to a deep meditative space. Now a civilization like yours needs this ability.

Hamalians, what can you do for my people?

The ability to focus, yet relax is what we offer. We offer a balancing in the brain function. Our role is to have the brain working in balance with both sides functioning at once. We are there for all imbalances in the head and neck region.

TAURUS (BULL)
APRIL 20 MAY 21

Star Constellation - Hyades

Corresponding Moon sign: Scorpio

Body Part: Shoulder, thyroid, liver, gall bladder

Element: Earth

The energy of the constellation of Hyades is one of inspiration and joy. You will feel that through this constellation's vibration, great freedom of expression, and a sense of upliftment. Nothing is too much to expect. The energy helps you to astral travel. Hyades lets in the light through the Crown Chakra to draw down the energies of the celestial beings. This vibration will make you feel lighter. There is freedom and expansion in this constellation, which makes for musical talents in all who attune to the frequency.

Hyadians can help in conditions of plethora, heaviness, throat, gum, jaw conditions, emotionally over judgmental, or dourness, as well as rigidity in thinking, materialism, or greed. The attunement can create a love of life, creative dexterity, coordination, artistic expression enhanced, communication as well as dexterity in creation.

GEMINI (TWINſ)
MAY 22 JUNE 21

Star Constellation - Pollux:

Corresponding Moon sign: Sagittarius

Body Part: Shoulders, arms, lungs, chest, nervous system

Element: Air

Polluxians what can you do for my people? We love humans because we see their potential for the expression of themselves through movement and light, dancing. Melodious, light filled, and charming are the attributes we bring. Think of us as a ballet performance.

This vibration is for communication between people, plants, animals, and universal beings. The Polluxians keep you opened up to the true communication process, and we are from the constellation, which allows the feeling aspect of communication to develop. If there is a need to help yourselves develop a resonance in the way you say things and how you say things, invite us in.

We are able to assist in all conditions where blockages occur in the body because of the inability to express feelings. If you find yourself holding back in the expression of your creativity, i.e. you need to really feel what you need to say, you will benefit from using our vibration.

If you sometimes experience chest or throat complaints, your body is jerky, clumsy, or holds nervous energy in your body we can assist in the true communication process, create a sense of gracefulness, and freedom in body flexibility.

CANCER (CRAB)
JUNE 22 JULY 21

Star Constellation - Prasepe Cluster

Corresponding Moon sign: Capricorn

Body Part: Abdomen, breasts, stomach, elbow, joints

Element: Water

The energy transmission from Prasepe Cluster is one of light. The light you will receive will help you to evolve very fast. We provide through our constellation a powerful connection with many sources of light. There are many of us able to assist you at this time. Through your utilization of our vibration with the elixir, you will feel complete freedom to be a part of the universal flow of light force for yourselves and your planet. There is a peaceful harmony in the transfer of light and a letting go of yourselves. You will feel that you are being very gently protected and your inner light glows. We dispel darkness around you and are particularly good when you fear the darkness and evil around you. Any primordial fears are addressed by us, especially fear which has no obvious cause. When you sprinkle us on you, you are being showered in tiny light dots, which will allow all fears of abandonment to depart.

Prasepe Clusterians, what can you do for my people?

Our role is one of releasing showers of light to Earth people at an important time in her evolution. We throw down the light like confetti at a wedding or rice at a holy function. Use us for all banishing of dark, evil, or stagnant energy. We ask for you to release to our light and we believe that if you do, your burdens will be much easier to bear, as you will be able to closely interact with the forces of light in your world.

When you feel fear, lost in a labyrinth where there can be punctures or holes in your aura, the Prasepe Clusterians bring protection from the beings of light, and surrender with the appreciation of all life and beauty.

LEO (LION)
JULY 22 AUGUST 21

Star Constellation - Zosma

Corresponding Moon sign: Aquarius

Body Part: Gall bladder, spine, heart, back

Element: Fire

You will find with this vibration the energy of total expansion and upliftment. Repeatedly you fail to acknowledge your own unique contribution to yourselves and your world. This vibration will bring the need for you to dismiss your own feelings of limitation in what you can create. See us being for all physical conditions, which result in you being unable to fully explore your own true capacity and self-worth. There is a tendency to find yourself physically unable to have the stamina and drive to complete your aims in your world. This lack of drive is self-created — of course, we know this — and our vibration will provide stamina for your pursuits. Your life is your own and too frequently you fail to see your potential. This vibration brings to you the feeling that you are able to achieve your destiny. Your life will be filled with joy and expansiveness and you will be filled with the desire to inspire others to do the same with their lives.

Zosmarians, what can you do for my people?

Taking control is what we are offering to you at this time, become established in your life, get direction; we offer the commitment to tasks and objectives and a renewed commitment to your life's purpose. With us life will bring you the capacity for endurance and you won't give in so easily.

When you feel you have no control over fear, feel self-centered, with limited beliefs about yourself the constellation's vibration will help you become an inspiration to others. You will develop drive and stamina. Commitment to your dreams will be the outcome of your attunement to our vibration.

VIRGO (VIRGIN)
AUGUST 22 SEPT 22

Star Constellation - Porrima

Corresponding Moon sign: Pisces

Body Part: Abdomen, small intestines, gastric system

Element: Earth

My vibration will allow your spirit to soar. See me as being like a bonfire and you will understand the energy and power our frequency will bring to you. The importance of the vibration is to make you aware of your own potential in your life and the energy of this is to create changes. You have to see yourself as a dynamic being, fully alive. Many of you get around half dead to your own potential. From Porrima you will wake up to yourself and not feel so lethargic and lazy. When you look at a volcano you see force and energy and light exploding through the top of the mountain. This is what this vibration will do for you. Physically, you will be released from tension, which hasn't an outlet, and you will feel a discharge of energy in your physical body. Utilize this vibration for all conditions in the body, which need to be released. Pollutants stored in the body will be released and the digestive system will be strengthened. Conditions, which affect the digestive system, will be relieved by this vibration.

Porrimarians, what can you do for my people?

Thank you for asking. We are very happy to be able to assist those on Earth to create a force field for themselves which will be very enlivening. Our role is to enliven the person and make them feel that they are connecting with the earth in a very powerful way to utilize the energy currents of the Earth and bring through to the body the currents to be released, heightening a person's force.

If you suffer laziness, are lethargic or your body feels polluted, you have digestive disorders our vibration will help you create awareness of your own potential. You will begin to feel connected to the Earth's currents for energy. A powerful energy will be transmitted for you to feel earthed.

LIBRA (SCALES)
SEPT 23 OCT 22

Star Constellation - Zuben-El-Genubi

Corresponding Moon sign: Aries

Body Part: Kidneys, loins, lower back, bladder, ovaries

Element: Air

My vibration allows the energy of light to pour into Earth beings. Our constellation attracts beauty to itself. We are known as the beautiful ones. We are beings who live with harmony and light. To those from Earth wanting this, we allow you to see beauty in everything: objects, plants, places, and people. We elevate the consciousness to bring you to a point where you are "above" the mundane and the sordid. We are beings who are literally able to "look through" ugliness and despair and embrace the "total" person, place, or experience. We can be utilized when you are struggling with your own self-image; the "I am not" thinking. We are able to assist when the situation you are in looks grim; we are able to allow you to experience a state beyond your perception, which brings on depression. This vibration is very good to use when you want to see colors in healing or to experience what true color looks like. We allow you to look at the bigger picture. We are very good for creative work where fear around creating beauty is featured, as is in much of your modern art. Allow for sight to be strengthened; inner sight, second sight, like clairvoyant experiences, which will embrace vivid color.

Zuben El Genubians, what can you do for my people?

We are able to assist where there is an inability to see beyond despair and ugliness. Our light keeps you protected and we deal with those who get depressed when there is no light in their lives, i.e. physically or otherwise; completion, being able to see through difficult tasks, light at the end of the tunnel.

If you suffer depressive states with poor self-image, your sight both inner and outer can be affected. Zuben El Genubi allows for devotion in your consciousness, strengthening the ability to bring color into your life, you will begin to see beauty in everything.

SCORPIO (SCORPIAN EAGLE) OCT 23 NOV 22

Star Constellation - Sargas

Corresponding Moon sign: Taurus

Body Part: Generative organs, prostate gland, bladder, rectum

Element: Water

The Sargas vibration will allow the qualities of giving so the closed secretive nature some people feel they must exhibit in order to survive will be diminished. When the energies are open in the giving state, more can BE GIVEN IN RETURN. Be aware of the vibration of equal exchange when the Sargas vibration is utilized. We bring to you the happy state of equilibrium in yourself, a feeling of not believing the world and circumstances are against you. Allow yourself to experience more of the love of your own humanity and that we have for you. You may have issues of shyness from previous encounters with people, places, and situations, which make you, feel vulnerable to being able to express your deepest concerns and private feelings. Sharing brings opportunities to grow and we will allow your full nature to flow. Bring to yourself your unique contribution and do not feel so secretive. Be bold in your expression and your beliefs; you are important. Because you are so deeply aware of the forces of the unconscious world, your unique contribution is to bring your own power and belief in yourself into being. We assist here in this expression, both verbally and spiritually.

Sargasians, what can you do for my people?

Belief in your own perceptions, those secret parts of yourself that need to be expressed, is what we offer you at this time. You will find that the release in not allowing yourself to be controlled by your society through manipulation of your thoughts, having respect for your own beliefs, and being able to stand up for your ideas is what we offer.

The Sargasians keep you in your ability to give and receive and allow you to be bold in the expression of your truth. Sometimes we find it hard to share our ideas or thoughts; this vibration will allow for freedom from manipulation of thoughts from others.

SAGITTARIUS (ARCHER)
NOV 23 DEC 22

Star Constellation - Kaus Australis

Corresponding Moon sign: Gemini

Body Part: Hips, thighs, tail bone, pelvis

Element: Fire

Kaus Australis is a constellation whose energy beings are committed to making change possible in whatever way imaginable for Australians or those wishing to attune to the country. We have an affinity with the continent of Australia and our vibration resonates with your country's people. We allow you to stand up for yourself, to take a role of leadership in your life. Your affinity to your continent is very important for a caring relationship to develop. There is a fear of embracing who you are and why you have incarnated in Australia (or feel you may have had incarnations in this continent).

Many people have no affinity with their land; this vibration addresses your need to feel part of your homeland and be proud of what you are. For people who show hostility and separation from their land; for people who cannot find their true home, adopted or native. You will feel, with this vibration, a sense of coming home, that you have a relationship with your Earth and its cultural and artistic life. In fact we aim to help you bring your best, so you can show the world that you have much to be proud of. We embrace the "big picture" of your life. When you feel lacking in inspiration, ideals, common-held beliefs with your group, we assist. We are the protectors of your evolution and we are shining our light toward you at this time. Alienation, indifference, self-absorption, "me only", I only do it for me — are all addressed by this vibration.

Kaus Australasian, what can you do for my people?

We aim to show you that you are inter-connected with your country, other countries, and the Earth. We help you to see your part in the "global village."

Allow yourself to feel inspired, become the love leader, and feel the love of your Earth with our vibration.

CAPRICORN (SEA GOAT) DEC 23 JAN 20

Star Constellation - Dabih

Corresponding Moon sign: Cancer

Body Part: Knees, skeleton, skin, digestive system

Element: Earth

Dabih will promote a feeling of expression in the spiritual and not make people fear their bodies being an expression of their spirituality. Their bodies become temples. The body is in fact a spiritual temple. This elixir assists in conditions, which are related to the knees and joints, particularly in the lower part of the back and stomach. There may be tightness in the lower body, and lack of flexibility in the lower joints. Definitely there is a release in the lower body. There is release and freedom knowing you can support yourself emotionally because spirituality is part of your essence.

Spirituality is made manifest in everyday life; there is an opening and expansion of your Heart Chakra. People who would benefit from the Dabih vibration are those who are selfish and stuck in their ways. They can have crabbed hands, a tight face, and a mean-spirited outlook. It is reflected in the way their body hunches; they eventually become bent over.

The Dabians help us to allow our bodies become an expression of our spirituality. We open up to unconditional love and release to our spirituality.

AQUARIUS (WATER BEARER)
JAN 21 FEB 19

Star Constellation - Sadulsud

Corresponding Moon sign: Leo

Body Part: Ankles, wrists, lower legs, eyesight

Element: Air

Sadalsud star brings the opportunity to feel expansion in your total life. It blows you up like a balloon. When you feel deflated and flat you need to utilize this vibration to give you life and buoyancy. Look at us being like a balloon and let us go. We are light, happy, friendly beings, and we are very playful. We bring children together and are wonderful for unhappy, lonely individuals; those who need to feel part of a group. The energy of our light is in bringing together people or concepts. If you experience difficulty in this aspect of your life or work, our vibration can offer the change of balance required. An adjustment in your perception and psyche takes place. Group cohesion is part of our function for human use. You will experience wholeness, like a daisy chain. We link you together. A wonderful vibration to work with in a small or large group situation where cohesion and cooperation are required.

Sadalsudians, what can you do for my people?

We love to see the whole picture. Our function and vibration is to make you see yourselves in a whole way — body, mind, and spirit. So if you are split off, isolated in any way, we provide the sense to bring a total picture. If a project appears too difficult and you can't see the woods for the trees, let us in. Relationships are particularly applicable to our vibration. We love being able to make people happy. Try us.

Sadalsud vibrations allows you to feel part of a group, brings balance in relationships you will begin to see the total picture for your life.

PIſCEſ (FIſH)
FEB 20 MARCH 20

Star Constellation - Petra also known as Eta Piscium

Corresponding Moon sign: Virgo

Body Part: Feet, stomach, intestines, body fluids, pineal glands

Element: Water

The vibration of Petra allows for surrender and release. The consciousness and energy of Petra is one of allowing the forces of light to come through and connect with you. Petrans are beings who are able to live with peace so they have the ability to offer assistance with the Earth plane addictions in every regard, especially the obsessions which seem to plague Earth people. There comes from us a gentle understanding of what it is like to be human, and a reminder that our world is not the only one. The beings of this galaxy have released the need for these conditions at every level, so they feel in their everyday existence a blending of all life — all of life is one to the inhabitants of the Petra constellation.

Petrans, what can you do for my people?

Thanks for asking us to be of assistance. We love to be able to allow you to understand your inner needs and not feel fear in your world. As our world is safe, we have special affinity with those of you who are plagued by self-doubt and self-criticism.

The Petrans allow for surrender and peace, the power to understand humanness. You will experience balance in everything, Karmic addictions can be addressed as you won't feel the need to hold on to fear, and feel buried in the past.

PART IV
THE HIGH PRIESTESS COURSE

THE HIGH PRIESTESS COURSE

Lesson One
Emotions

When you want to create a relationship with your High Priestess, there are certain emotions you may wish to reflect on and develop within yourself. Some of these emotional attributes are listed below. Please circle appropriate answer.

Have you ever been lost in love i.e. hurt, abandoned or betrayed?
- Never
- Sometimes
- Always

Do you suffer emotional anxiety or fear in any new situations, which see change?
- Never
- Sometimes
- Always

Have you ever felt fear in seeing the "truth" of a relationship, health, or financial issue?
- Never
- Sometimes
- Always

Do you need control in emotional situations, i.e. do you need to feel "in control" of emotional outcomes?
- Never
- Sometimes
- Always

Do you feel that you cannot trust your intuition?
- Never
- Sometimes
- Always

If you have answered "Sometimes" or "Always," you are ready to explore the world of the High Priestess.

The High Priestess is a spiritual being who is able to help you bring balance, love, and abundance into your life. In other words, she teaches you to like yourself and your humanness. To begin to develop your relationship with your High Priestess, you may like to consider offering Her a small gift or offering, such as a flower, jewelry, a pendant you have, or you might like to purchase a crystal. This is acknowledging respect for yourself and Her.

Would you describe yourself as a highly emotional person? YES / NO

Do you react emotionally in situations where you feel threatened or challenged in some way? YES / NO

In matters of love, most of us do to some degree; however, it is your emotional "reaction" that determines your ability to be able to create with your High Priestess. When you do overreact you are handing over your emotional authority.

(1) <u>List now</u>: Who do I hand my emotional authority over to?

This list can be as long as you like and can include "anyone" you hand over your power to.

| |
| |
| |
| |
| |
| |
| |

(2) Circle the qualities you would most like to have if you felt more empowered or felt you had an inner "authority" with this person.

a) Strength

b) Magnetism

c) Beauty (inner)

d) True Romance

e) Uniqueness

f) Empowerment

g) Other_____

Now prioritize these in order of preference from 1-7. 1 being the most needed and 7 being the least needed. What you need to do is to allow these emotions to happen energetically first within yourself. This is the most important thing, because you will be creating the

High Priestess in yourself first. It's a little like a rehearsal. Try now to imaginatively enter into the space where you feel you need to find your High Priestess's qualities. Breathe deeply, powerfully and rhythmically three times to establish this inner 'space'. Do this now.

Imagine the last encounter where you felt challenged. Visualize this scene with the person in front of you. Recreate the scene, detail by detail. Now feel yourself breathing in deeply, powerfully and rhythmically, creating with your High Priestess as an imaginary figure. Do this now, recreate the scene and feel the High Priestess inside you. Go through the scene again with 'Her' and feel yourself draw on 'Her' power and all the gifts you have allowed yourself to receive from 'Her'.

(3) I want you to describe, either through a fictional character, i.e. a movie star, myth, legend, or in someone you know who has these attributes listed above, while creating this new scene. If you don't know anyone or can't imagine anyone with these qualities, just create a fictional character and describe her now. (100 words)

Now that you have created your ideal character by doing this exercise, you can decide now how you want Her to behave when you are challenged by your own emotions and give your authority away. The next time you are challenged by a man or woman, you need to remember how your ideal character would behave.

(4) When you feel challenged you must remember to give yourself space to be you. In point form list five steps that you can incorporate into a situation where you find yourself emotionally challenged or over-reactive. How do you now see yourself reacting? What steps are you taking to give yourself this space, i.e. breathe, visualization, make an appointment to discuss the issue at a certain time and date, etc.?

(5) Ask yourself now, can the person who challenges you surrender his/her ego and let go to enter your space? More importantly, are you allowing yourself your own space first?

By recreating this scene, you will learn to trust yourself in the next situation you feel challenged.

Record, in detail, your responses below to see where you were challenged.

(a) I couldn't go through it

(b) I felt too much fear in doing it

(c) I achieved my aims and felt empowered

(d) Other

If you want to further develop your relationship with your High Priestess and bring balanced love into your life, you will now begin to make a commitment to creating with Her by asking your higher self's permission to begin your relationship with Her. Your High Priestess will create with your higher self. Your higher self is your "soul," or unconscious self. Establish this first. You can do this by going into a meditation and just feeling, or sensing the higher self. Your higher self is your first contact and will help you develop your soul's journey on Earth.

(6) Your higher self-exercise needs to be completed now:

- *Begin your breathing technique outlined earlier in this lesson and establish your connection with the higher self.*
- *Focus on the crown chakra now.*
- *Draw an indigo, or dark violet ying/yang symbol over your crown now.*
- *Feel the energy of doing this right now. Even though you can't see the results yet, the higher self will be activated and ready to give you the go-ahead for all you need in your journey with the High Priestess.*
- *When you sense a tingle, or a shift in energy, you will know you have communicated with your higher self.*

The High Priestess teaches you to nurture yourself. Most of us do a great deal for everyone else, but neglect "us," the "self."

We feel we must give and or be available to others, in order to receive. List the people you give to at the expense of receiving. Try to find a reason why you do this, i.e. fear of him/her becoming angry with me; I may be hurt, etc. <u>200 words max</u>:

Your High Priestess, through your higher self, teaches you one very important gift first. This is the gift to nurture the self. To nurture the self is to treat yourself as a mother would her new baby. To make a commitment to the High Priestess, you will need to establish a quiet corner in your environment and set up a small altar. An altar is a consecrated space or a space especially set-aside for your High Priestess.

(7) Establish a quiet corner in your environment and set up a small altar:

Establish a space in your environment, i.e. room, patio, by cleaning the space and using a table or desk as an altar.

Your table can be covered with a fabric in an appropriate color, i.e. blue, red, or any color reflecting your relationship with your High Priestess. You may choose an element, which represents, Fire, Air, Earth, Water, etc.

A pair of candles, incense, shells, flowers, oil and spray mists, can be purchased to begin your relationship with your High Priestess. Construct this with your High Priestess in a practical, focused way. Your altar reminds you that you have a unique and special relationship with your High Priestess. By constructing this small devotional space, you are developing an atmosphere for your High Priestess to be present. This devotional space can be used to reflect on your High Priestess daily.

(8) You can now provide a detailed plan for your altar. In diagram or point form, or in 100 words, describe your altar, e.g. its height, size, etc. One word of caution; don't clutter your altar with too many objects at once, keep it simple.

Personal magnetism is that special quality sacred to us all. Each of us has that magical ability to be able to bring to ourselves that aura which shines and makes us alive to all around us.

(9) To increase personal magnetism:

Breathe in: hold: gently release: building up to a count of 8 seconds.

Breathe in count eight: hold, count eight: release slowly, count eight: pause, count eight

To prepare yourself to create balanced heart-centered relationships, you should discipline yourself daily with this sequence of breathing.

To further reinforce the breathing sequence of 8x8x8x8 is to open and balance your energy belts, where the major chakras are located.

To do this, visualize yourself with your High Priestess: she is waving a large crystal over your aura. This crystal or wand can be changed to create different colors on your auric field. Prepare your quiet space. Light your candles on your altar and prepare yourself with your breathing sequence. Your High Priestess is about to arrive and balance your energy belts.

Your body consists of five energy belts, and they are associated with different colors. You need now to concentrate on the energy belt located at the pelvic area. You can help your High Priestess come through by concentrating on the energy belts one by one. Let's begin.

- 1 min for the energy belt at the Base Chakra Colors - Reds
- 1 min for the energy belt in the Naval Chakra Colors - Orange and Yellows
- 1 min for the energy belt in the Heart Chakra Colors - Greens and Pinks
- 1 min for the energy belt in the Throat/Face Chakra Colors - Blues, Turquoise, Purples
- 1 min for the energy belt in the Crown Chakra Colors - Gold and Whites

Do this for five minutes every day to bring yourself completely into balance with your High Priestess. By aligning your energy centers you stay connected to Her, and this provides your aura with valuable light energy, similar to food providing essential nutrients for your body. To do these rituals every day provides you with a framework for creating a deep relationship with your High Priestess.

Summary: You will complete this lesson by completing the following:

- Your list of authority figures
- Your list of preferences for your own power
- Your fictional character (100 words)
- Listing 5 steps to give yourself space
- Your 100-word response to being challenged, self review
- Your 200-word answer for giving at the expense of yourself
- Your detailed plan or description of an altar
- Your 5 min energy renewal, 8x8x8x8

Congratulations!

You have made a major step toward awakening yourself to the greatest gift: Yourself!

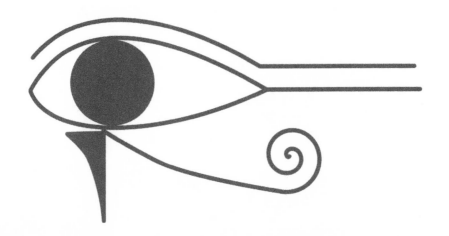

THE HIGH PRIESTESS COURSE

Lesson Two
Self-Nurturing

Your world will begin to change now that you have begun to establish your relationship with your High Priestess. You will find that you are drawing new people into your life and that your old life is shifting. Your world will begin to change now that you have begun to establish your observational of people and your responses to them.

(1) Describe either in point form or in a couple of sentences how your old world has begun to change.

| |
| |
| |
| |
| |
| |

(2) You might like to discuss your observations of your "new" self-nurturing self.

By observing and challenging your old patterns, you will begin to receive more from your High Priestess. Your High Priestess is growing inside you, similar to a pregnancy. By self-nurturing, your High Priestess can help you grow. This is a very important part of your journey with yourself.

Our previously held definition of the word devotion may have religious connotations or an association with guru worship. However, for you to experience your High Priestess fully you need to begin to explore your own relationship with the word "devotion." To be devoted means to serve someone with love and to have love returned. Devotion to your High Priestess is as simple as that.

Now that you have created your altar and have begun to feel the energy build in this space, it develops power and energy. Try to describe now a sacred space you have been to, which has this type of energy. Examples of this may be a spot in nature, a special beach, a grotto, or quiet, powerful space. Many people find this energy in churches, temples, and sacred places, like the Pyramid of Giza, or other ancient healing sites.

Now, you have established your connection with your High Priestess by being in a devotional space, which you have created by visualizing a sacred space. You now can visit this space anytime during the day when you are stressed and cannot go to your altar.

(3) I would like you now to describe this space in detail, really sensing the energy. What we are going to do after this space is described is to imagine yourself there with your High Priestess. You can begin the breathing sequence, and you will feel instantly peaceful. Describe the space now:

After you have written this description, you now can visualize your High Priestess in this space. This is your devotional space together. Really feel and be in the presence of your High Priestess. She will appear to you if you allow yourself to surrender in this space: What are your feelings, now that She is in this space with you?

(4) Give five separate words to describe this feeling you receive.

Remember your breathing!

This is a very powerful exercise because it is changing the cells in your body to help become all the things you want to be. Now that you have established your new life with your High Priestess, who is like a wonderful friend without all the emotional problems, She will help you create new opportunities to bring you a new life. Here are the lists of gifts she will help you achieve right now. Your High Priestess is ready to give you your gifts now.

1. A woman can be beautiful, but if she isn't powerful, she is like a Barbie doll: She can be manipulated. This is your first gift, the gift of power.

2. She now gives her second gift.

This is the gift of a glowing light body. Your body will feel and look lighter.

3. She now gives you your third gift.

This is the gift of being able to observe and find the source of emotional pain.

4. She now gives you your fourth gift.

This is the gift of peace. Peace makes a woman beautiful.

5. She now gives you your fifth gift.

The gift of expressing your sexuality freely to bring your duality in human form. Sex has no authority over you.

Now if you wish to accept these gifts, you must acknowledge in some way to your High Priestess that you will use and appreciate the gifts She is giving you. By accepting these gifts you are acknowledging to yourself that you are able to change your world of relationship self-abuse. When a woman doesn't acknowledge her power she gives it away too easily in relationships, work, her personal life, and her "pleasure-filled'" existence.

The only thing your High Priestess wants from you is your ability to love yourself enough to say, "yes" to Her gifts. Gifts always bring responsibilities. In your relationship with your High Priestess, the gift is the responsibility to really express pain, the pain of not allowing yourself to receive these gifts. We can be offered gifts, but the pain often stops us from expressing our gratitude for the gifts being offered. If you can honestly say, "yes" to the gifts, you will have to release attachments. In your life now being human brings attachments to everything. Your new gifts from your High Priestess will challenge these attachments.

Tick off the words that best describe how you are feeling when challenged by your attachments:
- Uncomfortable, fearful
- Terrified
- Isolated
- No security
- Other

Attachments mean just that. Attach. Your High Priestess challenges all definitions about yourself in your ability to separate from your emotional self, which is your attachment self. By releasing your attachments you bring your power to you now. By observing your attachments you know your vulnerable moments.

(5) Write a small description about your most vulnerable moments, i.e. when you feel most fearful or uncomfortable, terrified, isolated, or with no security. (50 words)

By contacting this fear and releasing it, you can see where your patterns are being held. These fears will hold back your High Priestess from fully creating with you the life you truly deserve!

Your High Priestess has different aspects which you need to recognize; in other words, She has the tools to help you look at those fears, for example, if the words "terrified" or "no security" appeared in your description you would look at the warrior aspect of your High Priestess such as Sekhmet the Egyptian Goddess who protects, avenges, and fights for you. Another way you can draw upon Her aspects for you at the moment will be for you to reflect on your favorite color, i.e. a piece of jewelry or a garment you would buy or wear right now. For example, deep blue lapis will connect you to the Isis frequency: Isis is the healer, mother, magician, and protector. Turquoise is associated with the Hathors: lover, sensualist, and creators through dance, sound, and the arts. You can combine the three aspects of Sekhmet, Isis and the Hathors for fighting, healing, and loving.

To bring Her into the world of yourself, you will need to feel if you are ready for the next most important commitment.

Just allow yourself to receive your High Priestess in your own, specially prepared space. Can you imagine coming home with a new baby or pet, and not having a specially prepared space for it? It's inconceivable. You may now begin your commitment to morning devotions, which link you to your High Priestess. Put on appropriate music (female vocalists) light, incense, and a candle, spray the area with appropriate oils. (i.e. ylang ylang, patchouli, rose, etc.)

You can begin your ritual time for 10 mins per day. In this specially prepared space by making this commitment, you are setting time aside to begin your world of devotion to your High Priestess.

You begin by:
1. Anointing yourself
2. Saying your affirmation:

"May the energy and protection of the High Priestess be with me now to protect me and aid my soul's path"

By saying this every day you are now being in the presence of you High Priestess who will wave their magic wand over your creations, and your world will change according to the amount of time you give her.

(6) You can give a brief description on how, after one week of using this ritual, your life has changed. Try to put into words your experiences, which may seem daunting. Writing grounds your experiences and provides you with a direction for your journey with the High Priestess.

Summary:

1. Describe how your world has begun to change.
2. Your description of your 'new' self-nurturing self.
3. Describe your new peace filled space when you begin to focus on the breath.
4. Five words to describe your High Priestess.
5. A description of your most vulnerable moments.
6. Creating a space for 10 minutes 'ritual time' each day.

THE HIGH PRIESTESS COURSE

Lesson Three
Relationships

Now that you have established your relationship with your High Priestess, you can create with Her to heal yourself, clients, friends and other relationships. By developing this relationship the bonus for you is to help not only yourself, but also others in your life. Remember the qualities She gives you will be transferred to others in healing too. Your High Priestess can be evoked through opening your heart wide to Her. Feel Her now in your body in your left breast.

Do this now:
Prepare your space (see Lesson Two for creating a space for rituals/devotions). Lie down in this comfortable space and make sure there will be no disturbances. You will now be ready to receive a healing from Her. This is indeed a powerful moment. Make the connection with your Higher Self by focusing on the breath.

You will evoke Her to the level of your Higher Self. Your Higher Self will reveal Her to you.

This is how you begin:
1) Open your heart wide; feel Her in your left breast
2) Offer yourself as a channel for Her power
3) Feel Her power through your body
4) Now feel Her life force through your hands and breasts
5) Let go to Her to heal you.

You will need to keep breathing consciously and with awareness for Her to enter you. She will enter your aura and stay there if you keep attuning to Her through breath.

As your High Priestess is more and more able to create with you, you will find that there will be changes in how you choose to represent Her in you. For example, you will begin to experience dressing for Her. This does not necessarily mean wearing long floating robes or frilly garments; it simply means that she is a representative of you in Her and Her in you.

Don't act, dress or do anything to please anyone except your High Priestess. Your jewelry selection, makeup and hair will also reflect Her in you. You must remember that how you choose to you present yourself to the world is how you are choosing to represent Her as well. Allow Her to help you decide: You always have the choice. Ask your Higher Self to connect with Her when you are needing to update your jewelry, clothes, accessories and hair: It's fun, and brings Her frequency closer and closer to you.

I would like you to draw or describe your High Priestess's choice of jewelry, clothes, accessories and hair etc. Give yourself a total make over.

Through evoking Her now through your Higher Self you go into a meditative space where you can meet Her. Find yourself settled and quiet, reflective and open to meeting Her. Begin your breathing sequence, by breathing in to count of eight - pause to the count of eight - release to the count of eight - and pause to the count of eight. See yourself meeting Her in a space that gives you a connection, i.e. a river, ocean, rainforest, or tropical retreat. Imagine your High Priestess in this tranquil environment, feel, hear and see the atmosphere. (100 Words/Drawing)

For the High Priestess you will begin to develop your own agenda with a man, and become more detached from his emotional issues with other women.

Please describe your definition of what being "in love" means to you in comparison to having a 'heart-centered relationship'?

Does being 'in love' have a big place in your world, why/why not? Does having a relationship with a man have a huge importance in your life?

Does identifying with the mother's role have priority in your world? i.e the need to look after others at the expense of yourself.

By challenging your definitions of being 'in love' and 'mother's role', you are really beginning to forge a deep commitment to yourself here. You need to be very clear and patient with yourself now as you unravel society's expectations of your role here. Often we project onto others what we can't bring to our own life. For example being 'in love' is different from loving from the heart, which is also passionate, but doesn't have an emotional agenda connected to it. Most of us have big issues with these definitions. For the High Priestess, being in love has no place in Her world. However she has the qualities that men adore: Power, life force, vitality, sexuality and above all she is her own woman.

This next exercise is designed to help you trust in relationships. Find a quiet space within yourself.

Ask yourself, where do I trust and where don't I trust in relationships?

List major betrayals and hurts:

Ask yourself now:
Who am I in relation to my relationship? Am I being loved? Can you say "I am loved. I am loved." Am I allowing myself to be loved?

List all the loving things you have done for yourself within your relationships?

| |
| |
| |
| |
| |
| |
| |

Now observe your relationships (or past relationships) with others and analyze where the negative qualities began to outweigh the positive qualities. Really feel where your scales are out of balance. Do the scales weigh heavier for betrayals, or loving things you have done? Did you do more loving things for other people than you did for yourself? If so, do you feel betrayed or resentful?

Now write a summary of your relationship with yourself, within these relationships. Find this feeling of self love within yourself first. Then spend five minutes recoding your cellular memory by saying "I am loved" out loud.

| |
| |
| |
| |
| |
| |
| |

Summary:
- Receive a healing from your High Priestess
- Drawing and Description of your High Priestess
- Refining your definition of love
- Evaluating yourself in relationships

THE HIGH PRIESTESS COURSE

Lesson Four
Love

This lesson allows you to experience the frequency of love and what it really means for you as a woman creating through The High Priestess. Try and see your High Priestess as a being who has one primary purpose, that is to love, to share, and to commit. Now if you feel comfortable with this role of Her in your life, you need to open your heart wide to Her.

After you surrender to Her, ask Her to recode your cellular memory where all our old patterns and thoughts are stored. One way to look at it is like having a computer upgraded. Re-code your cellular memory to accept the principle that "love" equals sharing and commitment.

"I now ask that my cellular memory be recoded to accept new frequencies. I now ask to receive in love, to allow myself to share in love, and to commit in love."

This healing exercise will probably take at least 30 minutes so please accept the time to allow yourself to do this self-healing for love, sharing, and commitment.

Please share your feelings in the space provided below after you have done this 30-minute healing.

I would like you to examine the last relationship or a current relationship, which is causing you, pain. Breathe in deep, powerfully, and rhythmically. You are examining yourself in this exercise. You cannot examine why a relationship with a person is causing pain until you bring your own emotions to the surface; however, for this exercise to be of any benefit to you, you must bring emotional control to the memories or hurts.

List your own weaknesses with the person, i.e. fear of not being good enough, abandonment, fear of breaking up, not trusting your partner, etc.

Ask yourself "Where am I vulnerable here?

Really examine your vulnerability. Try and source why you feel vulnerable. When did this pattern emerge? Perhaps there was something in your childhood or at high school? Or during the course of a relationship (or past relationship) which triggered this. What made you feel vulnerable? Was it a fear of abandonment? i.e. he cheated on me. Unemployment, loss of two incomes? I handed my authority away. Responsibility for another life. i.e. a baby or a death, loss, or similar situation can expose your emotions and make you feel vulnerable.

By washing out the hurt and really examining it (which is similar to washing out dirt from a cut or wound) you can seek to find the source of the karmic pattern in a relationship. All relationships have a karmic pattern. This relationship's pattern originated a long time ago. This pattern is repeated this lifetime. By sourcing the original lifetime and reason for this karmic relationship, you will begin to discover where and why your relationship first started. Be strong and ruthless in this examination and you will begin to determine the course of your relationships, which need examining every time you feel pain or hurt.

By sourcing the original lifetime in which this pattern emerged, you are then able to rebuild a new foundation for this relationship. Begin this meditation now to get to the source of the karmic relationship. Your meditation journey will be one of insight now, insight into your new relationship.

Breathe in deeply, powerfully, rhythmically. Examine your relationship in light of your new connection with your High Priestess. Ask Her now to find the source of karma.

If you really want to examine this source, ask your High Priestess to help you now. Visualize Her at your heart center. Count down from 20, 19, 18, etc. to 1. You may see or feel your High Priestess guide you to your karmic source. She is love remember, and only wants you to receive the best from the experience.

It is the dynamics of the relationship that must be noted, and the emotions that surface carefully and must be ruthlessly examined. It is only by really examining the situation that real change can occur for you in this relationship. This exercise will bring enormous change in the dynamics of your relationship energy.

Through Her guidance concerning your source of karma in your relationship, keep in mind that you are recoding the cellular memory. You are creating a new way of relating to the person. An experience such as this is life forever life changing.

Relationships are the most important avenue we have for learning about ourselves and growing heart-centered love. Try sourcing your karmic relationship with others now such as your mother, father, husband, wife, children, brothers, sisters, lovers, friends, etc.

When you have returned from your inner journey (give yourself 30 minutes), record your experiences and see how many glimpses you have received from Her. **Describe your experiences such as location, geographic details, smells, colors, textures, feelings and relationship dynamics.**

Here is a relationship checklist:
- **What can we do together now?**
- **Is your relationship one of shared truth?**
- **Can you be honest with each other now?**

Do you look back at the past to see what could have been?

Do you examine your relationships constantly and keep updating what your shared truth is? Why/why not?

What are you creating together now?

Do you feed your creations with love? i.e. When you are creating together, do you allow the love to flow into that creation? Why/why not?

How do you observe and witness yourself daily in all aspects of your life?

You cannot heal heart-centered relationships unless you release negative thoughts as part of your consciousness. You must witness yourself daily in all areas of your life, because they all are one. Give yourself good food, nurture yourself daily, and always give the best to yourself first. By loving yourself only then can this love go out to others. When you give to yourself you bring to your world love without fear.

Summary:
- 30 minutes healing to accept new frequencies of love and reflection
- Examine the cause of pain in a relationship
- 30 minutes Karmic Source Healing and reflection
- Relationship checklist for self examination

THE HIGH PRIESTESS COURSE

Lesson Five
Manifestation through The Atlantean High Priestess

This lesson focuses on one aspect of the High Priestess: The Atlantean High Priestess. There are many different High Priestesses, and they embody different qualities for different intents.

By focusing on one High Priestess's qualities in your life right now, you will have focus and direction for your creations. The Atlantean High Priestess will bring to you strong and beautiful power, cutting through illusion and negativity.

Imagine now what you want to magnetize. It may be a relationship, an event, or concept for your highest good. Ask; is this for your highest good? If it isn't for your *Highest Good*, it is merely perpetuating an old karma. There are many universal laws. What we are creating with is the law concerning your highest good. Holding an image for your Highest Good is now bringing to you all you need to manifest, for this is the art of manifestation.

True manifestation: A person who can truly learn how to manifest through her Higher Self for her highest good is a powerful human being.

You must feel you are worthy, and often we don't feel we are worthy to receive an amazing event, concept, or a relationship. Many good things are happening to us all the time, when we truly allow ourselves to receive these good happenings we are allowing our heart center to open.

You can achieve good things if you have power made available to you. What is power? Power for a High Priestess is controlled thought channelled through the third eye. Hold an image in your mind of what you would like to manifest for highest good. By using your third eye and your senses, feel the person, or event, etc. and see what you desire for your time with the person or event.

Say: In the name of my Higher Truth and with my (or insert person's name) higher self's permission may I forward that I now, _____ (describe or list your manifestations).

By stating clearly your intentions you are now creating your own image of your:

1. Event

2. Concept

3. Relationship

Surrender and ask that the life force of the (event, concept, relationship) to come to you. Distractions create barriers and all distractions must cease. Magnetize the event, concept, and relationship using the five senses. Imagine the image by writing it. I now magnetize this (event, concept, relationship). Also include your fears and limitations associated with your intent.

I want to manifest...

Event (100 words)

Concept (100 words)

Relationship (100 words)

This exercise can be used and mentally revealed every time you need to open your heart center.

Now see yourself as the Atlantean High Priestess. You are embodying the principle of love in its purest aspect. You are now the purest aspect of love imaginable.

Say: Through the Atlantean vibration in its highest aspect, may I embody the principle of love in its purest aspect.

Feel yourself as a cloud, a ball of luminous light, forever young, forever luminous.

You may have found many limiting patterns in your earlier exercise, i.e. limiting thoughts, deeds, actions, and words. List these limitations as they are keeping you in a pain-filled state. Release your own rocks of self-abuse. Self-abuse is mutilating the self. Take away the rocks. Now see yourself redoing the exercise, with all those limitations released. Sell it to yourself every day.

Share your journey in your response (150 words)

Your definition of intimacy is your next opportunity to further deepen your relationship with your High Priestess. What is your definition of intimacy exactly? How do you see yourself intimately with another person? i.e. friendship, love, mating partner. Intimacy is an emotion. Let's face it; our current definition of intimacy is based on the media and our society's definition of intimacy. Our media often insinuates exclusivity, i.e. I own you, you are mine. However, this is not necessarily a definition of true intimacy.

Examine now your attitudes toward intimacy as an emotion, and feel now in your heart your emotional attitudes to intimacy.

By needing an intimate emotional relationship you are bringing in two problems for yourself. An emotion can leave you feeling very vulnerable, i.e. my boyfriend has cheated, and my husband doesn't share or communicate with me. Now you see, by having and expecting emotional intimate exclusivity you are bringing intimacy as an emotion to the surface. Please witness this emotion, and see it like a bubble in a glass of champagne. Is the bubble big? What size is the bubble in the glass in relation to my totality?

This is a very important step in your evolution as a human being, because by loving yourself unconditionally, you are not expecting exclusivity in any aspect of your relationship with another human.

Define these attitudes and test them. This is very important to test for yourself. And imagine yourself loving someone just for the sake of you truth and their truth. No emotional intimacy or exclusivity.

Detail your responses, especially your first reaction to your negative emotion toward intimacy?

| |
| |
| |
| |

Thank you for allowing yourself the journey to create with your High Priestess. Everything in your world is changing now you have connected with Her in love. Your journey will give you even further depth to create an even more powerful and ongoing relationship with Her.

Summary:
- Magnetizing an event, relationship, or concept
- Examine your limitations
- Define your responses toward negative emotions

THE HIGH PRIESTESS COURSE

Lesson Six
Shifting Consciousness with The High Priestess

The next series of exercises will help you understand that The High Priestess is more than a superficial experience. It can be a life-changing one if you allow it, because you are diving into core beliefs about your relationship with your feminine self. You cannot imagine how you will be transformed by Her, because She re-codes every single cell in your body for self- nurturing.

Can you see, since the beginning of The High Priestess transmissions, how you have become more aware of balance and the need for emotional detachment in your life?

You may like to list some of the emotional extremes you have experienced, and ask yourself now how you have changed with your High Priestess.

We react emotionally to an extreme situation in our lives because of unresolved backlog, i.e. an event triggers off an old, unresolved issue. For example an emotional situation triggers an old unresolved event.

Up until now you may have reacted passively with "rage," "anger," or alternatively acted as a "victim," "I've been betrayed" scenarios.

Think of a situation in the past and examine your old emotional reaction. Explain your old reactions, and then explain how you think you would act now, with your High Priestess, if this situation reoccurred.

| |
| |
| |
| |
| |
| |
| |

You may be able to find a character to be a representative of The High Priestess. Draw on a character through a book, film, or myth who exhibits the gifts of a High Priestess. Finding a model for your High Priestess can be one way of triggering your feelings for how a High Priestess would behave or act in any given situation.

Write a story on this character, for example Isis, Cleopatra, or any fictional character. Make sure your character is a High Priestess archetype. Remember, a High Priestess is someone who is detached from emotional extremes in any given situation. Describe now the character you have chosen to represent The High Priestess.

All of us are challenged in enhancing and maintaining relationships every day. Your relationship with your High Priestess is no different. To develop your relationship with your High Priestess requires you to contain (literally contain) an emotion.

Visualize a container in which to place your emotion. What does this container look like?

For example:
A wooden box = could represent a coffin which can be burned

A plastic container = means that the emotion is not too tightly sealed

A steel container = means the emotion is a strong one and it is tightly locked up

A glass container = means the emotion could be quiet fragile

The choice of container can determine the intensity of the emotion being contained.

Now describe your container:

```
┌─────────────────────────────────────────────┐
│                                               │
├─────────────────────────────────────────────┤
│                                               │
├─────────────────────────────────────────────┤
│                                               │
├─────────────────────────────────────────────┤
│                                               │
├─────────────────────────────────────────────┤
│                                               │
├─────────────────────────────────────────────┤
│                                               │
└─────────────────────────────────────────────┘
```

Training the mind is one of the most essential factors in developing your relationship with your High Priestess. To train your mind you must feel a connection with your higher mind who is the instructor.

For example Veronica is about to hear how her employer will react to her demand for a bigger salary package.

I asked her to choose a container to place her emotions in. She chose a steel box to contain her emotions. This type of container suggests that she might let the un-contained emotion out of control if she doesn't get what she feels she needs.

Un-contained emotions need containers. List three emotional reactions you have had in the past, review them, and put them in containers. Describe the emotion, briefly, and the container you felt you could have used before your emotions ran away with you.

```
┌─────────────────────────────────────────────┐
│                                               │
├─────────────────────────────────────────────┤
│                                               │
├─────────────────────────────────────────────┤
│                                               │
├─────────────────────────────────────────────┤
│                                               │
├─────────────────────────────────────────────┤
│                                               │
└─────────────────────────────────────────────┘
```

Many of us do not like obeying instructions because of the emotional agenda others place on us to obey them. Obeying instructions from your High Priestess is far different because she doesn't have anything but pure love for you.

In your daily invocation, for one month, you may like to use this invocation:

"I now command in the name of love and light and in the name of my absolute divine truth that I be freed from emotional betrayal I place on myself through others in my life. I command myself to obey The High Priestess, at all times as I am being instructed by Her."

List all the problems you see yourself facing in doing this invocation every day for one month. Look at the language carefully. Make sure you understand it, and list the barriers to the commitment in developing your relationship with your High Priestess.

Now you need to examine the barriers, and then give yourself a contrasting statement to balance the barrier statement.

Example:
Barrier: I don't have enough time.

Contrasting Statement: I now choose to create more time for myself.

After listing your barriers, write a contrasting positive for your barrier.

1. _____

2. _____

3. _____

4. _____

5. _____

The Mysteries will teach you very specific things. The results from working with The High Priestess have changed others' lives. Choosing to work with the Mysteries will give you control and mastery over your "small self." Try working with these five affirmations for one month to help you overcome your barriers.

1. I now ask to access wisdom for a deeper insight into my reality.

2. How can I manifest a new reality for myself?

3. How can I change with The High Priestess?

4. I now connect to the "Universal Heart," the heart of the "mother."

5. I am now ready to be a student of the Mysteries.

Summary:
- **How do you react to a situation?**
- **Finding a role model.**
- **How can you contain your emotions?**
- **Where are the barriers?**
- **How to overcome the barriers.**

THE HIGH PRIESTESS COURSE

Lesson Seven
The Moon and The High Priestess

The Moon is not only a satellite but also the home of The High Priestess.

In developing your relationship with the feminine energies you need to observe and meditate on the Moon in her phases. We can observe the Moon in her five phases; New Moon, Waxing Moon, Full Moon, Waning Moon, Dark Moon.

Each Moon cycle is important and has a part to play in your relationship with yourself through The High Priestess. Have you encountered any particular experience associated with the Moon's cycles in your life? Have you ever been drawn to planting herbs and vegetables according to the Moon's phases? Or noted on the Full Moon that your emotions are amplified?

Choose one experience, good or bad, in your life where you have noticed the Moon's effect in your life. If you cannot think of an experience, you may like to reflect as to why the Moon's energy has been absent in your life.

Why do you think the Moon and the natural world are so important for the energy work with The High Priestess?

(blank lined space)

The New Moon creates a space within yourself to manifest your creations, then the Half Moon ripens your creative ideas. Outline your creations now that the Moon has ripened. You can be very specific in your creations, as your High Priestess will be growing rapidly now. This is a good time to really connect to your High Priestess intimately. The High Priestess also speaks of your separateness from your own small creations.

Ask yourself now if people have changed in their relationship with you?

(blank lined space)

Have you experienced a sense of your High Priestess as a presence around you at certain times in your day-to-day life? While bathing or when you are near water, ocean, streams, lakes, pools? Do you try to note Her presence consciously when you are out in nature? Do you attune to Her when doing your ritual breathing or while meditating on the Moon?

List your experiences when She has been present in these daily situations:

The exercises on the Moon's phases are created to experience properly the feminine energies. Breath work and rituals create this atmosphere. Do your daily breath exercises for four minutes. This will instantly connect you to the divine energies and create through the feminine. While doing breath work, observe your resistances.

CARMEL GLENANE

Set an alarm for four minutes and begin by observing your resistance during this time? Be kind to yourself here. Resistance is important; it is integral to growth.

How do you feel when you finally completed your four minutes of breath exercises? Did you gain anything from the practice? Outline your resistances. Where did they come from physically, emotionally, and mentally?

Why do you need a disciplined mind for these rituals/rules? Why do you perform "sacred rituals?"

By acknowledging and noting The High Priestess's presence in your rituals and daily life, and writing your experiences down you become more aware of Her presence in your life.

For the next Full Moon, research which astrological sign the Moon will be in. Describe the qualities of The High Priestess for the up and coming Full Moon. Focus on the attributes of the astrological sign in this Moon's phase.

By attuning to The High Priestess in a particular astrological sign on the next Full Moon you can bring specific qualities relating to that sign. i.e. If it is a Full Moon in Libra, you can attune to the properties of a Libran High Priestess. For example, you can attune to the attributes of the Libran Sign to bring the aspects of balance and beauty to all areas in your life. Draw on your High Priestess in this aspect.

Summary:
- **Moon-related experiences**
- **Relationships with others**
- **Noting your resistances**
- **Rituals and breath work**
- **Astrological signs and the Moon**

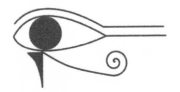

THE HIGH PRIESTESS COURSE

Lesson Eight
Recoding your Cellular memory with the Dark Moon

When we can see our potential and we become who we truly are we are ready to become "one" with The High Priestess. Your High Priestess is now fully unveiled to you. Ask for your cellular memory to be recoded to bring peace and space to you. In this peace-filled space your spiritual self will be revealed to you. The role of the water element helps this process in recoding your cellular memory by energizing your system.

How much energized water do you consume each day?

How often do you spend time ritualistically bathing or taking a sauna?

On a daily basis, how often are you in the presence of water? i.e. visiting rivers, lakes, or waterfalls; there might be a water fountain in nearby parks you can visit in your lunchtime, you might purchase a small water fountain to install at your work or living space. List where you may like to make adjustments in your intake of water if necessary.

For the next full Moon, make a list in your diary of the relationships where you have been giving too much emotional energy. The High Priestess cannot live in a space of emotional debris. This is why it is so important to constantly be in the presence of energized water. I suggest re-reading the section on the Waning Moon in this book. **Ask yourself in the dark Moon/waning Moon phase what is it that you need to let go of emotionally?**

Now record your experiences after you have done this exercise. You may like to do it several times over the Moon's waning cycle. The High Priestess will reward you when you surrender to Her.

The Moon speaks of personal creativity, purification, and, importantly, emotional weight. The source of being physically overweight can be linked to your emotional state. Try to get to the core of this emotion. Don't think you have to be overweight to examine "core" issues; underweight people need to address these issues as well.

List all "core" relationships in which you feel you may be experiencing a loss of power in relation to your core freedom? (i.e. Mother, father, husband, wife, lover, brother, sister, boss, co-workers, friends) **What relationships (relationship with food, exercise, loved ones, etc.) need pruning now?**

What lies at the core of YOUR issue with the relationships you have chosen to examine? (control, insecurity, fear, abuse, de-powered)

The Moon's energy can help you deal with frustrations and unmet needs. By asking for emotional protection, support, and finding your "core" freedom you are allowing yourself to experience more balanced relationships.

<u>Summary:</u>
- **Cellular memory and The High Priestess**
- **Water and The High Priestess**
- **Balanced relationships**
- **Letting go of overly emotional relationships**

THE HIGH PRIESTESS COURSE

Lesson Nine
Unresolved Grief and Emotions

What is your definition of "surrender?" Does the word make you feel uncomfortable? Describe what "surrendering" means to you. All emotions that are unresolved come to the surface at the time of the Full Moon. The Full Moon is magnetic and draws out grief.

Describe now what happens to you when you explore unresolved emotions and grief. 50 words

| |
| |
| |
| |
| |
| |
| |

Why do the body fluids and magnetic energy of the moon have in common? 30 words

Nature, the moon, and the High Priestess are the pain relievers for loss and grieving. Observe this cycle of letting go and allow yourself to experience letting go in all its aspects. Ask your High Priestess to be actively participating in this cycle. It is important now to look at one aspect of loss and how it can lead to depression.

Have you felt in your life a sense of depression? 30 words

Can you track this depression to unsupported grief? If so, which aspects of your life are you not feeling supported in? 100 words

Losses are often not supported and they can lead to grief. Have you experienced losses, which were not supported? **You may like to list losses in your life, which were not supported.**

Your High Priestesses is described as a living organism. **How would you describe your relationship with your High Priestess now? Does she feel real to you? 50 words**

Re-read the section on Nature Speaks. When Nature was channelled "She" spoke of many things. **What aspects or parts of nature do you observe every day? 50 words**

Why is attuning to the sacred elements in nature so important? 10 words

Describe now "by losing your mind in your creation" one aspect of nature, which has an unforgettable impression on you? 100 words

Can you see why the Dark Moon as a cycle is a very important one? Have you felt during the Dark Moon cycle any of the feelings mentioned? Can you understand that at times you could experience vulnerability during the Dark Moon? The Dark Moon is about growth because growth comes from observing the inner self, the emotional self, as a creative force. Rest and wait during the Dark Moon and examine our core fears. The Dark Moon's cycle is an intense one in so much as it reveals your own abandonment issues. The small child alone in the dark.

List your feelings during the Dark Moon as they emerge to be experienced and expressed. 100 words

As you develop your relationship with The High Priestess you can keep a lunar diary on your inner life during the phases of the moon for a month.

New Moon: Date:_____-_____ Moon in: i.e. Leo?

Waxing Moon Date:_____-_____ til _____-_____

Full Moon Date:____-____ til ____-____

| |
| |
| |
| |
| |

Waning Moon Date:____-____ til ____-____

| |
| |
| |
| |
| |

Dark Moon Date:____-____ til ____-____

| |
| |
| |
| |
| |

Congratulate yourself now on completing this most transformative experience with your High Priestess. By now "She" will be integrated into your psyche, and you now are invited to review your experiences with your High Priestess since the beginning of your Journey with "Her."

This is just the beginning, she is as ancient as time itself, and as patient. Be kind to your humanness in the process of having her reveal herself to you.

ABOUT THE AUTHOR

Carmel Glenane B.A. Dip Ed. Owner/Director of Atlantis Rising Healing Center™ and Mystery School. Founder of the philosophy of The Divine Feminine in 2002 and Senju Kannon™ Reiki in 2008, teaches The Divine Feminine Mysteries through her Mystery School Ascension Training program. A powerful interactive and dynamic motivational speaker, channelled writer, esoteric teacher, and sought-after healer, Carmel is known for her transformative tours to sacred destinations such as Hawaii, North, Central and South America, Turkey, India, Bali, Japan, Egypt and the great central heart of Australia, Uluru. With more than 20 years in business in personal development, Carmel's intent is to allow people to receive through the Heart's Intelligence through the mother's wisdom.

Carmel is the Australian Ambassador for HappyCharity.org as Director of Happy Spirits. She is currently writing training programs for all of her books to offer her courses online to a worldwide audience.

CARMEL GLENANE

Feminine energy teaching programs became a focus after 10 years of founding my business Atlantis Rising Healing Centre in 1992, which led me to spontaneously become a channel for "The Goddess of All Light," who guided me to establish "The Philosophy of The Divine Feminine" in 2001. Daily my consciousness is aligned to "The Goddess of All Light," where I receive written transmissions for my personal guidance and teaching.

Facilitating and leading my first teaching tour to Egypt in 2002; I have since taught in Egypt every year, as well as North, Central, and South America, Turkey, Greece, Hawaii Islands, Indonesia, India, and Australia. Each tour, book, and training has helped me "Earth" my body of Light; purging Earth attachments, as my ability to "Earth" (plug in) develops, holding more energy and light in my heart, for The Divine Ones to manifest.

In 2014, I was invited to open a Crystal Tones® Crystal Singing Bowl Sound Temple, and now incorporate these sonic Masterpieces into all my teaching programs.

I am in service to "The mother" and aim to have as many people as possible embody the teachings of our "Mother" through my books, teaching, and healing programs.

I am currently writing online courses to support The Atlantis Rising Mystery School ascension training program and creating new Guided Meditation mp3's to support the Ascension program.

To Connect with Carmel Glenane:
www.carmelglenane.com
www.senjukannonreiki.com
www.atlantis-rising.com.au
Ph: (+61) 0755 367 399

Recorded Meditations
By Carmel Glenane
Featuring Crystal Tones Crystal Singing Bowls

New Dawn Meditation
By Carmel Glenane
Feat. Crystal Tones® Singing Bowls

Set Yourself Free Meditation
By Carmel Glenane
Feat. Crystal Tones® Singing Bowls

Core Identity Meditation
By Carmel Glenane
Feat. Crystal Tones® Singing Bowls

CARMEL GLENANE

Today I am Receiving Love
By Carmel Glenane
Feat. Crystal Tones® Singing Bowls

Trusting to Receive Love
By Carmel Glenane
Feat. Crystal Tones® Singing Bowls

The Alchemies of Isis The Magician
Meditations
By Carmel Glenane
Feat. Crystal Tones® Singing Bowls

Embodying The High Priestess Meditations
By Carmel Glenane
Feat. Crystal Tones® Singing Bowls

The Immortals Meditations
By Carmel Glenane
Feat. Crystal Tones® Singing Bowls

Awakening The Intelligent Heart Meditations
By Carmel Glenane
Feat. Crystal Tones® Singing Bowls

The High Priest Meditations
By Carmel Glenane
Feat. Crystal Tones® Singing Bowls

The Miracle of The Mysteries Meditations
By Carmel Glenane
Feat. Crystal Tones® Singing Bowls

Embodying All Truth Meditations
By Carmel Glenane
Feat. Crystal Tones® Singing Bowls

All meditations are available on these and other fine retailers:

iTunes

DEEZER

emusic

OTHER BOOKS BY CARMEL GLENANE

Awaken Your Immortal Intelligent Heart, A Blue Print for Living in The Now **By Carmel Glenane B.A. Dip. Ed.**

ISBN: 978-1-938487-23-1 (print)
ISBN: 978-1-938487-24-8 (eBook)

In Part I: DISCOVER THE SECRET POWER OF YOUR HEART'S INTELLIGENCE

New scientific evidence reveals that your heart has an important role in supporting the Endocrine function of the entire human body. Read more as Glenane & Malcolm explore spiritually and scientifically the heart's important role in activating the Mitochondrial DNA (MtDNA). Discover how your heart's intelligence can be activated by initiating your five primary senses. Learn how The Black Heart, brings primordial power, pure peace and acceptance of all there is.

If you have a heart, you must read, "Awakening the Intelligent Heart"
Brenda Littleton, M.A. Ed., M.A.
**Contributing Author in Part I of *Awaken Your Immortal*
*Intelligent Heart***

Carmel Glenane does a magnificent job to remind the world that the center of our life is found by living from the center of our heart. In a time where consciousness is often mistaken for the mind, or even brain activity, Glenane presents a daily practice of heart-centered healing where weaving science, ancient spiritual disciplines, wisdom studies, and exercises of activation, provides the reader direct access to deep, personal growth. By integrating both light and shadows of the heart, this step-by-step process grounds the initiate toward a journey of realignment of purpose, of remembering one's true value, of rejuvenating energy, of regenerating the mystery, and of resourcing opportunities for the soul. Heart-centered healing is the language of love, and the application of Glenane's work will be useful not only to the individual reader, but also for couples working toward intimacy, for families wanting to communicate more effectively, and for businesses working through conflict resolution.

In Part II: THE IMMORTAL WOMAN

'*The Immortal Woman*' can be read sequentially or by opening up to any page for her message to be reflected upon for your day and see what 'She' reveals to you for your journey right now. Close your eyes, take a deep breath in, ask your question, then open the book up to a page. This book is your personal 'living guide' as the ancient secrets are revealed to you day by day. '*The Immortal Woman*' tests and challenges your previously held definition of Love and takes you to a space of truth for yourself where all of life becomes a multi-dimensional experience.

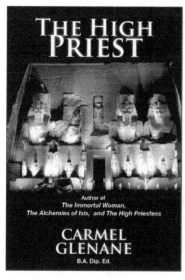

The High Priest, A Blue Print for Living through the Masculine Heart **By Carmel Glenane B.A. Dip.Ed.**

ISBN: 978-0-9873439-2-5

FEEL WORTHY TO BECOME A MODERN SPIRITUAL WARRIOR, SEEKING TRUTH AND CREATING A POWERFUL NEW REALITY IN YOUR LIFE!

Carmel Glenane, internationally published author of 'Awaken Your Immortal Intelligent Heart' and 'The Alchemies of Isis' brings to you 'The High Priest'.

- Are you worthy to become a modern spiritual warrior?

- Do you want to be a truth seeker?

- Are you ready to activate your hearts intelligence?

- Are you ready to release your attachments?

- Are you willing to really manifest and rip out your illusions about your creative masculine?

In The High Priest, Carmel Glenane helps you explore and take control of your creative masculine. The High Priest offers a practical guide to living powerfully, with truth, changing your definition of your current reality. Join Carmel Glenane as she explores your creative masculine and discover your power.

Allow yourself your truth through power, to bring protection, power and love!

CARMEL GLENANE TRAINING AND WORKSHOP PROGRAMS

Carmel offers training and workshop programs on the Activation of The Intelligent Heart in Australia and overseas.

Training programs are also offered for all levels of Senju Kannon Reiki™, through the Atlantis Rising Mystery School.

Carmel also facilitates tours to sacred destinations throughout the world. Carmel travels with Crystal Tones Singing Bowls and invites you to bring your own bowl to be a witness to your heart's remembering in all sacred sites.

If you wish to sponsor training programs please contact the Atlantis Rising Healing Centre™ office:
email info@atlantis-rising.com.au

For upcoming workshops or training locations or tour destinations please see our Website:
www.carmelglenane.com or www.atlantis-rising.com.au

Transformational Tours

Carmel Glenane Tour Facilitator

EGYPT TOURS

The essence of Egypt is in aligning your consciousness to the Ancient Deities themselves. The Hieroglyphics of the temples reflect, through the reliefs, architecture and atmosphere the energies of the Goddess's & Gods.

Egypt feeds your soul. Imagine being initiated to the frequencies in the Kings, Queens, and Subterranean chambers also known as the Pit in the Pyramid of Giza. Reflect on the timeless wonder of the Sphinx, touching the stele at the heart of its initiation chamber between the paws.

Discover old Atlantis again at Sakkara, as the desert winds whisper their secrets. Horus the Falcon hovers as he guides you to his temple complex in Edfu, revealing the essence of order, protection, and freedom—the ancient Egyptians were known for creating order out of chaos. Float upon the Nile, which reflects the starry body of the Goddess Nuit. Re-code your cellular memory with The Great Father Osiris as he resurrects your weary spirit in this most ancient of temples complexes in Abydos, healing you by the green Osirian well, where the secrets of the Ancient Flower of Life can be revealed. Be drawn to the mighty temple complex of Abu Simbel where Ramses II and Nefertari love was immortalized.

Allow our holy Mother Isis to enfold you in her wings of love as we sail to her sacred home on The Isle of Philae.

The magician High Priestesses and Priests of Karnak allow you to embrace your own magical powers in their home of balance and duality. Sekhmet the austere warrior goddess/mother of Karnak will receive you if you respect her power.

Explore where ancient rituals and offerings were given to the stellar forces at Dendara, home of the Hathors, Goddesses of Love and Pleasure.

JAPAN TOURS

Japan is a transformational, feminine and nurturing experience, especially Mt. Kurama known as the 'heart' of Japan. Mt Kurama, located 40mins outside the imperial ancient city of Kyoto, is the mountain where Dr. USUI received his enlightenment. Japan's delicate and very special spiritual energies reflect the beauty and power of Senju Kannon Mother of Japan and mother of our Feminine Reiki.

The Japan journey begins in the ancient shrine city of Kyoto, visiting powerful Buddhist temples, including Sanjusangen-do–The Thousand Armed Kannon Temple with 1,000 Kannon's (also known as Quan Yin) statues in the temple. The city's beauty is phenomena, featuring spectacular gardens, a geisha district, authentic Japanese cuisine, peace, order and tranquility. Unwind in traditional Onsen style bathing houses of warm mineral springs, relax in the peaceful retreat rooms or indulge in authentic traditional Japanese cuisine.

Our training program honors the Dr. Usui (traditional Reiki) but embraces 'The Mother' feminine heart of Reiki. Our programs are tailored to sacred sites and locations in and around the Temples at Kyoto and Mr Kurama. Travelling with our Crystal Tones Singing bowls magnifying and amplifying this incredible energy.

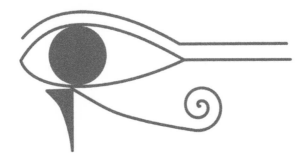